A Walk in the Physical

Understanding the Human Experience
Within the Larger Spiritual Context

Edition 1.0

Christian Sundberg

A Walk in the Physical
Edition 1.0

Copyright © 2021 by Christian Sundberg

Contact the author at:
www.awalkinthephysical.com

Cover art by Andrew Ostrovsky
Cover design by Lauree Sundberg Schloss

Proofreading and editing by Charley Sweet and Jörg Starkmuth

ISBN 978-1-7371970-0-3 (Softcover)
ISBN 978-1-7371970-1-0 (E-Book)

Table of Contents

INTRODUCTION

There is far more going on than meets the physical eye.

I existed before I was human, and so did you. Now that we are here, it is my honor to communicate with you while we are both human, to remind you of what the deeper parts of you already know. I wish to share some of what I have come to understand while human, so that others may be reminded of *our* true spiritual nature. I wish to encourage all my brothers and sisters so that we all might more effectively fulfill our divine purposes and grow together towards love!

You, dear reader, are a wonderful being of light! You have come to Earth to participate in one of the most ambitious endeavors of creation ever performed. It is my dear hope that these words will stir in you a remembrance of who we really are, and help you in your own very meaningful life walk. For though you may or may not be aware of it right now, *your* life is incredibly meaningful indeed!

My Story

My Pre-Birth Experience

Before I tell this story I think it is very important to say, as I will many times throughout this book, that the higher dimensions cannot be articulated with words. There is simply no language from our world that can possibly fully communicate the nature of the higher realms, the nature of our greater being, or even the nature of the incarnation process that I will attempt to describe below. Our physical universe is a very specific type of experience, and some of the most fundamental assumptions of our universe – assumptions like distance and linear time for instance – do not apply to many other reality systems. Our language is based on our local assumptions, so it falls very short of being able to speak to "higher" reality which transcends our local system entirely. In fact, language is an expression of

1

form – and our true being transcends all form – so as soon as a single word is spoken, we have automatically deviated from the deepest truth.

The following is a summary of my pre-birth and post-birth story. I am only providing a summary because this book is not about my story. Rather, this book is an attempt to describe the joyful truth of our shared spiritual nature and the larger spiritual context in which we live. I am simply telling my story so that you may better relate to me. You, too, may have experienced something similar, even if you do not currently remember it – perhaps my story then will help stir in you a remembrance of where we all come from!

You and I are beings of incredible freedom, joy, and love! We are sparks of the living Source of all Creation. As sparks of the Creator, our pre-human existence is filled with innumerable joys and adventures! We revel in many forms of creation, learning, expression, and play – many of which cannot even be imagined while we are human, let alone articulated! We engage in all sorts of creative activities and hugely varied experiences! Our being is of the stars, and far beyond. We celebrate our existence through the music and the unimaginably beautiful splendors of the heavens! We celebrate the very act of Being. And we do so in millions upon millions of amazing ways. That may not sound tangible or specific, but I can think of no other way to attempt to articulate the hugely varied realness of our higher natures, which transcend the earthly context.

One adventure available to us is that we can choose to commit to an experience of separation, contrast, and challenge. One of the ways we can help expand both our joy and the depth of all Creation is by diving deep into duality, to truly engage the constraints of physicality. This book is about the "why" behind that journey. You are taking that meaningful journey right now.

While the following pre-birth memories that I will attempt to describe do have a sequence, and while some are far more ancient than any Earthly memory, they also feel as if they are taking place right now. They are occurring with a simultaneity in the one Now.

2

I remember being inspired long, long ago by a great being of light who had himself experienced physical incarnations. When I came across this being, I was completely taken aback by the radiance, richness, joy, and power of his "nature" or "essence," which I could plainly see and feel. I asked this being what he had done to "become this" – and he telepathically shared that he had lived physical lifetimes. One in particular was exceptionally difficult for him because he had suffered from a chronic and painful physical condition. But through how he chose to meet that condition, and through how he "integrated" that experience, he "refined" to a degree that was utterly astounding. I was deeply inspired! I communicated to him definitively, "I am going to do that!" He was loving, but responded at first something to the effect of "That's what they all say. This is difficult in a way that you have never known before." But I was persistent. He encouraged me to approach my guides if I wished to pursue this path, and I did. Because of that initial inspiration I set out to embark on the long journey of physical lifetimes to refine the quality of my own being and increase my capacity for joy, creativity, and love! I have had many, many experiences since then.

I remember when the creation of this universe was being initiated! I remember the joy of being in knowing that "from on high" this creation, our universe, was being issued forth – for us, and also by us – as a new and fantastically rigorous level of expansion. I was not present at the moment of its creation. I arrived "soon after" (though as I will mention, time is not at all the same there as it is here), and I sailed joyfully among the stars and galaxies. I was full of bliss and profound excitement that here, in this place, we would actually get to "be" (experience being) these creatures of flesh, and more! What an absolutely amazing opportunity for Creation! What an absolutely amazing opportunity for the expansion of Being through experience!

Long, long after that, before incarnating as Christian but after many other experiences, I prepared for the next steps of my journey. Over the course of my physical incarnations, I had been people and I had engaged certain extremes. I now really wanted to experience a certain significant "distance" from Source and have the opportunity to confront and heal a specific

3

extremely deep fear – a certain deep low experiential vibration – that had been very difficult for me in the past. That fear had "bested" me in a previous life, and through it I had caused significant pain and distress for many others in that earlier lifetime. I was not a nice person in that lifetime. Working through to the end of it, my fear had caused me to suffer an agonizing physical death. I was terrified as I lay there dying, suffocating under the weight not only of my physical pain, but also this terrible fear. Though it is beyond naming, the fear was something to the effect of "I am powerless to avoid agony" mixed with "I am too proud to suffer."

Long after that death, from the higher spiritual vantage point of complete freedom, power, and joyful excitement, I wanted to confront that fear again! I knew that to do so would be a truly incredible opportunity for personal and collective expansion! Yet the task seemed daunting. The fear seemed so deep, so dark, that I wondered if it was even possible to confront such a low vibration.

From the glory and freedom of the realms of light, I asked my guides if it was even possible to integrate such a low vibration. I asked, "Has this ever been done in all of Creation by anyone ever?" And they replied, joyfully, "Yes – and you have all time available to you to do so!"

So I set the intention. That intention led me to where I am today.

But my current lifetime as Christian was not my first choice for this purpose. In fact, I selected a different human life first.

When we come to have a physical lifetime, we have to accept a set of consciousness constraints that we as humans call simply "the veil." The veil is an important and necessary part of the incarnation process. In order to actually be human and to have the full physical experience, we need to forget all of everything else that we are. The veil is the "spiritual mechanism," or perhaps even "consciousness technology," by which this is accomplished. It is like a great cloak the passes over your being, cutting you off experientially from your connection to all knowledge, and veiling the conscious awareness of your living connection with all things. From a state of both simultaneous individuality and blissful Oneness, you collapse into individuality only. You plummet from an extremely high vibration to an extremely low vibration as you interface into the physical reality system. After I accepted the veil, I experienced my "knowing" be cut off, and I suddenly felt separate, dark, and alone. Metaphorically, for me it was like going from rich, vibrant connectedness, straight into the airless, cold, and desolate vacuum of space!

Because the spirit is sovereign, the veil requires the individual's acceptance for it to "take." You have to "dive in" and commit to it, allow it to have power over you, in order to be "bound" to that physical experience for its duration.

The lifetime that had been brought to me was nearly perfect for my purpose of having an ample opportunity to re-engage this low vibration of fear! I really resonated well with the circumstances, biology, parents, and opportunity. But during and shortly after the veil acceptance process for that life, due to the extreme drop in vibration, I was quickly overwhelmed by fear. Immediately, I fought it. I resisted mightily. I was so terrified at the depth to which I was being cut off that very quickly I mustered all of my strength, and I rejected the veil.

I was immediately free again, back in bliss! But my rejection had killed the fetus; I had killed the unborn body that I was to inhabit. Then I had a life review (just like the life reviews reported by many thousands of near death experiencers), even for my very short life. Being back on that side, I knew that nothing was truly wrong! Yet I recognized fully the grief and negative impact I had caused not only the poor mother (her physical experience) but also many hundreds of others who were affected by the mother. I couldn't believe that despite my good intentions, my own fear was so strong that I could have such a negative effect. Despite my lofty goals, I had only heaped difficulty upon the physical experience of those beautiful souls whom I so wished to join.

I vowed to not let that happen again. So I "trained" for a while in a "veil acceptance simulator." It was something like a simulation room where I was able to practice releasing control and dropping vibration to a degree, so as to be ready for the actual moment I would do so again. I also took a long rest. Eventually, I was presented with the opportunity of my current lifetime – the life in which I would be known as Christian (a name that even during my pre-incarnation review of this life I recognized had the potential to be ironic).

This life as Christian wasn't as optimal for my purposes as the previous one would have been, but considering the specificity of my intentions, it wasn't bad. I remember very excitedly reviewing, all at once, a vast "flow chart" of millions of possibilities about what "being" this life as Christian would or could be like. I reviewed the possibilities with my guide and reviewed certain aspects of the life in detail. I knew who my parents would be. I knew that the confidence my father would nurture in me would be important. I knew that being male would be very helpful for my purposes. I knew that the body would have certain health challenges that other bodies do not, and because of that, many others probably would have passed on this experience. In fact, I knew that the biological limitations of the body would provide me with a certain "biological weight" on my day-to-day experience, which would be key to experiencing what I needed to experience.

I also requested to experience certain things or "be" certain things during this life. For instance, I asked the life preparation guides if I could be intelligent again, as intelligence was a trait I tended to prefer in many of my recent lifetimes. I also asked if I could retain just a very small amount of awareness this time, and not completely forget who I really was when I came. I was told that I could, but that it would add further contrast and make the experience even more challenging (and it has). Knowing that even this challenge added to the potential growth, I accepted!

In reviewing my "flow chart," I knew that it was likely that a traumatic experience would probably happen in my early or mid-20s that would allow me to deeply face my old fear. (It did happen – see below!) I knew that this life was potentially "biting off more than I could chew," but I preferred to take the greater challenge and do it all at once.

I was so very eager to be preparing for this life! I was so, so very deeply excited and felt so very blessed to have been given this precious opportunity! Being given the chance to be human was like being given one of the most precious gifts in existence! The feeling of excitement filled the entirety of my being!

Eventually it was "time to go," and a guide came to get me. He communicated with an abrupt and forceful message to the effect of: "GO, NOW!" The message needed to be abrupt because, as a spirit who was free from the constraints of physical time, something really needed to grab my attention so that I could catch the "precious window of opportunity" and accept the veil at the correct moment.

I was then in a staging area where a group of beings I can only describe as "technicians" or "tinkerers" helped fine-tune the veil to my specific energy. They asked me one last time: "Are you sure?" – because once I said yes, I was committed. I remember that I was instructed to accept the veil, and I did. I opened myself up completely, deeply mustering my courage to open and allow a complete "swallowing" of my being by the vast swath of the obscuring veil! My vibration plummeted. From the heights of the realms of light, my vibration collapsed lower, and lower, and lower, and lower, all within a breathtaking, shocking instant. I went from being connected to everything to being in what felt like a dark vacuum. My knowing was gone. I suddenly felt extremely small, dense, and alone.

The feeling was, again, intolerable. And once again I began to panic. But I chose to hold on moment to moment, letting it "sink in" for as long as I could. Through the darkness I sent a simple message, a "ping" back through: "Did it take?" And I was told simply, "Yes." And I let go. I let go into the darkness. I momentarily surrendered to the cold vacuum of the flesh. Time passed.

But not long after, my body still in my mother's womb, the panic returned. All my great plans seemed so distant and meaningless in this doleful state. It felt like my very being itself had been horribly reduced. I hated feeling so far from Home! I decided that I wasn't going to endure this, and nothing was going to stop me. Once again, I began to muster my great strength to fight free of the bodily shackle!

Just then, the great, powerful "I Am" presence of Source (which we also crudely call "God") came over me! To this day, thinking about this presence brings me tears of joy! The presence of God filled me, and for a moment, expanded me back out, showing me all the galaxies, all of the stars, and beyond. God reminded me that I *was* that! I knew that I *was* the stars, the galaxies, indeed the entire universe and more! I was joy, and freedom, and power, and love itself! I was a mighty churning symphony of bliss! And God said to me, "This is still what you are. You can never not be this."

The experience calmed me completely, and I surrendered into the simple and confining darkness of the womb.

My Post-Birth Experience

My next memory is of the day I was born. I remember the shock of physical birth. It felt like an overload of sensory data: light, sound, cold, touching, someone cutting my body (circumcision), etc. I had no idea what was happening, no concept of what this intense experience was about, but I was extremely curious. I could tell there were beings (the nurses) "taking care" of me, and I felt love and awe for them, even though I had no idea who they were. The experience was one of shock and wonder, but there was no intellectual context or understanding yet at all. I also remember one visual image of the layout of the birth room after I was pulled out. My mother later confirmed that layout to me when I drew it for her much later in life.

When I was a young child, I remembered my pre-birth existence, at least in parts. I was born in Pennsylvania USA in 1980, but I naturally sensed that I wasn't really just from Earth. I knew that none of us were, that we were just visiting. No one else talked about it, so I didn't either. It seemed right to focus on the physical, to relegate those memories to some distant corner most of the time. But deep down, I knew. I assumed everyone did.

One day when I was very young, young enough that I was still walking around in a diaper, a neighbor was over visiting our house. I asked her if she wanted to watch me dance to a song that I really liked, and she agreed. Now, in other reality systems, it is normal for beings to be able to feel each other's emotions, so I assumed that would be the case here, too. Really enjoying the music, I danced for her. I was feeling very funky! In the middle of my funky dance, she walked away unimpressed. Then it hit me: *She can't feel what I'm feeling!* Where the heck was I that people couldn't feel each other's feelings? Suddenly the entire world seemed very alien indeed!

In the first five or so years of my life, I would occasionally draw upon the "flow chart" memory to look ahead and gain information about what to expect. Eventually that began to close off to me. Physical reality seemed to become increasingly firm. And by the age of six or seven, I had completely forgotten my pre-birth memory. I was human focused, as it seemed I should be. I adopted the beliefs that were handed to me by the dear ones who now physically cared for me. I was raised in the Lutheran faith, and for a while I saw the world through that lens.

I grew up in a wonderfully loving family but was constantly beset by physical challenges, including the numerous symptoms of untreated celiac disease (autoimmune response to gluten), persistent migraine headaches, and a number of other chronic ailments. Despite growing up with constant fatigue, and despite commonly being the target of bullying in school, I was "successful" by human standards. I earned straight A's through all my schooling, and after high school I attended college for Chinese international business management.

After studying abroad in Beijing, China in my sophomore year of college, I attempted to move to China after graduation at the age of 22. Little did I know it then, but the trauma I had anticipated before I incarnated was about to happen. Emotionally distraught from the outcomes of my parents' divorce and the end of an important five year romantic relationship, and physically sick from untreated chronic celiac disease, I suffered a heat stroke in the humid 110°F heat of Cheng Du, China while teaching English. I spent four days in a Chinese hospital, and about a week in my hotel room. Somehow the heat stroke or the four days of straight potassium administered by the hospital triggered some kind of terribly painful neurological damage that lasted for months. I felt like every nerve in my body was being burned, and I could not escape an unrelenting and unbearable amount of pain. I experienced physical agony that felt like it would never end. The anxiety and terror I experienced during that time was also completely overwhelming. I suffered PTSD as a result of this experience, and afterwards spent years in counseling facing the deep negative self-perceptions I bought into during that time.

A few years later I also became bedridden from the celiac disease, until it was finally diagnosed. In that same year I also suffered a spontaneous hemopneumothorax (lung collapse due to internal bleeding), and I spent 10 days in the hospital, eight of those with a tube in my chest.

These experiences were significant personal challenges for me. But they were challenges that were, in fact, extremely valuable! All these illnesses mightily prompted one great response in me: the experience of that ancient deep fear. That very specific fear that I had come to this reality to face was being "pulled" up into my experience, time and again, day after day! For years I resisted it. I resisted it persistently, until after incredible amounts of suffering I seemed to have no choice left but to go *into* the pain. I spent five years going through EMDR (eye movement desensitization and reprocessing) therapy; and through that and other techniques, I faced my demons, one negative self-perception at a time. I became increasingly brave about actually feeling what I felt. I became a warrior of feeling.

I faced the darkness; I felt the pain – and through hundreds and hundreds of encounters with the reality of exactly the present moment that I had built up for myself, I healed! I healed far more than I ever could have previously imagined. And, even more importantly, I found the enduring light of being beneath the cacophony of my thinking human mind! That light of being was – and is! – far more real and enduring than the fears and pains that I thought were so real!

It wasn't until I was 30 years old that I began to remember how all of this fit with my pre-birth plan. It started when I discovered the impactful work of physicist and consciousness explorer Tom Campbell. I had always been a spiritual seeker, and I was initially drawn to Tom's work primarily because his reality model spoke at great length about fear, and the place of fear in the spiritual walk. That message really resonated with me. After only a few months of beginning a consistent meditation practice, as I became increasingly familiar with the nature of my awareness itself, the memories began to unexpectedly but naturally return to me. Those memories were so real, so vivid, so "now" – dissimilar from earthly memories – and so very personal. I not only had memory spontaneously return, I also began to have nonphysical experiences, including out-of-body experiences. These experiences were extremely eye-opening for me!

Bit by bit, over the next decade, I became increasingly tangibly aware of our very real greater spiritual nature! The veil remains over me, somewhat ebbing and flowing as my focus changes. My pre-birth experience is in mind almost every day, at certain times feeling extremely close, and at other times, distant. But always I feel that I remain at least somewhat aware of the greater context in which this earthly experience is arising.

A Few Brief Examples of Non-Physical Experiences

I am naturally skeptical, so I've also worked at validating my nonphysical experiences as much as possible. For instance, there have been four times so far that I have been able to meet another person whom I know physically in a nonphysical environment (while our bodies were asleep) and have been able to successfully confirm the interaction with them the next day, at least to my own satisfaction. There have been at least as many "failures" as well. I am yet a neophyte in nonphysical exploration, but the experiences I have had have been extremely impactful. Indeed, those experiences are even more real and clear than lucid earthly experiences! In general I tend to be careful about sharing the details of those experiences, because while they may seem very entertaining, the entertainment aspect can make them distracting for the ego.

Even so, I will share just three brief specific examples so that the reader may have additional points of reference regarding the types of experiences that have been personally impactful for me.

Once I was in a nonphysical environment that appeared in extreme detail to be the campus of Marietta College, where I had gone to school. My father was there. I knew it was actually him (not just a dream image or something), not only because of the nature of the environment and my own clear lucidity, but because of everything I could sense about him and his deeper nature. He was there with three of his dear nonphysical "friends," who waited for him while he met with me. I sensed their shared nature, their deep and ancient friendship, and how long he had known them. My father and I were conversing with great joy when I conveyed to him that I wanted to confirm the meeting was real when our bodies awoke. I firmly repeated to him, "You really have to remember! Focus on remembering! I'm going to call you in the morning and I want you to tell me where we are standing right now (on my college campus). Remember!" He said, "OK, I will!" Still I persisted, "No you won't, not unless you really, really focus on remembering!" I was very adamant that he remember. The next morning I called my father early in the morning. Despite having never tried anything like this with him before, I said simply, "So did you have any dreams last night?" and he quickly interrupted, saying, "Wait! I had a really strange dream that felt real and alien. I don't remember anything about it – but I just woke up thinking that I was definitely supposed to remember something. I just don't remember what that something was!" That was good enough for me!

Another time while my body was asleep I came across the soul of my wife's ex-boyfriend! Now, until this experience, in the physical world this person and I had not been fans of each other. But in this experience I saw his true nature – I saw who he really was, the living, unspeakably amazing soul who was "playing" his human character! It was so beautiful, so full of marvel and wonder, that I could not possibly express it here in words. His being was like an ocean – or perhaps a universe – of colors, energies, and vibrations! I sensed deeply that he and I actually shared an important part of our nature: an "ancient honor" that was dear to both of us. I also sensed how his nature overlapped with that of my wife's, in that they both were intrepid explorers of creativity. I sensed in a profound way what he was doing in his current life: how utterly "squashed" he felt from lack of love here, how he was like clay that had been smooshed incredibly thin by a car tire, and he was still attempting to manifest creatively from that place. I was overwhelmed by respect and love for him. Being certain of what I experienced, I physically called him the next day. Knowing now who he was, I risked saying directly, "I saw your soul last night!" And I continued to expound on what I had experienced at length. When I finished he said, "Well I have to say, if I was going to describe who I really am to somebody, that sounds pretty close to what I'd say." To this day, when I come across this man, I feel compelled to kneel to him out of respect.

As a third example, one time after meditating I suddenly saw hundreds of spheres of existence, which I knew were lifetimes I had experienced. I could see clearly that these other experiences were not those of "other people" – they were me! That is, the me that feels like me to me *was* those other people – the same "me" had those experiences. It was "me," just doing and being other things. I remember only snippets from some of them, but as an example, I remember being a woman who had given birth. As this woman, I then subsequently had the same fear I am now facing in this life. For me as her, the fear was a response to having experienced the pain of giving birth, and then being pregnant a second time and anticipating the pain again.

These experiences may seem interesting, but this book is about your experience, not mine. I share these experiences just to give you a little better sense of the path I am on, so that as you venture deeper into the book, you may feel that we're on this journey together.

Writing This Book

I am certainly no special person to be writing a book on spirituality. I have no special authority at all: Let my words speak for themselves. I am simply another deeply imperfect seeker, a single fellow spark of the great divine flame who is engaging this extreme human experience – like you! I have much fear and ego, I still suffer at times, and I have so very much to learn. And yet, I have come to know that there is no separate "I" in all of this. As strange as it may sound, there is no separate person named Christian. There is only "my" awareness – *the* awareness – having this amazing local human experience. I know in a tangible way now that my awareness actually transcends the human condition, and indeed this entire physical universe. I am overjoyed to proclaim that LOVE is the underlying power of all of existence, that there is nothing ever to fear! Love is the bedrock, the ultimate power, the undying foundation upon which all of this is built. *Your* life is built on it, too – and *you* are an incredibly important part of the great plan of love that is unfolding on Earth! I wish to remind you of that while you are here!

I feel it is important to write this book at this time because the collective consciousness of humanity is currently going through a great shift. I give thanks to our many friends in spirit who have guided me and helped me to bring this message into physical reality in this way and at this time.

I am writing this book as I feel called to share awareness of our greater nature, and to spread the message of fearlessness and love that is inherent to what we really are. We are not our human story! We transcend the human story. And yet, the human story is so very meaningful! I am not just the young man who collapsed in China from heat stroke. I am not just this body with its unique challenges. I can say with certainty that you, too, are far more than the confines of "your" story! We relate to each other by our human stories, but my intention with this book is to engage with you in a far deeper way.

I came to this side of the veil in part to write this book. I want to reach out to you – the real you! I seek to stir the parts of you that transcend your own

14

story, your own history, your own pain and circumstances. I want to remind you of the unspeakably vast love that exists for *you* specifically! And I want to encourage you as you are on *your* meaningful human journey so that you can seek to use this experience to its fullest while you are here!

A Special Thanks

I would like to sincerely give a special thanks to the physicist and consciousness explorer Tom Campbell, without whom this book would not have been written, and without whose work a great deal of fear would not have been processed. Also, I am thankful to borrow a few of Tom's terms in this book, as I find them most appropriate for what I am attempting to express. Thank you, "Uncle Tom"!

What This Book Is

This book is written with the intention of providing an encouraging mental framework for the spiritual seeker, so as to aid the reader in expanding his or her own personal understanding of the larger picture. I do not possess any special knowledge: I only seek to remind you of the truths that already reside deep within you. Your deeper being, beneath all the stories of your life, already knows! I wish to speak to that part of you, too. In fact, despite the intellectual nature of many of the ideas presented in this book, the content requires the reader to consider not just with the thinking mind but with his or her deeper being.

Every person is beautifully unique, and thus every individual's spiritual walk will also be beautifully unique! No one can hand "Truth" to you, not me or anyone else. Yet in what I personally know, I wish to support your unique personal journey and awareness of our very real greater nature by providing ideas and suggesting a structure for the human mind to approach aspects of reality which transcend the earthly context, especially those aspects that are often misunderstood by mankind at this time. I do this with the intention that you may then utilize whatever aligns with your experience and appeals to your reason, and discard the rest.

Part 1 of this book is a series of statements which attempt to succinctly describe "what is going on" with our existence on Earth in relation to the larger spiritual context. The intention is to suggest a concise framework of independent yet coexisting ideas for pursuing understanding of the larger reality and our place in that larger context. Part 1 is intentionally somewhat technical sounding (rather than narrative), so as to adhere to the goal of providing a concise series of statements as a framework. Throughout Part 1 are references to pertinent essays from Part 2 so that you may more deeply explore pertinent ideas as you wish. Those references appear in the following format after the period of a given pertinent sentence or paragraph: . (###)

Part 2 is a series of 160 short essays that speak to various important spiritual ideas. I have intentionally provided this content in short essay format because individual exploration often takes place in discrete steps or by "new idea" and not necessarily as a comprehensive intellectual endeavor. The Part 2 essays are organized by topic at the beginning of Part 2, and are also referenced beneath pertinent Part 3 Q&A topics headings.

Parts 1 and 2 are the primary body of the book, the contents of which are meant to be read independently and also meant to be considered as a whole.

Part 3 is an informal Q&A section where I attempt to speak to many common spiritual questions. I certainly have no special authority to try to answer the "big questions" that I have listed in this section! I do not have all the answers, and I also have no interest in telling anyone else what to think or how to live. I only wish to serve the higher currents of love that are at work by providing this information for consideration so that it might be helpful to somebody. Part 3 also contains some Part 2 essay references.

Part 4 is a short section containing simple ideas to consider as one pursues personal investigation of our higher natures. Part 4 also includes a suggested meditation exercise.

This book is not necessarily meant to be read front to back, but rather approached as the reader feels is best for them. This book is intentionally non-linear. Certain key concepts may be repeated many times, yet I feel this is important considering the depth of the current root assumptions about life on Earth that are being challenged.

It is my sincere hope that this book might aid you in your journey! The human experience can sometimes be very challenging, yet it is my hope that in reading these words and in sensing the intention within them, you will be encouraged in your own extremely meaningful walk through this physical world, and be reminded – at least in part – of who you really are!

Disclaimers

The Way Cannot be Named: An Ontological Disclaimer!

The Dao De Qing opens with the words: "The Dao that can be spoken of is not the true Dao. The name that can be named is not the true name."

As soon as we put ideas to reality, we are automatically incorrect about its full nature. As soon as we open our mouth and say something about what is, we are limiting it. As soon as we give reality a structure, we have reduced it to the structure we have named. Thus, nothing written in this book is the Truth. I can only write in the shadow of form, and then the mind of the reader can understand in the shadow of form. The greater reality of Being transcends all form, so no set of forms can fully speak to it. The thinking human intellect deals with forms, so the thinking human intellect cannot reach the full truth. Still, there is great value in pursuing intellectual understanding of both our local reality and the larger spiritual context! Our experience here is real, even though it is but a shadow of the far greater reality.

The joy of a loving touch, or the whisper of the wind, may speak more than any language can about higher truth. Art, poetry, and music can often convey more about our larger being than any words can. And yet, if I placed every great poem ever written into this book, and shared every beautiful piece of music and every art form ever created, they would not in total be able to hold even a small candle to the rich beauty of all that is within spirit. So how then can we with words? And yet words and ideas often have a most beautiful place, too – especially as perceived by the mind of the spirit who is genuinely seeking!

If the words of this book at any point seem intellectual or dry, please try to sense the deeper living joy that I am attempting to express through them!

I Am a Fool

I am a fool, and I know next to nothing. I say this honestly. While I may present ideas in this book in a definitive manner, I can say with certainty that in the context of the "Big Picture" I understand very little. I certainly do not have "all the answers," and I will not pretend to. The vastness of Creation is beyond imagining; the wisdom of Source is far beyond what any local mind can grasp. That includes mine, and yours too. Still, there is a lot that we can conceive of and master – and that process is indeed very meaningful and important!

Your Walk Is Your Own

No one can "hand" truth to you – it must be your own experience. This is because consciousness (your consciousness) itself is fundamental, not the limited objects that consciousness beholds, and not the limited ideas and discrete thoughts of the physically oriented mind. There are no ideas or beliefs that anyone can hand you that will be "the Truth." The Truth of Being surpasses and gives rise to all form. Your encounter with Truth must be your own personal experience – there is no other way.

Thus as you read the words of this book, I encourage you to try to evaluate not just with your thinking mind but with your deeper being. Examine and test these words through your experience itself, and allow your own experience and intuition to be your guide. You be the judge. If anything in this book is not helpful, please disregard it. If something rings true inside you, listen to that ring, follow it, and dare to investigate it, for in what is real there is nothing at all to fear.

You are responsible for – and free to choose – your own spiritual walk, your own life, and your own understanding. It is my simple hope that the words in this book will help you do that, even if in a small way.

Can All This Be Verified?

Yes! You do not have to take my word for anything in this book, and in fact you are encouraged not to. Please see Part 4 for some simple suggestions and a meditation exercise that may be helpful in your own investigative process.

"A true spiritual teacher does not have anything to teach in the conventional sense of the word, does not have anything to give or add to you, such as new information, beliefs, or rules of conduct. The only function of such a teacher is to help you remove that which separates you from the truth of who you already are and what you already know in the depth of your being. The spiritual teacher is there to uncover and reveal to you that dimension of the inner depth that is also peace."
– Eckhart Tolle

PART I – A REALITY MODEL
What is going on here?

I. CONSCIOUSNESS IS WHAT IS, AND CONSCIOUSNESS INTENDS

Consciousness is. Consciousness – also called awareness, or spirit, or life itself, but which cannot be identified by a word – is the living Beingness through which all experience occurs. Nothing occurs apart from consciousness. Everything exists as it is experienced by consciousness, through consciousness, within consciousness. (003) (155) Even intellectual modeling, like scientific theories or the contents of this book, only exist as a consciousness perceives them, and then interprets and works with them. (095)

Consciousness pre-exists. It just is. (099) Consciousness is the fundamental substrate of all existence. (150) It does not have a cause, a beginning, or an end.

Consciousness is the fundamental "substance" that exists, and the primary "action" that takes place is intent. (047) Consciousness "moves" in some way, and that movement causes occurrence within itself. Intent at the deepest levels of consciousness gives rise to reality systems.

II. THE SOUL AND THE WHOLE

Source, also called God, is sentient, purposeful, and unfathomably wise and loving. (037) (114)

The Whole of consciousness individuated Itself. We call those individuations souls. Each soul is indivisibly a part of the One, and yet is simultaneously a precious sovereign free-willed piece of the One. (056) (123) (152) There is no paradox in the simultaneous Oneness and individuation of the soul. (139) In the words of Rumi, *"You are not just a drop in the ocean, you are the mighty ocean in the drop."*

21

Through individuated pieces of Herself (Himself, or Itself), Source takes on numerous physical and nonphysical experiences, including experiences where She may veil Herself from Her own true nature so that She can have the experience of separate perspectives. (019) (065) (092) She does this for the purpose of the expansion of the joy and love of Beingness through Creation.

The soul is always full of the amazing life, power, vibrance, and profound abundance of Being. (015) (050) (110) (122) (144)

The soul contains many aspects of the self – different "personalities" or "characters" – that it has been and is, and yet it transcends them all. In other words, the human character is a small part of a much larger multidimensional self. The soul is the same "I" even when it engages the experience of being these different "personalities" or "characters," and they are each available to each other and inform each other. The self is unfathomably deep, and the individual can benefit greatly from personally exploring one's own depth of being.

Source vastly transcends the sum of its parts.

Source fully transcends all form, and yet is imminent within all form. Source fully transcends duality (a context where opposites and spectrums are experienced), and yet is imminent within duality.

From unfathomable wisdom and love, Source has established divine "laws" for how all of manifest Creation actualizes itself. (116) These laws form the foundation of all reality systems, and all activity takes place in accordance with them. The physical laws of our own universe are but a small subset of larger divine law that governs how all things operate.

III.   THE EXPANSION OF BEINGNESS THROUGH CREATION

22

Beingness is perfect as it is. And yet it chooses to actualize and expand itself through Creation (through manifestation of defined experience). (112) (141) (157) In the context of the whole creative process, at any given point the soul is only "so good" at expressing its true nature through a given context. (133) It develops its ability to do so through the integration of defined experience. (079) In that sense, it is imperfect. That imperfection is experienced as fear within a given constraint-set that has not yet been integrated. As Beingness integrates various experiences and develops its ability to express its true nature within a wide variety of contexts, its capacity for joyful expression increases. You, as a precious part of the Whole, are performing that important role right now, even as you read this book!

In order to participate in this Creative process, the Whole must apparently cease being the Whole and must operate from some specific experiential vantage point. (066) Depending on the reality system, that vantage point may include an experience of apparent separation, like we experience here on Earth. In other words, metaphorically speaking, the Whole must fall asleep to the fullness of what it really is, and have a dream of being something limited. (002) (008) Reality systems (universes) are like dreams within dreams within dreams, perspectives operating on a fractal scale of ever-increasing creative expression. Earth is just one dream – or rather, Earth is the shared dream experience of many millions of souls who are all a part of the One, which also experiences Earth from all perspectives. There are dream levels "above" our own in precedence (for example, astral levels or heavenly realms), or "below" our own (for instance, someone losing themselves while playing a video game in our world).

Images and forms are simply the tools and toys of creation. All manifest experience ultimately serves Life. (117) (121) (128)

Nothing is required of us at all. (009) (113) Simultaneously, we wish to expand our joy and creative power by participating in Creation, and we wish to "evolve" the quality of our being so we can more deeply experience and express love and joy in a variety of creative contexts. (130) The expansion of being that takes place is an enriching of the body of living consciousness such

23

that it can more fully express itself in a wide variety of reality systems, and more fully experience and actualize love and joy.

IV.   IT IS ALL ABOUT LOVE

In short, everything is about LOVE! (001) (126) In a sense, no further words are required! As reiterated by many thousands of near death experiencers (people who have technically died and have seen the other side and returned), and as taught by spiritual teachers throughout the centuries, we are here to give love, to receive love, to express and actualize love, to enjoy and share love, and to expand our capacity for love! (018) (027) (108) (131) Our entire human journey is ultimately performed in the name of love.

Love is our true nature, and we seek to express and expand that nature through our human context.

The entire experience of duality is a gift of love. (077) (117)

When we love the person next to us, we are impacting what is real. (004)

Love has the power to heal our world. (026) (084)

V.   WHY DO WE COME TO EARTH?

We come to Earth to have the experience of biological creaturehood. We come to Earth for the stark experience of "being" something specific. (075) (153)

We come to Earth so that our true everlasting nature may expand its capacity for creativity, joy, and love! (064)

The soul expands as its "experience vocabulary" expands. The soul adds to its potentials as it knows and works through experience. (079) That includes the knowing of duality. (077) The capacity of the soul to know, be, and understand some quality or aspect of duality expands as that quality or

24

aspect is applied within a context, and also as that quality's or aspect's opposite is actually experienced. The soul uses the experience of contrast as a creative tool. (128) The temporary dark is worth experientially knowing to expand the everlasting light. (083)

The soul also expands through choice making. (068) The soul seeks to express its true loving and joyful nature within a potentially challenging context. (071) The soul expands as it chooses *how* it meets the experience of limitation, and issues intent (makes choices) within that context. (032) Loving intent, which is reflective of the native unity of Being, supports personal and collective expansion, and is additive; fearful intent, which is reflective of the illusion of separation, is reductive or adds further layers of challenge (growth potential) for oneself or others. (149)

We also come for the purposes of serving one another and helping others fulfill their own individual or collective goals.

Physical incarnation allows us to intentionally put ourselves in a place where we are "forced" to deal with things that we otherwise may not have stayed to experience. (049)

In order to have the experience of creaturehood on Earth, we must accept the veil. The veil is a set of constraints in consciousness-space that temporarily but rigorously obscure our true nature so that we may have the full experience of being human. (002) (140) (148) The veil causes us to "forget" what we are, and generally limits our perception to the physical, so that we may "be" the human character. (008) (137) This is necessary primarily for two reasons. The first is because a significant part of the value of the human experience is in how the spirit chooses to operate and evolve through the very unique experience of separation that the earthly experience permits, and the veil permits that temporary experience of separation. The second is because if we fully remembered where we come from, it would be almost impossible to focus on and function in this dense and comparatively "low-vibration" physical universe. In fact, the longing to go Home would be unbearable.

25

Source so unconditionally loves us that It allows us to choose to forget that love for a time so that we can better truly know it forever! (005)

The entire soul does not incarnate – part of the self always remains Home. (085) The local personality portion of the self "contains" only a small portion of the entire self.

Earth is but a very, very tiny portion of All That Is. (070) Our universe is one of the most constraining types currently existing – but it serves an incredibly worthwhile purpose. Being unaware of that larger context can be a meaningful "part of the game," as the value of this experience often dwells in the "punch" of physical life. But underneath it all, unharmable true LOVE always exists, always presides. You are always totally OK; you are always completely taken care of.

VI.   WHAT IS THE PHYSICAL UNIVERSE?

The physical universe is an experience occurring within consciousness. (003) (008) (106) You are not "in" your body, your body is an experience happening within *you*. (124) (148) The physical universe is your experience of sensory data (sight, hearing, taste, touch, smell), perceptions, feelings, and thoughts. The physical universe exists in the contents of your local mind, and in the minds of all other participants.

When we ask what reality is, we tend to ask "what thing or things is reality?" because we assume that things – discrete matter and objects and ideas – are what is most real. (055) In fact, that which is most real transcends all the things, and gives rise to them. (072) (082) That is not just a philosophical idea but rather a tangible fundamental state of being that can actually be experienced and fully known. (062)

The content of the physical universe experience takes place in a consistent way per the "rule-set" of the physical reality. Our science is the investigation of that physical reality rule-set. (089)

26

Physical reality is not an objective material place, but is instead a real experience of a virtual environment taking place within the pre-existing consciousness of every participant. (132) Consciousness has been "folded and firmed" into the experience of the world and body. (134) The limitations of the body are an important part of that experience, but the body is not fundamental, just as the physical universe is not fundamental.

VII.   THE FRAMEWORK OF OUR LOCAL REALITY

We all come from a series of dimensions that "precede" our physical dimension. (113) Those "preceding" realities are generally thought-responsive. (154) Our physical reality manifests dependably in accordance with its rule-set as a result of individual and collective intention and thought form. (101) Thought form has a physical reality to it in higher systems, with its own type of momentum and density. Thought form is created and influenced by intent, thought, expectation, and belief. (109) (135)

Since consciousness is fundamental, change in consciousness-space precedes change in the physical world. (028) (087) Change in consciousness space (including change in the intent and mind of individuals) is valuable and important. (014) The individual's efforts to improve the quality of their intent towards love and to conquer fear are the active playing field for real change (see Tom Campbell's work). (026) (087) The name of the game is love, even in ways that may appear physically insignificant. Physical results naturally happen subsequent to a change in intent. (048) (059) (086) (146)

Distance and linear time are not fundamental. Linear time is a local experience of sequence taking place within "higher" systems. All of those experiences of time take place within the depths of Now, the ever-present moment. (103)

We are always connected to all other reality systems. We never truly leave the higher realms to come to be on Earth. Metaphorically, we sleep in Heaven to have the dream of Earth. (008) Generally speaking, the experience of the

27

higher realms is far more real, lucid, and magnificent than any earthly experience.

VIII.   THE PRISM OF THE HUMAN MIND

The physical universe is like a giant mirror provided to give us the opportunity to actually experience our beliefs, perceptions, and assumptions. (104) The contents of the human mind color the entire physical experience. (060)

Starting when we are children, the human perspective is formed from living within the experience of duality (the individual has little or no memory of his or her larger nature because of the veil, and thus may believe form to be everything). All ideas, objects, and sense data (the forms) are not fundamental, but while one is human they are experienced as real. The human mind then understands its entire world from the viewpoint of those forms that it bought into over the course of its local experience. (135)

But all interpretation is chosen. (057) (120) Consciousness places the meaning upon form. (022) The forms of our physical universe are neutral and do not possess inherent charge. Yet as beliefs are established, those beliefs become assumptions that appear to be fundamental characteristics of reality itself. Our deepest beliefs become invisible to us. (052) We then experience reality as exactly what it is like to be the one who has those beliefs, even if the beliefs are not consciously visible. (031) (105)

The physical universe is not strictly objective as it appears, but rather responds to, and changes as the result of, the intent and beliefs of the individual and the collective in accordance with the "rule-set" of our reality. (014) (086) Belief is not only a powerful lens that deeply colors the reality we see, it also affects how physical reality actualizes itself to us.

Fear and ignorance are the only obstacles to much more fully actualizing our true loving natures here on Earth. (151)

28

Regardless of the limited interpretation we are experiencing, all is always well in and through the foundation of Being from which it arises. (012) (050)

The physical experience does not need to be one of somber seriousness, but can be one of joy! (009) (061) (107) (127) (159)

IX. FEAR AND THE EGO

The ego is the part of the self that wishes to protect the self as the individual is having the alien experience of separation. The ego is not a separate thing, it is an internal structure that arises as a response to fear. The ego seeks to relieve the individual from fear by attempting to reclaim power that seems to have been lost (but in fact was never truly lost). The ego's main activities include establishing belief, claiming false power, and justifying the self. (038) (040) (052) (129)

Fear occurs when the soul engages an experience of form that it has not yet fully integrated. Fear reflects an opportunity for expansion. (111)

Fear occurs when the individual buys into perceptions that are not in alignment with the individual's fundamental true nature. (034) (084) (096) (143) The individual's true nature is immortal, powerful, free, deeply loved, and connected to everything. (016) (071) Fear can only occur when the individual's identity becomes "tied up" within the forms of the local experience (the illusion of separation). (051) (074) In other words, fear can only occur when the individual does not have conscious awareness of who he or she truly is.

Love, which is the truth, dispels all fear. (045) (158) Fear is not conquered by resisting reality or setting up divisions but by willingly experiencing reality exactly as it is. (010) (013) (033) (097) (148) Fear wanes or vanishes as the individual fully allows all experience, and as the individual experientially finds his or her true nature beneath the many stories of the local play of Earth. (156)

As fear is processed and overcome, love and joy naturally expand.

X. THE NATURE OF THE HUMAN EXPERIENCE

The human experience offers a unique opportunity for the spirit to make choices within a rich context.

The human experience is just one unique way in which the spirit may experience creaturehood. (079)

The human condition offers a unique opportunity to experience a specific set of biological limitations and a particular cognitive environment. (030) (088) (140) The only way for the spirit to actually know what it is like to be human is to be human; the only way for the spirit to experientially learn how to successfully exist through and express its true nature through being human is to be human. (137)

The human experience is heavily defined by the local physical body. Per the "rule-set" and constraints of the physical reality, the body's state colors all information experienced by the consciousness, and limits what the consciousness can do in the physical environment. Physical changes to the body can increase or decrease those limitations.

Our experience on Earth provides valuable feedback to help us experientially understand the quality of our intent. (033) (036) (142) Loving intent tends to yield a joyful experience (it is in alignment with our true nature); fearful intent tends to yield a negative experience (it is in alignment with the illusion of separation).

We never find complete satisfaction in the objects of the world, because what we really seek is the unity and wholeness that is native to our deeper being. (160) That wholeness is actually never absent, even when we are deeply "lost" within the thinking mind and within the forms and stories of human life. (093) We experience suffering when we associate with and "lose

ourselves" in the forms (thoughts, stories, beliefs, objects, feelings, etc.).
(074) But our very nature itself is always of love, joy, creativity, and freedom.

Even while we deeply experience separation on Earth, there is no true
separation. (065)

There is no such thing as privacy; all information is known and remains
accessible by spirit.

Death is the end of the physical experience and a lifting of the constraints
that consciousness bought into in order to be human. (053) Death is not the
end, but in fact is a wonderful transition to higher states of being. (006)
Metaphorically, death is like taking off a constraining space suit and
returning to the freedom of what one really is.

Health is our natural state of Being. Over time we always naturally return to
wholeness and health, even if physical death happens. (138) Oftentimes we
can encourage the healing process by locating and releasing our own barriers.
(024) (042) When Life can flow through us, healing can naturally occur.

XI.   INTENT VERSUS INTELLECT IN THE CONTEXT OF LOVE AND BEING

We come to wield loving intent. (115) Loving intent is not itself intellectual.
Love and fear can operate through an intellectual context, but intent itself is
deeper than the objects it works with, including both physical objects
(things) and intellectual objects (ideas or beliefs). (021) (040) (048) (073)
(125) Our deepest "being-level" motivation is what is important. (067) (074)

We come to Earth to execute and embody a quality of being. (078) We come
to *be* love! That can mean any number of ideas or actions. (027) (145) Love
includes a large number of qualities, including compassion, freedom,
vulnerability, responsibility, courage, humility, discernment, tenacity,
gentleness, strength, honesty, willingness, and caring. (010) (081) Love is
always about the other.

31

Human intellectual learning is generally limited to the objects and "rule-set" of the physical universe in which the human character resides. (046) (072) Since that physical system is not fundamental and is a subset of something larger in consciousness space, no object or set of objects in that physical system can fully speak to the Big Picture. (080) (082) (090) (098) It is not possible for the thinking human intellect, which relies on local system assumptions (like distance and linear time for instance), to fully intellectually conceive of the Big Picture. (102) (139) (147) However, the mind of the individual can know it personally when not operating within the forms and constraints of the physical, because the individual's consciousness is not separate from the Source, which contains all knowledge.

The "learning" that the spirit comes to do on Earth is not intellectual, it is experiential. It is a learning of the Being, by being. (137)

XII. HIGHER SPIRITUAL "NATURAL LAW" AND LOCAL "NATURAL LAW"

In the unfathomably vast wisdom and unconditional love of Source, Creation unfolds in accordance with divine laws, or what we may call "natural laws." (116) Just a few categories of the "natural laws" (or at least perceivable expressions of them), which are not separate but are interrelated, are only very briefly mentioned here:

The Laws of the Physical Universe
The laws of the natural physical world (including physics, biology, quantum mechanics, etc.) are one "layer" of natural law that governs how physical objects consistently behave in our local physical universe. The physical reality experience is transpiring because of processes that are occurring in higher dimensions, which are also in turn governed by "natural laws" of their own.

The Modifiability of the Physical Universe
The physical universe responds to the intentions, thoughts, and beliefs of the individual and the collective. Intent has the power to "nudge" the

32

probabilities of how physical reality unfolds. These processes do not conflict with the laws of the physical universe, but are a part of them.

The Law of Attraction

The law of attraction is the name we use for the phenomenon that energetically, and thus eventually also physically, we tend to experience what we resonate with, what we are focused on, or what we are intending. (059) (086) (135) This "vibrational attraction" occurs at the "being level" of the individual (true intention), not in the surface thoughts or ego stories. In our local physical experience, the law of attraction is helpful in part because it allows us to "get what we fear," which supports one of our universe's goals of allowing individuals to face and overcome their fears. Meanwhile distinction in higher systems is often not geographical but vibrational: similar beings or similar energies tend to group together.

Synchronicity

Synchronicity represents the natural flow of how events transpire when the spirit is "followed" ("permitted to flow freely") and greater intelligence can function naturally. (023) (159) Synchronicity happens naturally when we are "in the flow," which tends to happen when we follow where love guides us, when we follow our excitement, and when we practice non-resistance to the reality inside or apparently outside of us. The universe is always willing to work with us. (078)

Karma

We are fully responsible for every intent, thought, word, and action. (063) All choices yield a result for the individual. (094) This "energetic result" remains with the individual even past physical death. Love-based and fear-based choices yield a result that may lead to various heavenly or hellish experiences of form, whether on Earth, or in other reality systems, or in other incarnations. This "energetic accountability" is not a system of punishment but is rather energetic cause and effect and vibrational consistency for the sake of long-term being-level growth. This system is built on wisdom and unconditional love. This is true even as a given ego (a given "separate self") may suffer or reject a particular experience or circumstance. (083) (142)

In other words, we can't escape being what we actually are. And through "energetic logic," what we are guides us into future experiences. From the higher spiritual vantage point, we ourselves often choose to re-engage the "darkness" of what we have actually been, so as to evolve past it and expand in due measure.

XIII. THE SPIRITUAL "PATH" WHILE HUMAN

Spirituality is not about believing something or doing something, but about evolving one's consciousness and the nature of one's being towards love. (017) (040) (067) (078) (102) (125) (136) The doing comes after the being; intention precedes action. (028) (048) (146)

Spirituality is about one's relationship to the present moment. As that relationship becomes more genuine and less hampered by fear, one's experience of joy increases and one is able to be of greater service to others. (061) (145)

Spirituality is about finding exactly What Is. (044) (058) (070) (118) (134) Spirituality is not primarily a pursuit of any certain form, though we often do benefit from the utilization of form (belief systems, religion, spiritual practices, etc.). (062) (069)

True accomplishment is not a matter of achieving some physical end, but of the expansion and actualization of love. (004) (007) (025) (039) (043) (091) (131)

A spiritual person interacts more successfully with form. That is, an evolved individual is generally better able to wield a loving intent within various contexts of form, better able to utilize form for the expression of their deeper nature, and better able to use form for the betterment of others. An evolved individual's presence tends to be "net additive."

The state of the world is our responsibility – both collectively and individually. (063) (076) (094) (145) (146)

Meditation is a process by which the individual may move toward meeting the present moment as it actually exists unfettered beneath the associations with form. (015) (029) (041) Meditation is a process by which the individual may slow down their thought momentum sufficiently so as to be able to experientially know their deeper nature (allow their deeper nature to rise back up to them on its own). (011) (054) (150) Meditation is not truly an action or physical activity but a utilization of intent to meet the present moment for exactly what it is. (098)

Human society is currently largely ignorant of our real larger context, but the individual is never separate from our true source of knowing. (035) (046)

XIV.   YOU ARE LOVED!

You are profoundly, deeply loved! (056) You are loved, you *are* love, you love to receive love, you love to give love. (020) You are a creative, powerful, free being who has committed to all that this physical experience entails, and you do it all for joy, and freedom, and love. (100) You can never lose the love that Source has for you. (064) (068) (119) You are loved and celebrated not just by Source but by countless other beings who are your family and friends. Please remember that while you are here in the wilderness!

PART 2 – ESSAYS

Essays Organized by Theme

Love: 001, 018, 074, 108, 115, 119, 126, 149

Love as the healer: 045, 084

Healing through feeling: 024

Personal now (the individual's relationship with the present moment) to heal the world: 007, 014, 026, 028, 063, 076, 145, 146, 151, 159

The present moment as the point of power: 014, 026, 103, 156

Change in consciousness precedes change in the world: 014, 026, 028, 048, 059, 086, 087, 101, 146, 154

The small stuff is the big stuff: 027, 039, 094, 131

Challenge as a gift: 002, 013, 030, 032, 066, 077, 079, 083, 088, 111, 142, 156

Life as feedback: 017, 023, 033, 036, 042, 061, 071, 078, 079, 128, 142

Negative emotions as guideposts: 034, 083, 096, 104, 158

No enemies: 038, 049, 065, 084, 108, 121, 133, 140

Answer not in intellect: 021, 029, 041, 062, 070, 073, 075, 080, 118, 147

Truth beyond knowledge: 019, 037, 046, 062, 069, 082, 090, 098, 102, 132, 139, 157

Understanding as forms pointing to forms: 055, 058, 062, 072, 089, 139

Form vs. formless: 041, 075, 080, 105, 114, 118, 141, 150, 155

Seeking nonphysical answers while physical: 035, 044, 098, 150

Freedom from belief: 022, 040, 052, 057, 060, 069, 120, 125, 129, 136

Interpretation and belief appearing as characteristics of reality: 031, 071, 086, 135, 143, 154

Intent as the fundamental movement or "action" of consciousness: 047, 048, 067

Meditation: 008, 011, 015, 029, 044, 050, 054, 098, 150

Death: 006, 053

The power of vulnerability: 010, 081, 097, 121, 140

You are worthy and good: 016, 017, 020, 056, 064, 100, 110, 119, 133

You are always accepted: 068, 091

The importance of acceptance: 051, 084, 140, 148, 156

Playfulness over seriousness: 009, 061, 113, 127, 153, 159

Joy as native to consciousness: 071, 107, 138, 153, 158

You are already there: 085, 100, 113, 134, 155, 160

You (and we) cannot truly fail: 116, 117

Your true identity: 100, 106, 110, 122, 123, 124, 130, 144, 152

(001)

Love is the Answer

The great conscious awareness in which we have our being – that which we often call God – is also the Source of all form. That Source is unfathomably loving! Thus, the deepest root of all things – every single thing – is love. This can sometimes be extremely hard for us to see on Earth while our awareness is constrained to the experience of physical reality. Yet, no matter where we are, love is there!

When we totally let go of the form, and when we totally let go of all of our interpretations and beliefs, we immediately begin to move away from the confusion of form and toward the constant foundation of love that endures beneath every surface.

Love is our source and our nature. Love is the substance from which all experience is built. Love is our challenge, our desire, our unavoidable destination. Love is the answer!

(002)

The Allure of Vibrational Distance

As we exist in a nonphysical state prior to incarnation, our true nature is completely known to us. We fully know what we truly are: a boundless part of All That Is. The physical experience offers us the opportunity to fully experience a profoundly different "vibration." The experience of that new vibration permits the individual to engage and personally integrate a new level of being. And vibrations that are extremely dissimilar from our native state – those we might crudely call "low" vibrations – offer the greatest opportunity for expansion. In fact, the "distance" away that one can go is commensurate to the potential increase in capacity of the individual (if they can integrate that distance). Because the potential increase in the individual's capacity is commensurate to the distance, diving *way* in is incredibly enticing and desired. This is why so many souls choose significant challenges on Earth. The greater the challenge, the greater the opportunity.

Once we're here, though, we may be so dissatisfied that we even rage against reality itself. But that dissatisfaction and that rage are signs that the spirit is being engaged with an experience that it has not yet fully integrated, and are signs themselves that opportunity for real growth is present!

As all-powerful spirit, we actually *yearned* for the opportunity to experience such stark challenges! Now that we are here, now that "the rubber is meeting the road," we can recognize even in our perceived hardship that in fact we are being presented with a real opportunity. If you put aside your ego, let go of your fears and demands, and completely surrender to your experience of the present moment without any requirement or expectation, the deeper parts of you will always be ready to take you the next step towards the integration that you desired "so long ago." That integration may be an extremely intense process: You may have to face your deepest, darkest fears and actually feel your most poignant pains – but there is true healing and power available in doing so. It is often the very discomfort of our lives that finally pushes us to integrate the wonders of our depths! So we might as well choose to do so

40

when the darkness comes, and use the vibrational distance in the way it was intended. Nothing, ultimately, can change your true immortal nature – so embrace the adventure of the full experience of physical life while you are here!

(003)

Reality is an Experience

Our physical reality is not really a place – it is an experience. Consciousness beholds information and believes that experience to be an objective material reality, because the information is all that the local consciousness currently remembers, and the information occurs in a persistent and consistent manner. But that information, no matter how consistent, is not fundamental: It occurs primarily as an experience beheld by consciousness. Consciousness is always present for any reality to exist. In the case of our reality, consciousness does not arise *from* the physical reality (from a brain, for instance); rather, the physical reality and all the form within it only exists *as* an experience within that which *already* exists (consciousness).

This is an important distinction, because the vast majority of us are so deep into the "dream" of the physical universe that we have forgotten what is real. We typically believe that matter is what is most real. It is not. While we behold the shiny sense data of the physical universe, we forget to look deeply enough into the truer "substance" that is right beneath our noses: our own awareness. That awareness itself is a gateway to much greater forms of being than the one that you are experiencing as a human reading this essay! Your transcendent soul is ever present – it is You! – and it can be incredibly empowering to wake up to the fact that your awareness transcends all of the many subjective circumstances that you have convinced yourself are objectively real.

(004)

Impacting What Is Real

When you are impacting another person, you are impacting spirit, and spirit is real. Since spirit is real and enduring, by affecting another person's experience, you are "impressing upon" that which is real. You are having a real effect. This is in contrast to simply moving around the "props" of the physical simulation (the objects or forms) which are, generally speaking, local and transient.

The real spirit is interested in real impact. This is partly why from the perspective of the Big Picture, the success of our physical lives is not determined by our physical accomplishments or possessions, but rather by how much we were able to *love others*. Loving intention and interaction is successful in part because it furthers real change in the direction of our native state, which is unified and whole. That change is far more powerful than it may seem on the physical surface! In fact, since the spirit is multidimensional, by impacting another, you are *always* having an effect on multiple dimensions.

This is important to remember in a society that is obsessed with physical accomplishment, the allocation of objects, and the acquisition of temporary identities. Our society spends (we spend) a huge amount of energy focusing on the transient and pursuing the substanceless distractions of possession and identity. Yet we can remind ourselves of that distraction. We can remind ourselves of our inalienable power to make a true, lasting impact – by loving the person next to us! The genuine intention to love the person next to us, however we can, is all that is required to make an impact that lasts forever.

(005)

Unconditional Love to the Brink of Total Ignorance

You are so unconditionally loved by God that you are permitted to almost completely *forget* that you are unconditionally loved by God. In coming to Earth, somehow the truth of God's unconditional love that exists specifically for *you* has moved out of your waking awareness. Perhaps you have no recognition of it at all. Perhaps the concept of God's unconditional love has become simply an intellectual concept for you, as an aspect of faith. Or perhaps you have had tiny partial glimpses of it, through personal moments of surrender and dedication to the divine. In any case, the truth of the unconditional love that exists for each of us remains largely obscured while we are physical: painfully, persistently obscured.

Yet, being brought to the brink of total ignorance about how much love exists for you is an extremely important and necessary part of your purpose here. You could not have your adventures in physicality, with all of the opportunities for misperception and personal growth, if you actively recalled all of what you are! One of the primary purposes of physical life – growth of the spirit past fear and towards love – could not be accomplished with such recall.

But the love is still yours to remember. It is always yours to remember! Take some time, then, to simply sit in silence with yourself and the divine, and see if you can quietly feel even a glimmer of the real love that does exist for *you* (specifically you!), so that you may be encouraged. For you are what you are – which is a loved immortal spirit – even if you don't remember it. Even if you're so deep in your current personality that you cannot feel God's love – comprehend at least intellectually as much as you can that today, right now, you are indeed an incredibly adored, cherished, powerful, and irreplaceable portion of All That Is.

(006)

Death Is Not the End

From our physical perspective, death appears to be the end of the person. Our senses behold a body that is no longer animated by the spark of life, and we no longer can interact with the person in the ways that we know. What's more, we cannot typically see to the other side to have any certainty that the person continues on – so we linger with fear, doubt, and sorrow. To us on Earth, death seems merciless and final.

What has died, however, is not the person. What has died is the constraints they were bound to. The body and its crude limitations are shirked. The old coat is cast off and the spirit is set free!

Death is not the end. It is a beautiful new beginning! It is going home. It is a journey from the fog of the less real to the clarity of the more real. It is an awakening from the dream that we call physical life.

For those of us still dreaming, the absence of the person from the dream can bring us deep pain. And yet in a reality that is built upon loving consciousness, those who have passed from us are truly no more than a thought away. For unlike the body and its crude outcomes that are so temporary, the love between two people is real, and it cannot die. Love is never lost. Love transcends the binds of matter. Love supersedes muscle and bone. Love is the force of incalculable power that fuels Creation itself!

Thus, when someone we love experiences the death of their body, let us remember our love for them. Let us take consolation that we have not truly lost them, for they exist right now, not as less than they were, but in fact as much, much more.

45

(007)

Individual Choice Matters

Every day, every one of us is "casting votes" within consciousness space. Those votes matter. Every time one of us holds a thought or embraces an intention, both our reality and other reality systems are affected.

Most of us have been raised with the belief that the physical outcomes are what matter most. And since it often can seem like we have little power over those outcomes, we feel powerless.

We are not powerless. In fact, even if we are not consciously aware of it, we are connected to the Source of power itself, each and every hour of each and every day! We are creators ourselves! As participants who are deeply involved in this reality experience, we have largely forgotten that. But it doesn't change the fact that you and I are actually creating our world every day – not just with our hands, but with our consciousness itself.

Your individual choice to love the person next to you, matters. Your individual choice to face your fear, matters. Your decision to accept yourself, your decision to accept responsibility for this world that we live in, your decision to humbly accept the change that your own life has invited you to – matters. You do not need to move a mountain; you only need to genuinely work towards engaging your life with an intent that is more loving, open, and sincere! If you do that, you *are* changing the world.

Be encouraged in that power! Be encouraged that you are having a real impact, even if you cannot see it. For every choice that you make in the quiet of your heart is heard, and that is a power that will remain with you today, tomorrow, and every other day of your life, no matter the physical circumstances.

008

You Are Dreaming

Right now you are dreaming. You are having an experience in an apparently physical reality. You are receiving sensory data (sight, sound, touch, taste, smell) from an environment that seems external; your thoughts and feelings seem private; and you appear to be separate from those around you. While that's all a very real experience, it may be helpful to understand that it is also a fantastic illusion!

You signed up for the illusion. You made a choice to come and have this experience, to live in this reality for a time, with all of its rules and constraints. But you probably don't remember making that choice. You don't remember because that's part of the deal when you come here: You accept a kind of amnesia. It may sound all too convenient to explain away such incredible statements with "amnesia." But amnesia was a requirement, because this experience would be nearly impossible without it. In fact, this experience is *about* operating within some staggering constraints – including even, and especially, the constraint of not remembering all of what you really are.

Here in this reality, you experience yourself as – that is, you "are" – a human. You are male or female, young or old. You speak a language to communicate with those around you; you send symbols (words) to others who must interpret them in their own way and send symbols back to you. You get up in the morning, eat breakfast, do what you have to do during the day, and you use the toilet in the apparent privacy of the bathroom. You experience the pleasures and pains of the body. You have a name, a history, a list of things to do. You *are* somebody.

But in a far deeper sense, you are much, much more. You are an immortal being of conscious awareness. You are a spirit! You are unconstrained, unlimited, unharmable. You know on a deep level that you are an integral and fundamental part of the great all-comprising loving consciousness that

47

many call "God." You project your awareness into realities like this one to have the experience of *being* something within a special set of constraints, in order to grow your own being and participate in creation. Coming from God, the great foundational consciousness of unconditional love, at your core you also are profoundly loving, and you wish to expand and develop that capacity in yourself.

If these statements seem aloof and abstract, do not accept them! Rather, seek instead to simply discover for yourself if they are true or not. There are many ways to do so, and each is very personal and unique. But in general, meditation is a powerful first step: Gaining familiarity with your awareness as it exists beneath the thoughts and judgments is a window to actually experiencing glimmers of wakefulness. Don't take anyone's word for it – listen within!

009

Don't Take Life So Seriously – No One Makes It Out Alive

Creation is a phenomenon rooted in joy!

However, sometimes we do not experience physical life that way.

When we adopt the "veil" and become physical, we become bound to this reality's rule-set. That rule-set includes having a body and having to meet all its physical needs. We need things to protect us, shelter us, feed us. Since the objects needed to do so are so physically important to us for our survival and for our ability to live full lives, the control of objects – even by force – is constantly encouraged. The species that populate the Earth have evolved over millennia in this "kill or be killed" physical environment, constantly seeking to take from one another for their own survival. And in our own lives, there isn't a day that we don't experience the effects of that struggle, for even amongst our own kind we are constantly involved in a struggle for the control of limited resources (often in the form of money). Sometimes we are even involved in a struggle for survival itself.

That entire experience can lead us to take things very seriously. Indeed, just the concept of one's own body dying alone can seem like a very somber problem indeed!

From the perspective of immortal invincible spirit, the opportunity to experience such a messy, tough environment is a treasure. The decision to engage in such an experience is not done out of seriousness, but rather out of incredible excitement and joy! Every one of us knew the challenge we signed up for before we came. We knew that we were coming to a place where we would one day die. What joy we felt at the opportunity! For despite how serious the situation may appear on the unrelenting physical surface, such an experience is a most incredibly precious opportunity indeed!

That may sound untenable or perhaps even masochistic – but in fact, as creators it is *we* who have interpreted our experience here in that serious way. *We* have created this world and its perceptions. It can be very liberating to be reminded – if we dare – that none of our creation needs to be feared or taken too seriously!

In fact, there is nothing you absolutely "have" to do! If you feel there is, it is because you have chosen to buy into that belief for one reason or another. You may have bought into various beliefs and interpretations that lead you to feel that you "must" do this or that – and that is a valuable experience to have – but none of it is fundamental. Fundamentally you are free, joyful awareness. Fundamentally you cannot be harmed and you cannot die. Fundamentally you are more than all of the things in your mind, your life, and even your imagination. Fundamentally, you need nothing. Even if you die, it is not the end of the world – in fact, quite the opposite!

So kick back, relax, and enjoy the ride! Play the game of life with the carefree joy that is still yours deep beneath all the weight of your human identity. What's the worst that could happen?

(010)

The Power of Vulnerability

The ego is the portion of the mind that is devoted to defining reality in a way that will protect us. The ego protects us through presenting to us beliefs, justifications, and stories. We "buy into" those beliefs, justifications, and stories. Why? A primary reason is because we seek to avoid confronting the fears that those beliefs, justifications, and stories cover up. We withdraw ourselves from the *experience* of the darkness by building facades of light.

Sometimes when something threatens us, or our facade itself is threatened, we grip onto the facade even harder, even tighter, desperately demanding shelter within it. Sometimes the facade is all we've ever known.

The problem is not the facade itself. The problem is our unwillingness to face the darkness. If we let go of everything that is protecting us and simply surrender to experiencing the present moment in all of its gory glory, it will mean that we will have to be open and willing to *feel* everything. We call that willingness to feel "vulnerability."

Contrary to what our culture has taught, vulnerability is not a weakness. In fact, spiritually speaking, vulnerability is a profound strength! It is through the willingness to fully experience *all* of what we are, *all* of what we feel, *all* of what is around us and within us, that we can fully grow and mature in the way that God intended: toward Love. Love, the most powerful force in existence, is vulnerable.

It is OK, then, to relinquish your control. If you let go, the spirit will always be there to catch you! God is not a fairy tale or belief but a real, conscious force of profound love that dwells within and beneath every single thing in this universe – including you. That power is always on the other side of the fears and pains you may engage when you drop the facade and choose to be vulnerable, no matter how long those pains or fears may last, and no matter how long you may suffer the illusion of your own powerlessness.

51

(011)

Knowing Yourself

Really knowing yourself has nothing to do with whatever ideas are floating around in your mind. Fundamentally you are not your name, your body, your possessions, your affiliations, or your ideas. Rather than taking new ideas – even the ideas in this book – and adding them to your idea of who you are in order to define yourself, instead turn your attention toward full awareness of the Now. Even if you cannot sense it at this moment, your awareness itself – your consciousness – transcends the forms that it is currently beholding and identifying with.

Personally experiencing that is a matter of gently but consistently shifting your momentum of focus away from thoughts and judgments towards a quiet and full awareness of the present moment itself. We call that process "meditation." Yet, meditation is not an action; it is simply purposefully setting your alert intention toward being present in the current moment without judgment. In doing so, your awareness very gradually and naturally becomes less beholden to the "datastream" of the current physical reality. That may sound strange, but getting to know your true self is not a foreign activity. It is rather a subtle yet joyful movement toward that which is "most you" and most comfortable to you: Being aware is the most natural thing in the world! If you permit yourself to simply dwell with your awareness regularly, you will find that gaining familiarity with your true self is not only possible, it is one of the most rewarding and freeing pursuits available to you while you are here.

(012)

All Is Well

If all is not well, it is because you have interpreted that all is not well. Your evidence for all not being well may seem obvious to you. After all, it may appear clear that things in your life and world are not well. You may even feel disdain for those who don't see that things are "obviously" not well. How can anyone say "All is Well"?

In fact, consciousness places the interpretation and meaning. We come into the physical to experience the constraints of physical life, including the constraint of ignorance, which gives us the opportunity to interpret our experience from a very unique point of view. In response to our sense data, we "buy into" earthly interpretations, perceptions, and beliefs, and then have the resultant experiences that our interpretations, perceptions, and beliefs yield to us. That process of actually living through and working with our local interpretations, perceptions, and beliefs is what adds to Creation and is so meaningful to our soul.

At the fundamental level beyond all the interpretations, perceptions, and beliefs, the consciousness that exists is unharmable, and capable of nearly infinite creation! Its ability to have the *experience* of limitation is simply a part of its creative power. The brave soul that jumps in to experience the apparent darkness helps "All That Is" grow in its experience by providing profoundly valuable perspective. You are participating in that incredibly meaningful activity right now!

Beneath all the desires and drives, sickness and health, sight and sound, birth and death, ineffable Beingness exists deeply. From that fundamental state, it is totally and wholly apparent that All is Well, and always will be. That "All Is Well"-ness transcends and gives rise to everything else within it – including the temporary illusion of separation.

If you cannot sense that right now from your current state of awareness, don't worry – that's a part of the play of Earth! Allow yourself at least intellectually to consider that the pains and destruction that appear so unrelenting exist within something greater, something far more enduring. When you fearlessly listen quietly within, deep beneath all your own interpretations, perceptions, and beliefs, you will find that truth is always alive within you, too!

54

Pain Is an Experience Not to Be Feared

"There is no coming to consciousness without pain. People will do anything, no matter how absurd, in order to avoid facing their own Soul. One does not become enlightened by imagining figures of light, but by making the darkness conscious." – C.G. Jung

It is holy when you finally actually, actually choose to face your deepest pain with full commitment.

Pain cannot kill you. Pain may be profoundly challenging to experience at times, but your awareness cannot be harmed by it. Your body can and will die, but suffering will not obliterate your spirit. In fact, there is tremendous power to be gained by facing all of what you feel. Choose to accept all of your experience, including pain when it comes! Do not justify it away or tell yourself a story to temporarily ease its presence. Even when pain feels insurmountable and completely overwhelming, go *into* the storm. Even if you fear deeply that it will destroy you, plunge *into* the tsunami. Rather than being destroyed, you will come out far stronger on the other side.

When you make the journey into pain, do not judge the pain or its perceived causes. Rather, simply experience it and be present with the feeling itself. It is important that we feel our pain without any judgment at all. Often the stories we are telling ourselves about the pain only contribute to it, as they simply layer new negative self-perceptions on top of an original fear. The original fear root is available to be processed and truly healed if we are willing to actually feel our way through the branches (individual surface pains) one at a time as they surface. The Divine will always be there to guide and help us when we are truly willing to face our own darkness. To feel it is to heal it.

(014)

You Have the Power

Fundamentally what we are is conscious awareness. Fundamentally what we do is exercise intent by making choices. Put another way: The fundamental substance is consciousness; the fundamental force is intent. These statements are true no matter what reality system we are in and no matter how things may currently appear "outside" of us.

Consciousness may elect to participate in experiences that provide rich constraints in which difficult choices may be made. Physical reality is one of those meaningful constraint-sets.

Yet even here, because focus is a part of intent, focus itself is a creator of momentum. When we focus on a certain perception, that perception grows. Physical reality is meant to give us the opportunity to have the experience that our nurtured perceptions yield to us.

It is valuable to recognize this phenomenon because it allows us to take back our power. How? We can move away from perceiving the world as a place that happens "to" us, and gradually shift our perspective towards recognizing that in fact the power lies within us. This may seem like a big leap in such an immersive and challenging environment; indeed in this reality it can take time to institute substantive internal or external change. But we do have the power to change our momentum in every single "now" moment. "Now" is always the moment! We can choose *now* to focus on the good instead of the "bad." We can choose *now* to dwell on the love in the world, and not the fear.

We are not powerless to our circumstances, but are in fact powerful creators who are able even to commit ourselves to the temporary illusion of powerlessness. Despite the appearances, we always have the power to change the stage of the play.

56

If you have relinquished your power in your own mind, it is OK to take it back! Become familiar with how you are perceiving your experience. Choose to focus on the positive, even as you fully acknowledge and allow what you might have identified as the negative. Your awareness is at the root of all of it. Change the momentum of your experience by intentionally choosing what you focus on and how you decide to interpret what happens in your life. You as consciousness have that very real power – it's time to remember that you do!

(015)

The Treasures Within

We are taught to constantly focus outside of ourselves. We have things to do, places to go, bills to pay, appointments to keep, and people to interact with. We need to eat, sleep, walk, talk, and move. We think we are our physical bodies, and we perceive others as theirs. We even tend to believe quite firmly that what is most real is that which is outside of us that can be verified by others.

Yet through meditation one begins to get profound glimpses of a much larger truth: All that is taking place "outside" of us is in fact taking place "inside" of us!

You are not the objects of your experience that have held your attention for so long. (The objects of your experience include both your perceptions of physical objects and your thoughts and emotions). Rather, the objects of your experience are taking place within your awareness. The sense data that you experience even when others verify what is "outside" of you is also taking place within your awareness of it.

When you gently and gradually quiet your physically focused mind-self and you permit yourself to sink deeply into simply "What Is" in the present moment, you will eventually find without any effort that there are treasures within you that go beyond all the treasures of the physical world of form. How remarkable it is that such fantastic treasures go unnoticed by us while we are on Earth! Indeed, they often do. Yet, they do not have to. Take a few moments today to allow yourself to take even one gentle step towards actually dwelling quietly with your own awareness. If you can quiet your thought-momentum sufficiently, when you least expect it you may just sense the incalculable and unspeakably precious treasures that are, in fact, within *you*!

(016)

Original Sinlessness

We are fundamentally beings of freedom and love. We are not born into the world "sinful" – meaning in any way opposed to or separated from God. In fact we can never escape God, for that which we call God is our very root and nature, and nothing in all Creation exists apart from It/Her/Him. In fact, we have come into the world for the very purpose of making hard, messy choices within a set of constraints that permit us to experientially learn to operate lovingly within a hard, messy environment. We are *encouraged* to use free will, in order to grow and participate in Creation. God knows we are making choices. We are not punished for making choices, even if they harm others. Punishment is not needed: As countless thousands of near death experiences tell us, after our life we will inevitably experience a "life review" process in which we will come to understand and actually feel the full effect that *all* of our choices had on others; and with that full clarity, we will be able to judge ourselves. Also, importantly, God in His loving wisdom has set out certain "universal laws" of operation that naturally and inevitably guide each individual in growing toward love. The ability to make mistakes is a necessary part of that process.

Some may say that the sinful and narcissistic nature of man is evident. Yet narcissism is no more than a natural consequence of a yet undeveloped spirit seeking to make choices within challenging constraints. (And the constraints of existing as a human on Earth are very significant indeed!) Ego – the erection of self-protective justifications, beliefs, and identity – is no more than a great castle of illusion built by the individual to protect himself from facing his own fear. One who acts narcissistically is acting from ego and from fear. He does so because his spirit has not "grown up" enough yet to make the more loving or fearless choice within his current history and constraint set, not because he is inherently bad or separated from God in any way.

When my children are whining or fighting, I do not think, "what sinful, selfish people!" Rather, I see joyous and loving beings who are befuddled by

59

a situation. We as adults are not much different. Our ego structures and beliefs may be complex, well justified, and built high over a lifetime; but beneath it all, we, too, are beings of love and light!

Original sin, then, is a myth. The truth is original sinlessness – followed by very real conscious beings making very tough choices in a very real simulation called physical incarnation.

(017)

You Are Where You Are

You do not need to be hard on yourself for being where you are. Wherever you are, whatever you have become – you are at an OK place now, and the universe understands fully why you got to where you are. You made a lot of choices to get here – both those you remember and many you do not – and it is OK that you made those choices.

Simultaneously, oftentimes spiritual growth is only possible when we recognize where we have failed. In response to our fear and the negative self-perceptions that we have bought into over the course of our lifetimes, we commonly tell ourselves stories about why we are worthy or justified. In fact, we are already worthy and justified; none of the stories are required! Meanwhile, those stories often prevent us from seeing where, in fact, we could be more loving. We can become blind to where we need to grow when we think we are already grown up.

Being both totally OK with where you are and also simultaneously aware of your shortcomings requires a profound amount of both full self-love and humility. Self-love and humility are not opposites; we can and should develop both simultaneously. The path for doing so is a complex and personal journey that is not easily articulated. Yet wherever you are, allow yourself today to recognize it is OK that you are where you are, no matter the circumstances you may find yourself in. Accepting ourselves by accepting our circumstances and our part in those circumstances is a powerful step toward lasting peace.

(018)

You Need Love

Love is what you seek! You may not even consciously remember the love that you seek, but as it is native to your being, you seek it every day. God's love – however you may or may not identify it – is your substance, your life blood, your desire and drive. It is the place from which you've come and to which you will return. It is what you yearn for. It is your ultimate strength and your motivation. It is the purity of being that rests beneath all your interpretations. Love is the fountain of life from which you spring.

It is OK to acknowledge your deep, deep longing to truly be loved and accepted. Yet doing so may mean acknowledging to yourself how very much you have *not* received the love you have yearned for, because doing so would mean facing your deepest wounds and mistreatments. But that is OK! You do need love, and it is OK to turn into a sobbing wreck and surrender to the divine (however you may conceive of it)! It is even OK to be angry about how you feel. If you are truly open, you will find that the spirit is always there for you, and can take any "venting" that you might dish out. The love that exists specifically for *you* is very real, and it transcends all the pain you have suffered. You may feel abandoned and unloved at times, but in truth you never are.

Just as you need love, recognize that it is also the thing that everyone around you needs. We all need love! Yet we are so tangled by a lifetime of thoughts that we have become lost in the deep illusion of separation that is physical life. We turn to forms around us to fill the void – to substances, to entertainment, to possessions, to ideas. We have forgotten that we are searching for love. Those who are around *you* have forgotten.

You are here for a purpose. That purpose is to love! Be the reminder. The being who is next to you right now needs what you have to give. Shine God's love back into the world! For as you need it, give it!

(019)

The Author of Duality

All the experiences of individual perspective, and in fact all experiences of duality (duality meaning experiences of contrast like "up versus down," "hot versus cold," etc.), exist within the larger reality of consciousness that "contains" everything. All individual perspectives and all cause-and-effect events and choices that led to them are all "accounted for" within that great awareness. Absolutely everything is known and accounted for. And yet that great awareness is not simply a sum-total of individual perspectives, it is a potent living consciousness that far exceeds the sum of its parts.

From an individualized perspective within a dualistic universe such as ours, we simply cannot grasp what that means. God as the Author of duality is beyond it – so we cannot define all of Him from within it.

Stated differently, it is impossible to describe Source with the earthly dualistic intellect, such as the one you are using right now. Since form cannot describe the formless, God – the author of form – is beyond description.

Fortunately, however, the spirit of which we are primarily comprised does exist beyond duality. It is a part of God. Your earthly personality, steeped high in the experience of duality, may not remember it; but because your spirit is irrevocably a part of God, you do fundamentally transcend the duality, just like God does.

It is OK, then, when you wish, to let every single thing in your life go: to relinquish your death-grip on forms, responsibilities, and ideas and simply allow yourself to be fully present, exposed, and surrendered to the current moment. God, the great Author, is always there.

(020)

You Deserve Freedom

You deserve freedom. You deserve love. You deserve admiration, adoration, and respect. These statements are true! And yet, on a deep level, you may not accept them. If you're like the majority on Earth right now, you have established a system of beliefs and justifications to convince yourself that you are worthy, when in fact, you already are.

You've been conditioned to do this by society, or family culture, or perhaps by religious beliefs. You may believe you are a good and worthy person when you perform the right tasks, or go to church, or act a certain way, or believe a certain thing, or maybe even when you pay your bills on time.

But the fact of the matter is: You are an awesome, precious consciousness that is a part of All That Is. You are *intrinsically* worthy, a creation and fragment of God. You don't need any earthly words, actions, or justifications to establish your worthiness.

Except when you believe you do. Except when you interpret your reality within a system you've bought into that says you do. Except when you meet the constraints of physical reality with fear, and respond by setting up a system of action to justify yourself to yourself.

Loving brother or sister, please be gently reminded: It is certainly OK to embrace your own worthiness. I am not speaking about the empty worthiness we convince ourselves of when the ego tells us a story. Ultimately there is nothing to be found there. Rather, I am speaking about the inherent, intrinsic worthiness of your Being.

Within that context please also be gently reminded that it is certainly OK to question your beliefs – including those that make you feel less than worthy. It is certainly OK to change interpretations that cause you or others pain. It is certainly OK to evaluate even the most cherished of what you perceive to be your "core understandings." Even your "first principles," or the basic "truths" you establish for yourself by which you understand reality itself, can – and sometimes should – be up for interpretation. You are worthy of doing even that. You are fundamentally free enough to do even that. No one can take that ability from you – though you can quite easily take it from yourself.

This reality is an experience simulation, built so that your awareness can truly experience what it is like when you "buy in" to certain beliefs and then make free-willed choices based on those beliefs. Yet recognize that free will choice is at the center of the game: You get to choose how you will see this world! And the world will respond to your choices.

So as you make your choices about how you will see the world, just remember: You do deserve freedom! And if you bravely let yourself have it, truly, you will!

(021)

Love Is More Important Than Knowledge

One of the main jobs of the ego is to try to prove one's worth to one's self. For much of my own life, I justified my worth to myself, at least in part, by establishing intellectual capability. I learned facts and skills. I grew my knowledge of various subjects and learned a foreign language. I earned a near-perfect GPA in college, worked hard to excel in my career, and became "the best" I could be at various activities. Eventually I had a long list of intellectual accomplishments to present to myself to prove my worth to myself. It worked for a while.

Eventually I made a profound personal discovery: In the Big Picture, intellectual accomplishments are largely unimportant! Sure, they have some effect in the physical – and of course there is in fact certain spiritual value to my having achieved them. But in the Big Picture – from the view of the larger reality that supersedes the entire environment and "rule-set" of this physical reality – my local knowledge, skills, and abilities actually mean little. They are not the reason why I am here.

I found that what is important is, in fact, intent. What is important is striving to have the truest quality of intent – meaning genuinely loving intent – in all the choices that I make. Put crudely but succinctly: Love is more important than knowledge.

You and I are living in a "virtual" reality that is, metaphorically, like a giant video game. Our world is an experience constructed within consciousness. When the human body dies, the character's body dies, but we do not. That's OK because fundamentally we don't need the skills, or the body.

What we do take with us, rather than the character's skills, is our own increased ability to actually play the game with higher-quality intent (intent that is more loving and less fearful). We learn how to actually *be* more loving and less fearful. Every time we play, we tend to get a little better at seeing past the illusions and making loving choices. Every time we play, we conquer some fear. As we integrate experience, we evolve.

Our knowledge does not survive in its current limited form, nor does it need to. However our wisdom, our genuine love – that survives forever!

022

Belief Is Not Fundamental

God does not require you to believe anything. He/She/It is All That Is – the profoundly loving conscious foundation of reality that has given you the opportunity to make choices, including the choices about what you believe. You are not punished for making the wrong choices or for believing one thing or the other. Countless reports from the other side (NDEs) reiterate this.

Love, on the other hand, is paramount to our reason for being here. We do always inevitably experience the results of our choices – whether they be loving or unloving. The true nature of our intent is never hidden from God. We often tell ourselves that we have loving reasons for doing things, but often our motivation is rooted in fear rather than love.

Being able to successfully navigate this phenomenon sometimes requires taking a hard look at what we believe. This is because belief often arises out of the need of the ego to protect the individual (or group) from their fears: fear of the unknown, fear of powerlessness, fear of worthlessness, fear of death. It is not *always* the case that belief is a tool of the ego: Indeed, we are currently creatures of form, and so we often require form (symbols, specific ideas, religious frameworks) to somehow understand or pursue the divine. Beliefs can be profoundly valuable – and oftentimes necessary – to many who seek to rise above the brutal nature of our world, to grow spiritually, and to seek God. Beliefs can be used to orient or motivate a person in loving action. But belief itself is not the "active ingredient." The active ingredient is the quality and direction of one's deepest intent: whether it be motivated out of genuine love, or selfish fear; whether it is pointed toward the other and to the whole, or to self. Intent transcends context but actualizes through it. When one seeks God truly, God *always* responds, regardless of the physical metaphor or form used by the individual. The consciousness is primary; the symbols used by it are secondary.

It is very important to recognize that many are not ready to question their beliefs down to their foundations. That is totally acceptable! Re-establishing a lifetime's worldview can be an incredibly personally destructive process, and many simply do not need such a radical belief-overhaul to successfully express love or pursue their relationship with the divine (whatever they call it). Do not try to push over someone's apple cart with new ideas when they are not ready – rather, respect and uphold each person's place and beliefs. The spirit will always work with each individual as they are ready, and the individual will always eventually utilize their actual experience to grow in their own way.

Others, however, can benefit greatly by permitting themselves to examine the nature of their beliefs so as to discard that which does not serve love, and so as to better pursue their own "next steps" on their genuine spiritual walk. Indeed, at this time in history, this is happening right now all over our world! Oftentimes the individual and the group both are greatly benefited by releasing old fear-based thought systems that include ideas such as condemnation, group favoritism, shame, and sin. Such ideas are, in fact, completely OK to release when one is ready – because in the very real larger context, belief itself is not fundamental. Genuine Love, however – that is the stuff universes are made of!

023

Following Life's Natural Dynamic

There is a natural way that events tend to unfold. From the highest orders of magnitude to the lowest, life follows similar patterns of development at every level. Seasons, cycles of birth and death, cycles of development from low complexity to high complexity: Patterns emerge and repeat under the ultimate direction of the universal laws that God has laid out in Her incredibly deep wisdom.

Those laws include feedback mechanisms both "outside" of us and "within" us. When we listen to those mechanisms, we live life more smoothly. When we resist those mechanisms, we experience struggle and difficulty. Oftentimes we choose the latter, and we do so with great effort and resolve! We do this because we think we know what will be best for us. We deeply trust the intellect to lead us toward the situation that we believe, for one or many reasons, will be optimal.

In fact, we are far more than our limited human intelligence, and the knowledge and wisdom of the spirit from which we come is far greater than that of our earthly intellect. Spirit has a much better vantage point.

Furthermore, the universal laws established per the wisdom of the Whole are ultimately perfect in their operation – and so, properly and honestly interpreted, they can be trusted.

Thus when making decisions in our own lives, it can be beneficial to recognize the "place" of the intellect – and instead try to listen to what life itself is telling us. We can always listen from the "being level" and turn to spirit for guidance. Oftentimes in silence and genuine humble surrender, the divine will indeed reach out to us. But even if we cannot hear it, we can still look at the "currents" in our lives for guidance. Which way is the current flowing? It might be easier to recognize than you may think: God's way is the way of love, stresslessness, creativity, understanding, forgiveness, acceptance, and joy!

(024)

Healing Trauma Through Feeling

We are integrators of experience. Here in the physical we have experiences (receive sense data), interpret the experiences (attach thoughts, meaning, and judgments to the data received), and then react to our own interpretation (even if we've forgotten it's our own interpretation). Through that process we grow as "successful integrators of experience."

Some experiences are more challenging than others. In general, this physical reality offers to us uniquely challenging constraints: The fact that this reality around us "stays firm" and appears to not yield when it pushes on us makes the "force" of the circumstances we face very strong. As the consciousness seeks to integrate such a challenging circumstance-set, the stress of the experience can potentially enable profound spiritual growth.

Alternatively, it can also potentially stress the individual to a "breaking point." Psychological trauma cases are examples of where a personality has been "forced" to experience a constraint-set and resulting interpretations that are too severe to handle in its current form. Often the consciousness "buries" the experience somewhere so that it does not have to fully confront what it felt as a result of the experience.

Yet in the long run the consciousness always seeks to integrate – always seeks to "assimilate" experiences and their interpretations – into its own "big picture" of knowing. For trauma sufferers, the old fears, "unanswered whys," negative self-perceptions, and pains may continue to come up time and time again – often very disruptively – in the effort to be "processed" (achieve integration). I myself have experienced this, and it can be unspeakably painful and challenging.

But ultimately and eventually, *any* experience *can* be fully processed and healed. However, in order to do so, we must be humble enough to admit our many weaknesses and negative self-perceptions, and we also must be brave

72

Part 2 – Essays

enough to be willing to fully *feel what we feel in the now*. We must actually feel our feelings in the present moment, as they come up, no matter what they are, without judgment! Healing always takes place in the now; our power is always in the present moment.

You can always decide *now* to face and feel your old wounds – especially during the precious opportunities when those negative feelings have risen to the surface for you to feel. It can take years, decades, even lifetimes to heal certain old wounds – but when you truly commit to undertaking that process, the powers of the higher realms themselves come to your aid!

(025)

Respect in a Capitalist World

In our modern society, others tend to respect us when we succeed in making money. Our system of capitalism holds up as successful those who can earn and spend material wealth. Indeed the word "successful" itself typically means "financially capable."

The entire capitalist system of our society exists within a reality of constraints. Limited physical resources are required for survival. We have evolved within a stark "kill or be killed" environment in which stealing food from someone else meant survival and the success of one's self and one's progeny. Our capitalist system is a more sophisticated version of the same process of controlling resources. As the current system pushes most individuals to work hard in order to acquire the resources they want and need, total physical output is relatively great (relative to living in the wild), and thus many can physically survive and enjoy material comforts that they otherwise might not have had. However, it is still a system of force and aggression. It may be a largely invisible force, but the lives of billions are very heavily influenced by this system's power over physical resources.

Yet success in the larger reality has very little to do with material success. Indeed, we are not even physical beings, but beings of conscious awareness who can take many forms! Our success is not derived from the material possessions or even the bodily survival of any of the avatars that we play. Ownership of physical objects and the power to allocate physical resources are almost totally insignificant in the Big Picture.

True success goes much deeper, to matters of the being: to selflessness, to the conquering of fear, to creativity, to love. As we spiritually grow we should take note of this, so that we might gently redirect what we value in our earthly lives. As we all do this, we will begin to respect each other for what matters – for Love – and not primarily for our ability to control the allocation of a bunch of transient physical objects.

74

(026)

Healing a World of Broken Systems

We live in a world of imperfect human systems. The political systems, economic systems, legal systems, and nationalist systems all end up failing countless individuals in myriad ways. One fundamental reason: Our systems are primarily driven by self-interest rather than love. Most human systems are built to protect one's self or one's group at the expense of other individuals or other groups. Capitalism is a clear example of this: It is a system that capitalizes on selfish motivation to produce economic output. It generates tremendous activity – but the motivation of the activity is often selfish rather than loving.

Love supports the optimal way that individuals can interact and support one another; selfishness does not.

Because the fundamental motivation is not optimal, the human systems themselves can never function in optimal support of the experience of their participants. The systems themselves are not the problem: The quality of our intent is the problem. The answer to the world's problems is not a new leader, new laws, or even a new financial system. The answer is love.

Love means full individual accountability and commitment to act with loving intent (intent that supports others over the self) in *all* things – even (and especially) in how one deals with one's own weaknesses, fears, and needs.

While the universal application of loving intent would heal the world, it has also proven to be the very hardest thing for us to do. In fact, as a species we have a pretty long and dark history of how we have neglected one another, the animals on our planet, and the planet itself. But learning how to actually embody loving intent in such a constraining environment is not something easily mastered by any given individual, let alone a few billion of us! Indeed, the mastery of selfless loving intent is not something that typically can be

75

experientially learned even in several lifetimes! Fortunately, all of us are beyond time, and have been graciously given all the time in the world to really grow up and get it right.

It is important to recognize that our opportunity to grow up is happening *right now*. Our power to change the world is right now – by actively working on the quality of our intent towards being more loving with whomever is around us and by confronting our own fear and ego, today. Every one of us needs to own the responsibility. Every one of us can take a hard look at where we have been selfish and can strive to put others above ourselves. That step *is* a step toward healing the entire world! *You are* an incredibly important piece of the solution. You do have the power to advance the entire world one step closer to love by the choices you make! So the next time you turn on the news and see something challenging happening in the world, instead of worrying about it, look to yourself to take just one step toward grace and love. The power to heal the world exists – through your love, right now!

The Small Stuff Is the Big Stuff

In near death experiences it is often reported that the most prized and celebrated accomplishments of our lives are moments motivated by love. The smallest of actions, when motivated by concern for another with no thought of personal reward, are the greatest triumphs. Accomplishments that society may deem successful are not necessarily seen by spirit as important at all.

Yet often we go through our lives thinking that our success is rooted in material prosperity, social status, or physical impact. We celebrate CEOs, politicians, surgeons, and actors. We hope to be "successful," too.

The entire realm of the physical is subordinate to the realm of the spirit. You are in both right now – you're just focused on the physical, which is the one that will pass away. In the realm of the spirit, where you will always exist, love is what matters. The physical will pass away; love will never pass away. The physical dirt or money that you moved around will not last; the spirit that you moved through love will last forever.

Recognize today, then, that your true success resides not in your great physical achievements but in the small matters: in making selfless choices, in helping others in small ways, in facing your own failings in simple quiet moments. Great spiritual work is done even when nothing is seen in the physical world. Follow where your spirit leads, and embrace the wonderful treasures that are the smallest decisions – for indeed in the Big Picture, even though we cannot see it, the small stuff is the big stuff!

Change Through Action Versus Change Through Consciousness

Often when we wish to "make change" in the world we perform tasks that seem pertinent but may in fact not be very effective. For instance, perhaps we care about a local cause, so we join a committee or fill some leadership role to support it, only to find that instead of effecting great change, we spend much time and energy bogged down in procedure or politics. Or perhaps we are sick and wish to be healed, so we go see a doctor – when in fact the doctor may have limited understanding of what could actually help us. While our actions are of course always meaningful to some degree within the Big Picture, in the physical arena sometimes our allocation of time and activity may actually be pretty inefficient at effecting change. This is a natural part of living within a system of very limiting constraints.

It is important to recognize, however, that the very real all-powerful Source of our entire reality itself is always present. In a fundamental sense, the power of physical action is crude and paltry in comparison to the power of the spirit, and the power of the spirit is mobilized by intent. Intent is deep at the root of all events. The entire rule-set of this experience on Earth – this experience that *seems* physical – has arisen from higher divine intent, which we are connected to.

We are connected to the Source of the most awesome changes possible! And as pieces of that Source, within our own consciousness itself *always* lie the keys to unfolding a new reality around us. Rather than some abstract idea, and despite how it might appear on the surface, this is a real and practical engine for change. In fact, it is the primary and most powerful one.

Yet collectively, in consciousness space, we have "dug this reality deep." There is a humongous precedent, a monumental amount of vibrational history, that has set us to where we are, both in how our physical world has evolved and also in how the human psyche typically expresses itself. But we can change it. We, individually and collectively, have the power to bring the light of the higher realms into this reality frame.

How do we do this? The answer is complex, highly personal, and not expressible in language. But here are five ideas for consideration:

First, we relinquish old ideas that make us fearful or powerless and embrace the power that is inherent to us. For even as we do so in mind-space, we automatically begin to do so in the world.

Second, we change our focus toward celebrating the light instead of accepting and feeding the negative systems and ideas of our world.

Third, we accept responsibility for exactly who we are and what the world is.

Fourth, we recognize that how we see the world is primarily a reflection of *us* – not a statement about how the world actually is.

And fifth, we work on ourselves to conquer our own fears, to bring forth our own love, so that the world shines back to us the love that *we* really are. Real change comes through love – for when the spirit loves, the physical solution naturally unfolds.

(029)

The Jungle of Confusion

We live in a jungle of confusion. The veil of amnesia and the illusion of separation cause a profound state of "limited information" in which each individual must use limited data to decide what is true. Seven billion people on Earth, and each has his or her own perspective. Most think they generally have the world figured out, and many spend an incredible amount of energy trying to tell each other what to think. Advertising, religion, social media: All add to the cacophony of individual and group messages to other individuals and groups. As technology proliferates, the volume of the jungle increases.

Yet, so very much of it is confusion, because none of the messages sent in metaphor or word can successfully communicate the full scope or deeper truth of What Is. Forms (words or ideas) cannot fully describe that which is beyond them.

Since conscious awareness is fundamental, the *only* way that the individual can encounter deeper truth is by personal experience. Striving to experience deeper truth is a very individual and unique process that certainly cannot be articulated in words to you by someone else. But one important channel *can* be identified: the unadulterated experience of the Now (rather than the consideration of some idea). The more one is able to be fully present with one's entire actual experience of the present moment, the better one will become at being able to see past the deep construct of one's own thoughts, judgments, and beliefs. The more one is able to see past those thoughts, judgments, and beliefs and simply experience the Now itself, the closer one will be to *allowing* one's self to be touched by glimmers of the ineffable truth which transcends all the metaphors of the world.

The sounds of the jungle can be very distracting; but fortunately, nothing can thwart your free-will ability to choose to focus inward to the silence, rather than outward to the noise.

80

(030)

The Hard Class

From the other side, the spirit actually excites at the prospect of having to deal with such constraints as we experience here in the physical. When we're here, though, the incredible challenges of our lives often seem insurmountable and crushing.

And yet, the spirit does transcend them!

Thus we can approach our deepest challenges with an understanding that we can in fact rise above (and through!) that which seems to thwart us, no matter what it is. We can embrace our difficult experiences and use them as the counter-pressure they were meant to be. Metaphorically, we are on the weight bench – so we might as well lift the weights!

Doing so is a process not just of intellectual willingness but of a deep commitment to have the intent to actually embrace our current experience, whatever it may be. We must be willing to feel. We must be willing to be honest with ourselves. We must be willing to be fully present. We must be willing to face our fears. We must be willing to remove the blame from others and the outside world, and instead accept responsibility for our own state of being. We must choose to experience what we are experiencing. In doing so, we may find that physical life is not just a challenge; instead, it is an amazing and precious opportunity for peace, love, and joy!

(031)

Embracing Personal Reality

Our deepest personal beliefs that are fueling our experience don't appear to be beliefs at all. Instead they appear to be obvious observations about *how reality is*. When it appears obvious to us (while physical) that reality is "a certain way," that is often our own belief about it. And that belief about it is significantly contributing to the nature of our own personal experience, both in how we interpret what we experience and also in how reality itself physically manifests our experience to us.

In fact, this physical reality is neutral, and we are each imposing our own meaning upon it. For the soul, this is a critical aspect of why the physical experience is so valuable: It permits us to experience and expand our deepest powers of interpretation.

And yet, let us not confuse the current experience of personal reality with a lack of an absolute reality. Indeed, absolute reality exists! That absolute reality contains and greatly transcends the personal reality. It's just that living a personal reality in the physical *necessitates* that our perspective temporarily not include the perspective of the larger reality.

In other words, we are here for the full experience of "being human." Thus while we are here we should fully embrace our current personal experience with all its confusions and limitations, for there are great treasures available to us when we do so!

At the same time, we can also always relinquish ourselves and choose to surrender – even by a few steps – back into the ever-present and much greater reality of the love of God. For even as you embrace the experience of personal reality, you are never, ever outside of the transcendent larger reality of Source's love. Existence itself at its root is creative joy, even as in its creativity it has chosen to exercise its power to transcend personal darkness.

82

(032)

Accepting Your Physical Path

We who are physical are blessed with the opportunity to be physical. Near death experiencers and other sources from Spirit remind us that we, the physically incarnated, are particularly blessed! It is also said that there are many more spirits who wish to have the opportunity to make it *into* this reality than there are those of us who are already here. It is ironic, then, that so many of us here seem to want out!

Having the opportunity to walk the challenging path of physical life is a tremendous gift. Being physical is not primarily a walk of trial or judgment or sorrow. Being physical is having the precious opportunity to love when it is sorely needed, to grow through and shine in the face of challenges that may seem insurmountable, to participate in and experience Creation in an extreme way.

Thus instead of resisting your path, permit yourself to let go and accept the beauty of the messiness. Whatever is happening in your life, recognize your power to view it how you wish, or to drop your judgments altogether. Are you able to look past your own judgments and see with the ever-wondrous eyes of your spirit? Are you able to sense the profound opportunity in the challenge?

If so, recognize that your challenges are, in fact, gifts! As gifts, you might as well accept them while you are here! For when you accept your challenges and surrender to your own experience, rather than to your ideas about it, you will find the fruits of the spirit are ever available to you. True power and freedom lie in acceptance.

(033)

The Erosion of the Ego

The unrelenting weather of "What Is" will always eventually erode the ego. That is, reality itself is built in such a way that, over time, each conscious participant will naturally work their way through their fears to greater states of freedom, creativity, and love. That process may take a long time or a short time, but the duration of time required is not hugely relevant: Space-time itself is an invention.

The quality of your experience speaks to you about "how you are doing." If your personal experience is one of peace and joy, you are following the natural way. If your personal experience is one of stress, pain, and suffering, in many cases you are experiencing the counter-pressure necessary for you to grow. Anxiety, negative emotions, and stress are symptoms of having bought into perceptions or beliefs that are contrary to your true nature. Regardless of how much you believe the limited story you are telling yourself, and regardless of how much you blame others, you cannot escape the feedback that is your own personal experience.

The story of the ego is sometimes one that is not easily challenged, especially in the context of such a constraining universe as this one. But over time, that story does inevitably get challenged: Beliefs that don't seem right ask to be challenged; or self-doubt that leads to pain demands to be challenged; or our possessions and accomplishments do not ultimately satisfy us; or hurtful action leads to retaliation against us; or we fail to find fulfillment when our intentions are primarily selfish. Useful feedback abounds in our lives, if we are humble enough to listen.

Allow yourself, then, to acknowledge, and consciously play along with, the game of life! When your experience is positive, allow yourself to be fully present with it and thrive in it. When negative feedback arrives into your experience, allow it to reveal to you what needs to be healed. Pain can be a useful warning. Remain alert to the feedback and be honest with yourself

84

regarding what it is telling you. Be willing to be shown. When your own stories are challenged, allow them to be. The erosion of the ego will happen one way or the other – this universe that you are committed to is made to facilitate it – so you might as well play along! When you do, and you surrender your deep need for control, you will find true freedom is waiting for you.

(034)

Following Your Fears

Any time we consider perceptions that are not in alignment with the fundamental truth, we feel a negative emotional response. Thus negative emotions can be used as a tool to locate what untrue perceptions we are holding onto. If you feel fear when you consider an idea or belief, then follow that fear. See if you can identify what negative self-perception or negative interpretation about reality itself may exist in you as a result of the idea or belief.

When we enter this world, we adopt the constraints that come along with being human. Chief among those constraints is a constraint on our knowledge: We no longer have access to the knowledge of the larger reality systems to which we intrinsically belong. This means that when we consider ideas as humans, we do so from a place of artificial ignorance. The state of *not* knowing permits us – provokes us, even – to consider possibilities that are frightening to us, and thus gives us the opportunity to experience firsthand a new perspective that would otherwise be impossible for the all-knowing spirit. Sometimes that new perspective we are entertaining is one that is contrary to our true natures; and when that happens, we experience a negative emotional response.

For instance, regarding one of our most prevalent fears, if you consider the idea "what if there is no afterlife and I die for real?" and you feel fear or resistance as a response, go find out why. Follow the sensations sufficiently and see if you can discover what negative self-perception or negative state about reality itself that belief would mean. If you consider the possibility that no afterlife exists and you are simply destroyed at death, then the resulting self-perception you may be entertaining is one of powerlessness, or nonexistence.

86

But in fact, the spirit is never powerless and cannot not exist. Consciousness can only temporarily buy into those perceptions, and experience the result; it cannot actually fundamentally be powerless or lifeless.

Nevertheless, in our example of the question "what if there is no afterlife?", it's likely that in fact you don't actually know right now if there is an afterlife or not. Note that the state of not knowing itself does not cause discomfort: It is the resulting *negative interpretation* we quietly entertain that triggers our fears.

Our fears are meant to be explored. No matter how deep they go, the sensations that come with them cannot harm us. In fact, those negative sensations are valuable guideposts that lead us to discover the untrue perceptions that we have adopted during our human experience!

Permit yourself, then, to actually welcome your negative emotions as the fear-messengers that they are. Following where they may lead often requires great humility, persistence, and courage, but the pursuit is incredibly worthwhile. Find out what negative self-perceptions or negative perceptions about reality you are buying into. When you find those negative perceptions, spend time with them and with the resulting negative emotions they cause you to feel. Let them rant and rave, hear them out in the now. Feel them. Rather than listening to the *story* you have spun around them over a lifetime, just allow your awareness to be with the sensations themselves, without judgment. The light of your awareness is powerful: Its mere presence, backed by the power of your intent to actually experience your emotions for what they are and to let go of your control, will naturally melt the illusions. With sufficient humility and bravery, it is possible to peek through the ego-structures of our lives sufficiently to see that in fact, everything negative is an illusion; only light and love are fundamental!

(035)

Society's Misunderstanding

In the context of the larger reality around us, our society currently has a lot of things wrong:

- We are taught that possessions will make us happy, when in truth they will not.
- We believe that matter is the most real thing there is, when in truth it is not.
- We believe that the Earth and the outer space that we can see is all there is, when in truth they are not.
- We believe that God is judgmental and "angerable," when in truth He is not; or alternatively we believe God doesn't exist, when in truth that which we crudely call "God" is more real than everything we know.
- We are taught that we are harshly judged for our mistakes, when in truth all things are understood.
- We are taught that we are only worthy if we do or achieve certain things, when in truth we are fundamentally worthy.
- We believe that we are unloved, when in truth we are profoundly loved, cherished, and adored.
- We are taught that humans are the only beings "with a soul," when in truth we are not.
- We are taught to fear the dangers of the world, when in truth there is nothing to fear.
- We are taught that we have no power to change the world, when in fact we are incredibly powerful.
- We fear that death is the end, when in truth it is a fantastic beginning.

With so much misunderstanding "out there," it is no wonder that clarity often eludes us. And yet, your greatest source for knowing is not external: Your own experience, your own intuition, your own knowing, your own

88

inner connection to Spirit will whisper answers to you when society's constant messages fail you. God is always speaking to you in one way or another, if you are humble enough to listen. Listen within openly, and with pure loving intention, and you will find that a light is always available to lead you through the almost ubiquitous misunderstanding of this apparently physical world!

The Gold Mine of Your Experience

Your experience is what it is for a reason. You cannot escape the nature of your experience – because what you are experiencing is always *exactly* an accurate experience in any given moment, based on the many natural laws that Source in Its incredibly loving wisdom has laid out. Thus the nature of your experience *itself* contains precious keys to your own development and your own life. This includes "negative" experience, which actually contains rich messages for us, if we are willing to listen.

In order to properly excavate the gold mine of your experience, you need to surrender to it. Surrender to your experience itself, rather than to your ideas about it. You have to be willing to actually feel whatever arises, to fully dwell in the present moment with whatever it is presently offering you, and to do so without any intellectual judgment whatsoever. The more you do that, the more you will be able to see the contents of your intellectual mind – and the resultant emotions – for what they really are.

The Ineffable Nature of God

The wonder of "That Which Is" is far beyond any description. The creative power of the spirit is beyond imagining. The beauty of Creation is vastly beyond that which can be quantified. The Love of God is more beautiful and desirable and perfect than anything we have ever articulated in any form in this entire universe!

All things, including everything we've ever considered or felt or experienced as humans in the sum of human history, is but an infinitesimal speck in the grandeur that is God. God's nature is totally ineffable, undefinable, and sublime!

How then as humans of such limited intellects can we believe that we can define "All That Is" in our petty language? How can we announce that we have grasped the truth while we are here? How can our rituals, our metaphors, our forms and understandings, our symbols, books, names, identities, beliefs, or stories ever capture the truth? How can our fleshy brains, our failing bodies, our limited minds, our imperfect organizations and systems ever profess to have the truth?

No word, song, voice, symbol, person, place, story, or any other form in all of Creation will ever be able to quantify the great, awesome, awe-inspiring, limitless, boundless, perfect nature of God!

91

(038)

Relinquishing Judgment

Judgment pervades our society. We constantly label, categorize, and place blame. When something that we deem "bad" happens, we quickly seek to identify who is at fault. The ego is deeply attached to the idea that there are enemies somewhere out in the world.

But in truth there is no enemy. There is never truly an enemy.

All of us are integrally spiritually connected to one another. We may be currently entertaining the deep illusion of separation, but nevertheless fundamentally we are all individuated facets of the same Great Spirit. How can there ever be an enemy when the other is always a part of us?

Those among us who are acting hurtfully are simply doing so out of ignorance caused by being on this side of the veil: ignorance of their own undiminishable power; ignorance of their inherent worthiness; ignorance of the unspeakable love that exists for them! Everyone who acts hurtfully is suffering themselves, for lack of love has prompted them to act out of fear. Can you forgive your brother and sister who is suffering, as you have? Can you forgive them for being afraid?

Relinquish your need to place blame or to be on the "side of right." For the sense of empowerment one may gain in doing so is only a false illusion set up by the ego. It is fake security. The ego may proclaim, "I now have power over the situation because I have identified the cause of my duress," or "I now affirm that I am good and justified because of the group I belong to," or any other personal justification of power – but such proclamations are illusions. Like all illusions of the ego, they are created to give us a false sense of comfort, which we often embrace wholeheartedly rather than facing our fears and feeling our discomforts.

You do not need the securities of the ego, including the security that judgment seems to provide. The truth stands firm and strong, always: You are loved, you are cherished, you are divine – and so is the person next to you! That truth, when actually recognized, is far more comforting than the false comfort that any egoic judgment can provide!

Physical Versus Spiritual Accomplishment

The primary thing we are accomplishing is not anything external, like producing, consuming, amassing wealth, or creating something physical. The primary thing we are accomplishing is in consciousness space: the development of the quality of our intent toward love, the addition to creativity and to ideas, the broadening of awareness that occurs as one has experiences and makes choices. *We* are the substance of what is happening in reality; the things we see around us are not. We can turn materials into finished goods, build a thousand cities, direct resources by spending money for decades and centuries: None of that has any meaning except through the experience of, and resulting evolving nature of, those doing it and those affected by it. When the Earth has passed – and pass it will – the objects we moved around effortfully will matter very little. However, our experience, our love – that will be incredibly precious and eternally enduring!

You and I will exist past the death of our bodies. We will exist after the roads have crumbled to dust, the skyscrapers have fallen low, and the languages of the Earth are no longer spoken. Someday, eventually, all the things we have built will be gone – but *you* will remain.

Should we then, while we are here, spend our energies primarily on physical production and acquisition? Or should we instead work towards building up that which will never pass? Are not the treasures of the spirit worth far more than any possession? For wisdom endures! Joy lifts up all of Creation! Creativity adds to What Is in an eternal way! The growth of the spirit cannot ever be lost, and love never, ever dies or diminishes.

Work, then, for love! Work to conquer your fear, to fully face whatever your experience may be. Work to create. Work to add to the experience of those around you. Work to serve, to humble yourself, to make the world better for someone else. Work to expand your understanding, your perspective, your willingness. Work to surrender. Work to face yourself and be the best you can be. Work to allow the love of the divine to flow through you. And know that your "work" is not work at all – it is the gentle calling of your spirit to be the loving being that you are at your core, wherever you are. Let go of all concern, follow the quiet asking of your spirit, and know that "all is well." For *you* are the brave one who has decided to come here, not to accomplish the transient ends of the physical but to add to yourself, to love, and to Creation!

(040)

Faith Transcends Belief

In the context of your belief system, especially a religious one, if you are feeling doubt it is a sign that your reason is compelling you to explore. It is OK to follow your reason. "Big Truth" is not make believe and does not require your belief to exist. (Only your ego requires things to be a certain way.)

If you genuinely seek truth, you will look fearlessly into your own history and experience and your own reaction to it all. If you look close enough, you will see that your beliefs have deeply colored and created your experience. In addition, if you consistently take the time to explore deeply into the present moment, beyond your thoughts and judgments, into your awareness itself, you will find that your awareness is fundamental to every experience you have had, while your intellectual justifications and beliefs are not. "You" have (your awareness has) persisted and endured, while the thoughts and forms that you have entertained have come and gone. You are not the thoughts.

Faith, then, is not about simply finding an idea and holding on to it with tenacity. Faith is setting your deepest intent in the "right direction" – which is toward Love and God (no matter what you call it or don't call it). The words *Love* and *God* attempt to encompass many aspects of truth that vastly transcend all human language; but we might say they include actually setting your intention toward: fearlessness, personal responsibility, active relationship with your Source, peace, acceptance, humility, surrender, joy, creativity, being fully present in the current moment, and striving to put the needs of others before yourself.

Genuinely pursuing all of that is both much more challenging and much more rewarding than tenaciously holding on to any human intellectual dogma, creed, book, name, or idea! God vastly transcends the forms you may identify Her by anyway, so your selection of the form itself is not critical.

96

That being said, admittedly we are physical beings living in dualism – so the form or belief pursued *can* in fact be extremely meaningful and important! Religion often serves this extremely meaningful purpose. But when you are ready it can also be liberating to realize that the form or belief itself is not the "active ingredient." Spirit – which we might also call "life" or "awareness" – is the thing that is real; and the "active ingredient" is the mobilization of that spirit – including *your* spirit – by intent! Intent transcends the forms of your mind, even as it works through those forms.

You *can* at any moment let your faith transcend belief!

When you glance upon truth, there is no doubt: You know it in a way that resonates perfectly with the true goodness in your soul. This is because at their deepest root all things – including you – always exist within harmony, love, and perfect beingness. If you feel conflict, resistance, pressure, or fear, in that moment you are not operating from a place of higher truth. And that's OK! You, as a part of the Creative process, utilize your experience of duality and contrast to expand and create. Nonetheless, *your* personal decision in any and every given moment to choose loving intent versus fearful intent is truly important! It is the very reason this reality exists – to give you that opportunity to choose love and to conquer fear! Faith, then, is always striving for the divine however you may personally identify it. Faith is choosing to embody pure loving selfless intent. Faith is *allowing* the greater truth and mighty river of Source's ever-present love to flow through you in whatever your circumstances, regardless of the forms involved!

(041)

Thinking as Distinguished from Being

When you are *thinking*, you are lost in a dream of form. When you are *being*, you just "are": No distinctions are necessary, and all possibilities actually exist.

The intent to dwell "in the now" is often referred to as being "present." Being present is like looking at a sunset and fully experiencing its beauty in the moment: You are simply being present with the experience, rather than quantifying or judging the experience with thought. The sunset admirer does not begin to think "the sunset should be more pink," for as soon as she does, she is no longer experiencing the sunset but is instead judging it. God often speaks to us far more clearly in simple presence than in thoughts and judgments.

If you slow down the momentum of your thoughts and go far enough into the present moment and allow yourself to completely surrender to it without judgment, you will find that rather than nothing being there, everything is there. You will find your awareness exists beyond the boundaries of your body, and that you can experience your being that transcends your entire physical identity and all of its thoughts and judgments. The only things that separate you from that native transcendence are the thoughts, judgments, and beliefs that *you* have decided to cling to and formalize over a lifetime.

This present moment, this very moment right now, the great depths of your own being are available to you. While the momentum of your thoughts and judgments may be great, and may seem to keep you far from being fully aware, recognize that at any time you can take one step away from the thoughts and toward awareness of the present moment itself. Who you really are is much bigger than who you may think you are right now, and it is completely OK to explore that!

98

(042)

Your Pain Wants to Be Heard

When pain shows up at your door, let it in. You do not need to fear it. It is not necessary to open your door and go looking for pain to let in, nor is it necessary to be excited that pain has showed up at your door. But when it shows up – open the door, let it walk in, and be with it. Let it be your guest. Listen to the story it wants to tell you. Be a good nonjudgmental listener. When pain has shared all that it meant to express, being empty of anything else to say, it will leave happily, often to never return.

Survival Is Not Your Goal

Your goal for being here is not to survive. In fact, your body won't survive. Your goal is to shine joyfully as your true self, to bring the light of love into this experience, to grow toward genuine love, to process your fears, and to add to creation by being the real you. You are here to be genuine and to exercise true loving intent in common moments wherever you are, not to protect yourself at the cost of others.

In this context, financial success is not enough. Fitting in and being comfortable is not enough. Achieving stability in a world where the normal way of doing so is by primarily thinking of yourself and not those around you, is not enough.

It is enough to simply be. It is enough to put another before yourself in whatever small way is available to you in the present moment. It is enough to create something, even if no one else will see it. It is enough to have fun! It is enough to follow the calling of your spirit, even if you abandon comfort.

The universe is built in a spirit of playfulness, joy, and pure creativity. Thus, while your body here won't last, you might as well enjoy the rigorous environment of this physical universe and use it in a way that satisfies your soul!

Spirituality: The Search for What Is Real

True spirituality is the dwelling in what is real. It is not primarily adherence to ideas in the mind. This is an important distinction because as beings living in duality we commonly feel that truth is to be found within certain ideas, and not others. Yet all ideas and all form exist within the One Thing That Is, or what we sometimes call "God" or "Source." Source transcends all the ideas and forms. And at the most fundamental level, Source is the most real thing there is. Spiritual truth, then, *ultimately* does not need to be taken on faith: We are talking about something that is actually real. In fact, it is far more real than that which we commonly experience day-to-day. Because it is real, we have absolutely nothing to fear in honestly searching for what is real and in exploring what *we* feel is real.

Many people find it terrifying, however, to explore what they feel is real, because they *believe* that the world is a terrible place or that life is terrible. Indeed, they have much evidence to convince them of this "fact." In fact, this reality will always give us evidence to support what we believe. This occurs because what is fundamentally true is not our beliefs themselves but our *awareness* itself. Nothing is ever believed, conceived, or experienced without our own awareness of it. And thus in order to actually discover what is real, we must be willing to truly and deeply explore the most challenging thing there is to explore: ourselves.

Spiritual growth can occur when one commits to the honest pursuit of *what is real in one's self*. Doing so, however, takes considerable personal courage, because it means one must be willing to feel what one actually feels and face what one actually is. It is far, far easier to place the blame on certain ideas or to cling to long-held beliefs for safety, than it is to drop the charade of the ego and allow one's self to actually experience everything – including the experience of uncertainty about what is real.

But the whole charade of the ego is ultimately an illusion. It is not real, except that we have made it to be.

Truth, on the other hand, will stand up to scrutiny, because It Is. But since the truth transcends the human mind, the human mind alone cannot fully discern it! Because consciousness transcends the objects of the mind that it beholds, the window to true discernment is a deep familiarity with that which is more real than one's mind: one's awareness itself. This is why meditation is such a valuable tool: It is simply exploring "what actually is" by dwelling fully in the present moment, instead of being lost in the many thoughts of the illusory mind.

(045)

Shining Through the Shadow

All experiences of darkness are temporary manifestations that occur as a result of experiencing non-native separation, or lack of love. Love is our native state: complete, perfect, and whole. When we agree to become physical, we do so knowing that we are agreeing to participate within a set of constraints wherein the native love that exists for us will be temporarily obscured. We do this, in part, because how else could "What Is" *know* what it is, other than to actually experience what it is not?

The constraint-set that we have adopted permits us to actually experience the ability to make hard and meaningful choices, even under duress, within a context. Physical life is the context.

The very natural result of making choices in obscurity, however, is what we often call "negative" experience. We experience the effects of selfishness and greed. We experience misunderstanding, judgment, and violence. We experience pain as we are misunderstood, as we are mistreated, and as we even buy into misperceptions about what we really are! We are hurt ourselves, and we often retain that hurt and then pass it to others: person to person, parent to child, we perpetuate the pain that is in us by operating out of our pain. All of that pain is rooted in fear-based choice making – choice making that naturally occurs within the context of being obscured from the complete and total love, power, joy, and acceptance that is our native state.

So then how do we heal this cycle? *Love!* The solution is to love the individual who is experiencing obscurity – in effect, to seek to remove the obscurity by reminding the individual of the greater truth that always exists beneath the surface: that he or she is wonderful, accepted, taken care of, adored, powerful, free, and worthy! For ultimately we are accepted, we are adored, and God's Love is always, always available to us – it's just that we have undertaken an experience wherein we have forgotten it.

103

Love is the ultimate healing power in the universe. It is the expression of the wholeness and unity that is native to what we truly are. It is what we yearn for, and what others here so desperately need. We are called to be beacons of love while in this place, to personally express the divine love that exists for us *to each other*. That is our mission while we are on our walk in the physical.

Know that regardless of the fact that you are having an experience in a place where love often appears to be obscured, you can never truly be separated from the incredible love that exists *specifically for you*. Be assured that one day you *will* return to the loving foundation of your existence, and you *will* be healed fully by that love. However, we do not need to wait until the end of our time in the physical to experience healing! In fact, we are here in this place to take a shot at seeing how *we* can do under these challenging constraints in the name of love for each other! Since the love of God is often not immediately apparent here, *we* have the precious opportunity to actually shine that light to each other!

(046)

Acknowledging Human Ignorance

The process of attempting to establish an intellectual framework to understand one's reality is, in itself, natural and healthy. However, as we seek to intellectually gain control so as to allay our fears, in our clamoring for answers we often collectively or individually institute assumptions and beliefs *as if* they were knowledge. Since the dawn of our history, ignorant man has ever concocted ideas about how reality works, and then declared those ideas to be truth.

As we evolve, we will need to be humble enough to recognize how very little we truly understand. The old stories we've been telling ourselves – even the old stories about physical matter being what is "most real" – will need to be deeply examined and then put aside as necessary in the honest pursuit of truth. We will need to recognize the limitations of our materialist science, which will not be able to answer the Big Picture questions from within the physical. We will need to be bold, humble, and brave enough to confront what is within us, so that we may truly grow our understanding of both the "internal" and "external" worlds, and more consistently bring the truer nature of love into this reality.

That can't be done, however, until human ignorance is recognized for what it is. Being ignorant is not a vice. But claiming knowledge where there is none is a hindrance. Human knowledge currently is extremely limited. Sure, we understand a lot more about the physical rule-set of this reality than we did a few hundred years ago. But our understanding about reality itself, about our place in not only the cosmos but within the greater dimensions in which we exist – in that regard, as Tom Campbell once so eloquently put it, we barely have even one foot out of the cave!

105

(047)

You Can't Trick Your Intent

Your most fundamental power, the one that exists beyond all of the boundaries of realities, is your intent. Your intent is a force that always belongs to you. The context in which you are able to make choices may change drastically: Your constraints may change, your environment may change, your body or your knowledge or your circumstances may change; but your power to choose and to wield intent always remains. The effects may not be obvious, depending on what reality rule-set you are participating in, but your intent always has an effect of some kind.

Interestingly, though, what we are actually intending is not always obvious to us. This is because the portion of ourselves we call the "ego-mind" has often buried our true intent deep beneath a complex pile of beliefs, judgments, and justifications. We are often not ready to examine the true nature of ourselves, because we are full of fear: fear of the unknown, fear of pain, fear of negative perceptions that we have consciously or unconsciously bought into along our walk in the physical. And because our true nature is currently obscured, many times we believe we are making choices from one motivation, when in fact our true motivation is something quite different. Many times we believe we are motivated by love, when in fact we are motivated by fear.

No matter what your mind says, you cannot ever trick your intent. Your intent is always exactly what it is. It is a fundamental force. Your intent is *you* – it is the very deepest ultimate "what and why" of your motivations and choices, the reason and movement of your spirit. It is not the choices themselves. It is not necessarily the intellectual reason you can produce for why you are making the choices.

We are here on Earth to develop the *quality* of our intent by being something within a context. We are here to actually experience what it is like to live in a world where billions of conscious participants exercise their intent

106

within a shared environment, and to grow in a real way toward becoming beings who genuinely make choices out of love rather than fear.

Since that is why we are here, it is very beneficial for us to take time to genuinely search for what our intent really is. Doing so takes remarkable courage, but for the individual who is ready to accept responsibility, face their fears, and truly serve others, the universe itself will respond.

(048)

Intent Versus Action

From the divine perspective, what is important is not necessarily what we do but why we do it. Our deepest intent is what matters. And our deepest intent is always totally unobscured and plainly obvious to the spirit. In fact, every intent we've ever held and every action we've ever taken in our entire lives is clearly remembered by the Whole. When our lives are reviewed after their completion, what is applauded is not necessarily what we did but when we truly acted from selflessness and love. Genuine unconditionally loving intent is the key, not necessarily the actions themselves.

But loving intent *will* lead to loving action. Intention causes action. Personally mobilized action cannot take place without intention.

When we pass we will be fully aware of the full impact that we had on everyone we ever affected in our entire lives. That impact will include the many effects that our physical actions had on others. But furthermore, our impact far surpasses even the effects of our actions: Our intent *itself* – our love *itself* – has a tone that rings out through Creation! We are communicating with and "nudging" this reality and each other with "who we *really* are" every day, and that is also a significant part of the impact we have while we are here! In that sense also, intention *is* action.

Be brave, then, while you are here, not only to discern the many effects of your actions but also the quality of your intent. For what you really are, the love or fear that you really carry, has far more impact than you can see with your physical eyes!

108

(049)

You Can Trust Reality

You can trust reality, and you can trust it completely. The reason you can trust reality is that absolutely nothing takes place outside of the "natural laws" established by Source, and those laws have all been established from a place of incredible wisdom and love.

The ego typically has serious trouble with this. It thinks, "How can I trust reality when it is so dangerous? Reality is cold, merciless, unrelenting. Reality has cruel people in it. Reality is unfair. Reality is full to the brim with suffering!" And thus the idea of actually trusting reality seems impossible.

Reality was built for Source by Source, so that you – as a part of Source – could experience exactly all that you are experiencing now in your life. Reality is not some ship adrift out at sea ready to sink unattended, or some happenstance, or some forgotten creation – it is perpetually and indefinitely and completely within the loving Source that created it. You are, too, even if you are not consciously aware of that fact.

How can such a loving Source permit us to be in a place where we may experience so much lack of love? You are so loved by Source that you have been given the opportunity to temporarily forget that you are unconditionally loved, so that you might actually experience real contrast and thereby better experientially understand what that love truly is, forever. You have been given the gift of the opportunity to "play real life," the gift of being able to make meaningful choices and to experience the results, the gift of being able to live as someone experiencing defined perspectives – and this physical reality is simply the stage. Its purpose is being fulfilled, and that purpose is ultimately meaningful and loving.

All the laws that govern the workings of the world do so for the ultimate purposes of Source, which are all motivated by love – which means ultimately for our benefit! For instance, even the most horrendous pain can

109

be a profoundly valuable experience in the grand scheme. As we learn to trust reality for what it is, it can better work with us to further the grander divine awareness-expanding intentions that often elude our limited human minds.

Recognize also that the entire stage of reality takes place within your awareness of it. It is not an independent external thing, as it appears on the surface – it is something that takes place within your awareness. The reality you experience, then, is a reflection of what *you* are, right now. Allow it to function as the mirror it is meant to be! You can trust the mirror – it is only faithfully serving the purpose of reflecting back to you what you believe about it.

Happiness Is Always Within You

You do not need any single thing to be happy! Happiness is available in every moment at the root of experience. Yet we experience unhappiness. We experience unhappiness because we buy into thoughts and beliefs about the current situation or stimulus that are counter to our true nature. It is never the situation or stimulus itself that causes us to be unhappy – it is our interpretation of the situation or stimulus that causes us to be unhappy.

The Source of happiness is within you! You do not need to go anywhere to find it. You do not need to do anything or attain anything to *be what you are*. What you are is conscious awareness – and awareness, when it hasn't been obscured by getting lost in the illusion of form, is profoundly blissful! When you allow yourself to let go and just be what you truly are, joy is always the natural experience. Joy is the native and natural state!

In order to refamiliarize yourself with what you really are while you are inside this "dream" of physical life, you can allow yourself to completely let go – at least for awhile – of all that you are not. You are not your thoughts, you are not your judgments, you are not your expectations, you are not your beliefs. You are not your responsibilities, you are not your abilities or disabilities, and you are not your pain. You are the *awareness* that beholds those things. You are the you that feels most like *you* to you! You are the awareness that is "wearing" those thoughts, judgments, expectations, and beliefs for a while. As awareness, you *always* have permission to let go of your thoughts about the present moment and to just fully experience the present moment for exactly what it is without any resistance or rejection. If you do so deeply enough you will find that beneath all the pain, there is always joy!

Rejection Closes the Door; Acceptance Opens It

You are immortal awareness that surpasses all form. That is not a metaphor or just an abstract concept – you actually surpass the entirety of your physical experience and all the form in it. The only reason you may not be aware of that fact is that you agreed to be bound to the constraints of having a defined experience within form, and that experience *requires* a limited physically focused stimulus-set, understanding, and memory. The fact you agreed to have this experience does not change the much more fundamental fact that you actually *are* an immortal spirit who surpasses all of the form!

The experience of form can be very rich, very convincing – and at times very painful. We end up quite naturally believing that the scenery of the stage is real. We go very, very deep into the illusion. As we do, we *artificially define ourselves* by choosing some form (ideas, identities, thoughts) over other form (contrasting ideas). This is all expected and natural, except that we have gone *so* far into the illusion that we have "lost sight of the forest for the trees"! As the world challenges us deeply, we end up taking shelter within the illusory forms of the ego to stay safe and avoid pain. And as we do that, we naturally end up rejecting parts of our experience.

When you reject your experience, you are choosing illusory form over infinite formlessness. This is because when you reject something you are choosing to stand against some form, and that can only be done as a form itself. Your consciousness ends up lending credence and solidity to the form that it is trying to stand against. As the form strengthens, so does the (typically negative) experience that comes with it.

For instance, if someone perceives what is occurring in the world as terrible, and rejects it, then he or she will be giving energy *toward* that negative perception and will experience the negative constricting emotions that go along with that rejection. If someone perceives that they must struggle, then they will experience struggle. If someone rejects their body, then their

112

experience in it will be more difficult. Rejection is a "low-vibration" energy, because it is an occurrence of some part of All That Is temporarily turning against itself. Acceptance – also called Love – is a "high-vibration" energy, because it aligns with the innate natural unification that exists at the deepest level of our connection with All That Is. Rejection is an expression of fear; acceptance is an expression of love! (Yes, there are times that it is proper to "reject" something unloving, or to intercede to stop violence – but here I am speaking about rejection at its most fundamental.)

The source of all power lies beyond all form! Acceptance, then, is *regaining* power: By relinquishing your need to resist "what is," you automatically take a step *away* from the illusion of form and naturally move closer towards the infinite, powerful, and peaceful formlessness that gave rise to the form in the first place.

052

Growing Beyond Belief

No matter what the belief, people will tend to find data to support it. In fact, over a lifetime we tend to assemble complex fortresses of data to support what we already believe. As we do this, most of us believe that our viewpoint is "true" and that others' viewpoints are "false" (or, at least, not quite as correct as our own). Furthermore, many believe some forms (ideas, beliefs, identities, or actions) are inherently "good" while others are inherently "evil." To those who are so deeply accustomed to living in a universe of duality, this can seem natural.

At the deepest level, there *is* fundamental Truth. But that Truth transcends *all* of the form of the physical universe. It transcends all of the ideas, all of the words, all of the beliefs, all of the objects, all of the contrast. While there is no word that can name it (since words are also form), perhaps we can attempt to speak to what that Truth is by using this one simple word: *Love*!

While forms themselves are not innately "good" or "bad," since a consciousness must always *assign* meaning to them in order for them to *have* meaning, the *movement* of consciousness through intent *does* either align more closely or less closely to Truth or Divine Love. This is why it is so very important to deeply explore the nature of our own motivations and to act from loving intent (which aligns with Truth) rather than fearful intent (which temporarily does not). Loving intent might also be described as: selflessness, personal responsibility, humility, and acceptance. It includes the willingness to be wrong, to seek out truth and grow in the acceptance and service of others, even at the expense of one's self or at the expense of what one has previously believed.

One of the main challenges is, our beliefs tend to become invisible to us: They tend to appear to us to be *assumptions about how reality really is*, rather than beliefs. In other words, once our beliefs are set, the data that arrives *almost always* appears to support the existing belief. But in fact, the

114

same data is being utilized by different conscious participants in different ways.

We often don't think about spiritual growth in this way. Instead, we fight for the form. We try to make sure our way of seeing the world is furthered. We worry about it, we fret and fight to make the rest of the world adapt to the correctness of what *we* believe to be right. But the correctness of belief is *not* what this universe is about. We are here to develop the quality of our intent, the quality of ourselves as truly loving and authentic beings. We are here to face our fears and to accept personal responsibility. We are here to actually accept and support one another! That, far more than any claim of form, will further Source's plan (the ultimate loving intent) for this universe!

115

(053)

Death Need Not Be Feared

Being afraid of death is like the dreamer being scared to wake up, because the dreamer doesn't remember waking life while he is asleep. Metaphorically speaking, you are in the dream right now, reading this book. You may not remember what is it to be "awake," because such "amnesia" is a necessary requirement of buying completely into the dream. Nevertheless, you are not just the dreamer: What you truly are is too vast to articulate, and entire other reality systems much more real than this one are available to you when you "wake up."

Does it hurt when you end a dream and wake up? No, the transition is very natural. Every day we wake up from our previous night's sleep, and we typically think nothing of it. Physical death is a similarly effortless transition. Countless near death experiencers confirm that there is no pain in the transition itself from physical life to the nonphysical one. In fact, just the opposite – the transition is incredibly liberating and full of unspeakable love and joy!

Living in the physical – dreaming that you are actually form – is the much more constraining and potentially challenging state. We are free to thrive here, to fully enjoy the contrast and all the experiences that this human life has to offer, but we do not need to fear the end of it in the least.

Death is release, the great liberator, a joyful awakening into our much more native state! Not only do we not need to fear that, we can in fact look forward to it as the wonderful, expansive, celebratory return Home that it is! And indeed when we dismiss the specter of the fear of death, we are able to live our lives more in joyful alignment with the immortal spirits that we truly are!

116

(054)

Letting Go of the Desire to Think in Meditation

Meditation is not ultimately about piling one thought (the thought "don't think" or some other) on top of a stream of other thoughts. Meditation is about removing the *momentum* behind the thoughts, so that their arrival will diminish, so that awareness itself can rise without falling asleep back into thought.

Thought is not the same as intent. Thought is a form beheld within the mind; intent is the fundamental movement of consciousness. In order to slow down the momentum of thought, intent must first move to change the *desire* to behold the thought. Our desire to listen to our thoughts feeds their momentum. If we want to experience our truer nature, we have to decide to actually "let go."

Most of us who experience constant thought do so because we care about those thoughts. We truly believe their content is important. Or perhaps we find comfort or pleasure in them. The thoughts arrive to serve us. Perhaps we've been propelling the same thoughts so consistently and for so long that they've become almost all we know. The following is not to be misconstrued, but in order to fully meditate and experience our greater awareness, we have to allow ourselves to "not care" about the content of our thoughts. We have to allow ourselves to let go of the *need* for the thoughts to serve whatever purpose they are serving. We see the thoughts arrive, but we pay them no heed.

If you sit down to meditate, and you actually want to be doing something else, your intent and your meditation experience will reflect that. Meditation, then, should be done at a time when you are ready to let go. When you invest yourself in letting go, when you give yourself permission to deeply release all expectations and needs and desires, then your momentum of thought will reflect that, and your greater awareness will naturally rise to

117

Part 2 – Essays

the surface. Indeed, incredible relief is available to you when you finally "put down" the needs that your thoughts are faithfully serving.

Meditation is ultimately not an action. It is allowing awareness to be more fully in the present moment without being lost in the dreams of the mind. That allowing means letting go – even letting go of the need to listen to our thoughts, and letting go of the wants, needs, and desires that those thoughts are serving.

(055)

The Inherently Limited Understanding of Form

Until you can understand all phenomena, you cannot fully explain any one part of all phenomena. In other words, you cannot speak to fully understanding why something is if you cannot speak to why everything is. Everything is ultimately connected – and identifying *relationships between* forms does not convey a true understanding, which is complete.

In our world we often identify "why" something has happened when we can point to some other thing that caused it. We believe identifying the relationships between various forms means we understand them. For instance, that ice over there melted because its temperature rose above 32°F. Why did the temperature of the ice rise above 32°F? We may identify a cause for that, too. Science helps us to follow a logic chain and understand physical laws further and further, until we understand many complex relationships, at least between how physical objects interact. But eventually and inevitably, we arrive at a "we don't know *why* that is; it just is," and that means the understanding remains incomplete. Yet we tend to believe we understand the true cause of something when we comprehend some level of the cause-effect relationships that relate to it – in other words, we are satisfied when we can explain one form by identifying its relationships with other forms, to some subjectively sufficient degree of complexity. We also tend to do this with more nebulous topics, such as religion or social phenomena. For instance we may ask, why is there racial inequality in America? And we may point to historical context, political events, or even to groups of people or to their ideas to explain. Or we may ask, why do we suffer? And we may embrace a religious idea that may seem reasonable, such as the idea of original sin. We buy into the explanations. Soon enough, we believe we "understand" reality, when in actuality all we grasp is but a tiny subset of the perceived relationships between its forms.

The word *form* here means anything that is commonly perceived as a unique, individuated thing – whether it be an object, a person, a thought, an

119

idea, an event, a sensation, or any combination of these. A form, by definition, is not everything. And because it is not everything, no form (or forms) can contain all the answers and explain all phenomena. These statements might sound like nothing more than silly word play, and it may sound daft to say that "something that is not everything can't explain everything" – but in fact this is an important spiritual truth. It is important because we do not *truly* understand something only by comprehending its relationship to other things, even if we do so to what *we* consider to be a high degree of complexity.

In order to truly understand what is happening, we need to look *beyond* all of the forms. We need to look to what is most fundamental if we want to understand that which is not fundamental.

All the answers for all phenomena do exist at the level of Source. And if for today we might attempt to pick one word (one form) to identify what Source is, we might use the word *consciousness.* Nothing exists that isn't consciously experienced! Consciousness is the foundation; the forms it beholds are but "dreams" – subsets that it experiences within itself. The dreams are not everything. But ultimately, consciousness itself is.

You are consciousness. If you are reading this right now, you are a conscious part of Source! And through that inseverable connection between you and what you are, at the deepest levels you always have access to All That Is. Many people who physically die and come back report that they experience "knowing everything." This is because all knowledge and all form exists within Source, and once they are "removed" from the form experience of this physical reality and the "rules" that go with it, they return to the deeper state of awareness that is native to them. True understanding is always available at the deepest levels – but it vastly transcends all human language and all human ideas. Even the entirety of all of human history and all the experiences of the Earth are but a tiny subset of the forms that exist within All That Is.

We who are yet human need to embrace the humility necessary to fully recognize that our forms (our ideas, our physical understandings, our beliefs) do not hold all the answers. Yes, we can and should expand human knowledge and broaden our scientific capabilities and understanding, and indeed there is true value in that. But such understandings will never be complete. Form itself by definition is inherently limited. But the wonderful, amazing, and loving boundlessness of All That Is contains *all* understanding, and it is something that can never be further from you than your own breath – *except that* you behold, believe in, and participate *as one of* the many forms that are a part of its Creations!

(056)

You Are Treasured Beyond Comprehension

You are a completely unique and irreplaceable portion of All That Is. God (Source) loves *you*, specifically and personally, so much – far more than any love you have likely ever experienced on Earth! You are more wonderful and precious and valuable to Her than you can even conceive! The reality of those statements cannot be articulated in words, or even thoughts – it can only be personally known and deeply experienced.

And yet we live in a world where for many of us that experience is not commonly known. Why?

Neale Donald Walsh shared a great metaphor to answer this question, which I will paraphrase here. Imagine that everything that existed was light and love. Imagine that a small bright soul rejoiced and existed as a single light within the ocean of light, which was God. The soul said to the ocean of light of which it was a part, "I am the light! I am the light!" And God replied joyfully, "Yes, yes you are!" And they rejoiced together and reveled in existence. But eventually the soul said, "But God, what does it mean to be the light?" For as it had always been light amongst light, it knew nothing else! It could not conceive of that which it had never been; no contrast existed for it. The soul in its joy innately wanted to do something, to add to the light, to participate in Creation! And so God said, "I love you so much that I can provide a way to you that you can better understand what it means to be the light." The soul replied excitedly, "Wow! How?" And God said, "In order to be more fully of the light, you must experience and temporarily become that which you are not: darkness." The soul was ecstatic that such an adventure and opportunity existed for it, that it could become even more by experiencing contrast, and add to the light – so it excitedly agreed to participate in the experience! God said to the little light, "To experience what you are not, you must temporarily forget that you are the light. And yet even while you have forgotten, you cannot ever truly be other than what you are – for you *are* the light." And the little soul set out on a great adventure, to see

122

how much it could actually be and engender the loving Source from which it came...

So it is with us here on Earth. We have chosen to have an experience of contrast and limitation, to have a context within which to make choices and exercise our intent, so as to participate in Creation and evolve the quality of our beings towards love! We seek to exercise love even in the face of great challenge. We have received an amazing gift! We don't often think of physical reality with all of its hardships as a gift – but indeed, a precious gift it is!

You may have forgotten the wonderfulness that you are; but truly, you are a cherished, marvelous, powerful, bright soul in the ocean of All That Is. What's more, by choosing to participate in this experience – and so many other experiences – you have undertaken the brave and deeply respectable task of participating in the *very real* process of actual Creation, however messy or painful it may (temporarily) be.

Take a moment to listen deeply within yourself beneath all the thoughts and beliefs of this lifetime, and in the quiet presence of your own spirit you may sense a subtle but enduring reminder that indeed, no matter what this walk in the physical may hold, you are the light, and you are *loved*!

123

The Authority of Awareness

The fact that you are aware gives you authority to explore what is real. The fact that you are aware gives you authority to interpret what you perceive.

In the individual sense, your awareness itself is "what is." Its powers of experience, interpretation, and choice are fundamental to it. You can bind yourself to a much more limited choice-set or interpretation-set based on your own beliefs (which are typically beliefs passed to you and "hardened" over a lifetime), but fundamentally you are free to interpret absolutely everything as you will. You may temporarily wear the clothes of limited interpretation within a defined experience, but on a fundamental level you cannot be anything but utterly free!

In the Big Picture sense, God's awareness is ultimately "what is." It doesn't have to answer to any other system or entity – it *is* What Is. You are a part of that. Metaphorically, you are a drop in the ocean – and yet still the ocean itself. Your very being is rooted in and seeks to be in loving creative service to the entire vast ocean that you most fundamentally belong to; and yet simultaneously and without contradiction you also, then, as the ocean, ultimately report to nothing except what you are (the ocean itself).

This authority of awareness is important to recognize, because we live in a world where our own fundamental power to interpret how we choose has been obscured beneath an extremely deep history of disempowering belief. We are so free, you see, that we have created even this experience of such a deep history of disempowering belief! And yet now many are choosing to wake up: to wake up to their power, to their profound personal responsibility, to their true nature that transcends the physical illusion. If you wish to participate in that awakening, you deserve to know that you have the authority to question and explore *everything*. If you believe otherwise, it is because *you* have bought into that interpretation.

(058)

The Desire to Make Everything Fit

As we try to understand reality, we innately sense that everything should "fit." The desire to make things "fit" is not just ego-derived, it also stems from our inherent spiritual desire to integrate all experience. This is because at the deepest level, in truth, everything does fit – and we naturally seek to reach for that and to integrate everything that we can while we are physical. Yet as we attempt to understand and integrate our current physical experience, often the ego gets in the way: Our intention quickly strays from genuinely pursuing truth (which is all encompassing) *wherever* it may lead, to trying to avoid pain and make ourselves *feel* like we have control or understanding. Understanding only a subset of relationships between forms, and then deciding to "believe things" to close the gap, is not a true pursuit of truth. Pursuit of truth requires full acknowledgement of that which we do not know – and there is a lot of that.

Because we live in a universe of duality, we often seek truth in the objects of duality themselves: ideas, objects, names, definitions, actions, or concepts. We believe "this" object is the truth, while "that" object is deception; or perhaps "this" object is good, while "that" object is bad. And yet, truth transcends *all* of the form. Since truth transcends all form, when we "buy into" one form – and resist another – we are embracing something that is not the full picture, which is completely unified.

Thus if we wish to honor our desire to make everything fit and genuinely pursue truth, we need to be willing to look the one place we may have never looked while physical: *beyond all of the things that we are trying to fit together*. What does it mean to look beyond all of the things?

The things only ever exist as beheld by your awareness. Thus, to look beyond them, you need to train yourself to look beyond the objects to your *awareness itself*. Doing so is not an *action;* we can say it is an exercise in intent to focus away from your many definitions and thoughts such that you can

125

truly *experience* the infinite and unadulterated present moment. We often call that exercise "meditation." Meditation is just the word we use for allowing ourselves to move closer to fully experiencing the present moment, without the participation of the physical mind. The present moment is the doorway. The experience of the present moment itself transcends the objects and the thoughts. And in that transcendence, it is possible for each of us to take one step closer to truly *experiencing* the unity that exists at the root of All Things. That unity is real, and as it contains everything, everything fits.

Focus and Expectation Have an Effect

Whatever you focus on, you get more of. And, you get what you expect. These two statements reflect what many spiritual teachers call the "Law of Attraction." We might say the Law of Attraction is a term for the phenomenon that, since consciousness is fundamental, when it "pushes" reality responds.

Children naturally focus on what they want. When you tell them they can't have something, they respond naturally with, "But I want it." That response is not simply immature – it reflects that the child is instinctively responding in a way that *does* work more immediately in other reality systems, where desire alone has historically produced an immediate change in circumstances. Our reality is the shockingly different place where desire itself seems to be insufficient to bring us what we wish.

However, that is not entirely the case. What we call the Law of Attraction still functions – it's just that the constraints of our physical reality make it such that the "manifestation" of our focus and expectation can seem impossible or delayed. This physical reality is "dense," because it takes a lot more "thought momentum" to result in a physical change than may be the case in other reality systems. Also, the rule-set of our reality system is relatively strict – but within and through that rule-set, change does occur.

We do create our reality, both individually and collectively. Recognizing that fact is not only liberating, it is also an important step towards accepting personal and collective responsibility for our world. Not only is the responsibility ours, the power is ours, too: We *can* actualize the positive changes that we so deeply desire! Recognizing the role of our own focus and expectation is a key step in that process. For many of us, in order to fully recognize that role, we will need to work past the many disempowering beliefs that have been so deeply engrained in our minds, for our expectations follow our most deeply held beliefs.

127

(060)

Awakening Through Freedom from Belief

There is nothing you believe that you didn't first decide to buy into at some point. Even your deepest assumptions about how reality works are viewpoints that *you* had to establish.

Physical reality is a defined context that provides a neutral mirror through which you may experience the nature of your perspectives and beliefs. Physical reality is such that through its constraints, you may very richly experience your unique perspective. In a reality like ours, that perspective can get incredibly "deep" over the course of a lifetime – so convincingly deep that you can forget entirely where you have come from, or even what your assumptions are! This in fact is one the reasons the physical experience is so very valuable to the soul: It allows you to truly experience a defined and unique perspective first-hand. Another reason is that such a deep perspective allows for a very rich place from which you can make choices, so that you can ultimately evolve the quality of your intent toward love.

As we undertake our exceptionally long journeys across space and time, we seek to grow towards love. An important part of growing towards love is growing past fear. And as humans, our beliefs are often put in place to protect us from our fears. Thus, in fact, we are doing a great service when we decide to confront our beliefs and face the fears that they were protecting. That awakening process is a very meaningful one indeed! When we face our fear, not only are we able to free ourselves from its shackles, we are able to then actualize a more loving presence in our world for everyone else!

Even as deep and convincing as this physical experience and its resulting beliefs can be, if you remove or look past all of the thoughts and beliefs, you will find that beneath them is always what you truly are: your awareness itself. Your awareness is the silent witness to all of your thoughts and beliefs, the presence that beholds your entire physical experience. Your awareness is *you;* your current beliefs and identity details are not. In fact, you do not need

128

to believe anything, or think anything, or do anything. If you feel otherwise, it is because *you* believe so.

You do not need to fear changing your beliefs or viewpoints at any level. You are free to do that! In fact you will find that as you let go of the assumptions that have bound you and truly face and process your fears, you are more free than ever! For the spirit itself is much more than the forms it temporarily beholds, and there is always great joy when you take a step closer toward what you really are.

(061)

Choose Joy!

We are not here to struggle, suffer, and merely survive. We are here to thrive as the beings of joy that we truly are!

But oftentimes, what we perceive to be the "demands" of the world cause us to fall into seriousness. Our worldview requires things of us, and in heeding them we quickly get bogged down by the responsibilities that we have heaped upon ourselves.

None of it is required. None of the seriousness, heaviness, or stress is required. At the most fundamental level, nothing is required of us – for awareness itself is perfectly free, and in fact awareness fully transcends the forms that it allows itself to get lost within.

Thus while you are here on Earth, allow yourself to let go and to choose joy! There is never a circumstance in which you are not allowed to choose joy, should you wish.

130

Seeking Truth Beyond the Intellect

When deciding whether something is true, especially when it comes to philosophical or spiritual topics, we tend to immediately consult the intellect. We think: "Does this information jive with my own understanding?" or, "How does this information fit with my existing beliefs?" We tend to seek and interpret truth through intellectual understanding, or through intellectually held beliefs.

And yet the larger spiritual context fully transcends the human intellect. Truth transcends form.

Thus, if we wish to seek out what is true, we need to do so with more than just our minds – we need to do so with all of our being. Our being lasts. Our being is actually connected to All Things. But our human intellect is only a narrow, specialized subset of what we truly are, the portion of us focused on processing the seemingly dualistic nature of our physical world. We are much more than that. We should be careful not to confuse the shadow of man's understanding and metaphors with that which transcends them.

Because the physical universe is not fundamental, it will not do to try to understand all of reality with the physical mind. Consciousness is fundamental, so to explore reality, look there.

(063)

The Responsibility Is Ours

"You are not just a drop in the ocean, you are the mighty ocean in the drop."
-Rumi

We are "what is." We are the experiencers and the interpreters of our experience. We are the *creators* of our experience. Every single element of our world, every single experience that any being ever has here, is ultimately our collective responsibility.

Collective experience is rooted in individual experience. As an individual experiencer, *you* are a fundamental and key part of the play that is occurring. Never overlook the importance and the power of individual responsibility – it is the root of all responsibility.

There is never anyone other than "I, the experiencer" who is making the choices that affect others.

And thus the responsibility for everything is yours, mine – ours. There is no other group out there, no other individual, or government, or idea, or location, or force that can be blamed. We are the only ones that can be blamed. And the "we" is rooted in you and me, the individuals.

Some may say, "But I cannot change other people" or "I cannot change the entire world." Here are two responses to that. First, you are not responsible for every other soul's choices – but you are responsible for your own. Very importantly: From the spiritual perspective, taking personal responsibility *is* enough! Second, you are far more powerful than you imagine! You are intrinsically connected to every single other thing in existence, everywhere. You are connected to every single other person, animal, and rock on the planet, and every star in the sky. When you change, reality changes. When you grow toward genuine love and conquer your fear, the world is positively affected. That is true even if you do not see the effects visibly. A change in

132

consciousness space always precedes a change in physical space. Thus the outlook of the world is not one of gloom but of hope – for you do personally have the power to bring about meaningful positive change.

So take responsibility! Take responsibility for your intent. Notice your thoughts, your actions, your reasons. Why in fact are you doing what you are doing? What can *you* do to make things better? What personal fears can *you* take ownership for and confront? What one single step can you take to help make the world a better place for someone else – today? You will find that as you accept responsibility, rather than being burdened, you are in fact *freed* – for acting from love always moves us closer to our true Source of freedom and joy!

(064)

Brave One, You Do Not Need to Prove Yourself

You are unconditionally loved by God. You can never lose that love. Source accepts you entirely. You have nothing to fear, nothing to prove, and nothing you must do to be accepted. You are loved! Nothing can take that away from you.

That is true even considering the fact that you will make suboptimal choices while you are on Earth. It is understood that you will. All things are understood – so how could your "mistakes" not be?

In fact, the act of being human, even in all of its messiness, is recognized as a profound and meaningful contribution. Why? Because as the soul expands, so does the ocean of which it is forever a part.

The soul "strives." It has everything available to it, and yet (on a post-fundamental level) it is not flawless or perfect but can in fact evolve in love toward the perfection of God. To participate in that process, the soul immerses itself in a context so it can have the opportunity to make choices.

The soul can always "be more." That "growth" is very meaningful to the soul. It permits it to be and express itself in new ways. The soul can develop by being something within a context and striving to forever improve the quality of its intent toward love by working through the experience of that context. It can conquer fears. It can better understand duality: It can better know the light if it first knows the darkness. The experience of unique contrast is useful. Other realities are affected by the soul's decision to become physical, too! Incarnation is an absolutely amazing and precious opportunity for the soul! We are so unconditionally loved that we are permitted to choose to have the *experience* of *not* being unconditionally loved. For in so doing, love – the nature of God itself – is that much better understood. Indeed, every detail of our lives is a unique setup within duality that helps the soul better know itself, and helps All That Is gain new meaning and insight – and

134

Part 2 – Essays

that *adds* to Creation! You are participating in that very valuable activity right now!

Thus you did not come to Earth to prove yourself, or to earn the love that is already given to you. In fact, you are the brave one who has embarked on the great journey of being human so as to participate through experience in the expansion of Creation itself! That is not only forgivable – it is admirable!

(065)

We Are All Family

"Us versus them" thinking currently prevails in our society. Because of the physical rule-set of our reality, life on this planet evolved in a "kill or be killed" environment, and it was physically beneficial to ensure that one's self and one's group succeeded even at the expense of other individuals or groups. Our cultures enshrine the importance of supporting one's group, whether it be a tribe, a sports team, a nation, or – especially – one's family.

And yet, where we truly come from we are all family. We are all intrinsically connected to one another. That statement is not just a nice-sounding platitude, it is a statement of actual fact. Spiritually, all of us are a part of one incredible whole. We are all not only connected, we are a part of one another!

This is true no matter what role we temporarily come and play on Earth. This is true of every single person we meet. The cashier behind the register at the grocery store, our best friend, the person collecting our trash, the worker in China who made our clothes, even the next-door neighbor's dog – we are a part of one another.

Thus we do not need to differentiate between "our people" and "other people." It may have been natural to do so in the context of our long history on Earth, but it is not fundamental to what we are. Our true nature is one of love! In fact, we have come here to this place partly so that we can explore what that means and to learn to truly love *everyone* more fully, even within a rich and challenging context. That means learning to genuinely love and accept others even when they are not a part of our immediate group.

The next time you interact with someone who seems like a stranger to you, take a moment to be present with them and try to peer into what they really are. Can you drop all of your preconceptions, all of your identity labels, and truly see them? Can you sense that you are indeed connected to them? Can

136

you feel the wonderfulness of their unique presence? If you look close enough, past all the ideas of your human mind, you just may sense their brightness, and it will speak to something in you, too. For none of us are truly separate from each other – we are *all* family!

(066)

The Gift of Choosing to Be Human

Imagine for a moment that you are absolutely free and absolutely powerful. Imagine that nothing can limit you, nothing is impossible, and nothing can thwart your every desire. Imagine you are everything –you and those who are a part of you are all that is. How would one, in such a state, truly create and expand? How would one in such a state be able to choose something even greater, be something even greater? If absolute freedom were already yours, how tantalizing would it be to have the choice to experience a true challenge, so that you could fully personally know unique contrast, deepen your experience, and in so doing, become even more? How exciting would it be to be able to experience a new level of limitation, that you could once again see how well you could exert your incredible powers of choice?

What would it be like to be so free that you could choose to be so constrained?

This is what we really are. We are really limitless, absolutely free beings. In absolute freedom, we have chosen to participate in a truly incredible experiment to push the very boundaries of freedom and expansion: We have chosen to forget what we truly are for a while, and to *be* mortal beings on Earth.

From the perspective of man, the choice to be frail, challenged, powerless, and decaying can seem almost impossible to comprehend. But from the perspective of spirit, having the opportunity to actually experience those things, and actually impact others while they are on their own rich journeys, is an incredibly profound gift. How much greater a gift could be given by the Creator to spirits who are already absolutely free than the ability to fully experience contrast, that they may in fact exercise their freedom even more, actually *be* more than they once were, and learn to express the *love* that they really are in new and very real ways?

138

(067)

True Growth

True personal growth is not done in the intellect, or through action itself. True personal growth is a change in one's very being. While "right" ideas and actions do emerge from that, they are not growth in themselves.

It is the quality of our intent that must grow, not the correctness of our ideas. Like dream settings, ideas and environments change. What remains is *us* – the consciousness that experiences those things, and the quality of its ability to make choices from love rather than fear.

Too often we believe that we are growing when our ideas change, or when we do certain things, or when our circumstances change – when in fact what matters is when *we* change. The forms that we play with (ideas, sensations, objects, circumstances, beliefs, and even bodies) are temporary; but improving the quality of our intent itself is growth that endures *beyond* all of the form.

Thus rather than finding new ideas or simply performing some specific actions, we must strive to actually *be* more loving! We must strive in every choice to accept personal responsibility, to face our fears, to allow ourselves to be vulnerable, and to put others before ourselves. If we truly pursue that every day, we will fulfill our purpose for being physical.

(068)

There is Nothing You Can Truly Do Wrong

You exist. If you explore that existence sincerely enough, past all of your beliefs, you will become aware that your fundamental nature is pure, worthy, and good. You just *are* something that is, unto itself, wondrous!

When you as a conscious awareness decided to come into this experience of limitation, it did not fundamentally change what you are. You committed to seemingly being bound to having the human experience. Meanwhile then, within that experience, it was fully understood that you would make choices. It was known that you would have to make very difficult choices, and often those choices would be made under ignorance, fear, or duress. It was known that you might act out of selfishness or cause others pain. Even now, then, everything you've ever done is understood. All That Is fully understands everything, and so the reasons for your making imperfect choices are always fully understood.

Does that mean you should be selfish or cause others pain? No, of course it doesn't, not at all. You've come here to experientially grow so that in fact you can be more effectively loving, more selfless, more fearless, more powerful for the good. You've come here to actually experientially learn not just how to perform loving actions, but how to *be* more loving within a rich context. Selfish or fearful choices do not fulfill that purpose, are not in alignment with your true nature, and often lead to eventually having to experience certain challenges so as to grow past that selfishness or fear.

But nevertheless, there is nothing you can truly do wrong. All of your choices, even the "suboptimal" ones, are understood completely for what they are. Your fundamental nature cannot be less than wondrous, no matter what may happen in the play of life. And Source always, always loves and completely accepts you with a profundity that is beyond imagining.

In Neale Donald Walsch's *Conversations With God,* Neale is told this, too. He responds by asking, "If there is no punishment, then what prevents people from doing bad things to each other?" And the response came, "Do you need punishment to not do bad things to each other?" Perhaps many of us on Earth *do* currently need to believe in consequences to prevent us from harming others, because that is where we actually are in our own development.

And yet when we are ready, it can be profoundly meaningful to relinquish the fear of judgment and to embrace the unimaginably deep and forgiving love that exists for us! For when we know that love, we can act out of gratefulness, out of true deepest desire to do good, out of the joy of grace – rather than out of fear of punishment! We *can* drop guilt and shame, and allow ourselves to shine bright, knowing that we are *always* completely loved and accepted – no matter what!

141

069

The Two Sides of Human Religion

For a long time humans have relied on belief to explain that which was unexplainable. Humans have generously extrapolated that which they perceive and understand into that which they do not perceive or understand. This is a common practice of the ego: We draw conclusions about that which we actually do not understand and proclaim our conclusions as truth.

Yet it would not be accurate to categorize religion strictly as a phenomenon of ego and belief, because in fact religious phenomena also arises from the individual's very real personal experience with the greater reality and with the divine. God is real (whatever you call God or don't call God); the spirit is real – in fact, whether they are recognized or not, God and spirit are more real than the objects that appear to be around us. And as the individual processes experience, including the very common and natural personal interaction with the spirit, the physically oriented portion of one's awareness seeks to intellectually and emotionally *secure form* for that experience. The form that one seeks to secure then is sought within the context and history of what one has experienced in the physical, including what one has learned or been taught, which can include a religious context.

We might say, then, that our physical religion has two parts to it: first, the human-derived mythology (comprised of ideas, which are a type of form experienced within the physical universe); and second, the individual's interaction with the transcendent, loving substance of the spirit (the divine in and through all of us, which transcends the physical universe). (In fact, these two elements of mythology and spirit are intertwined and not ultimately separate, but to the human intellect which seeks to understand reality through dualistic ideas, the distinction may be helpful.) Differentiating the former from the latter has proven to be very challenging for humanity! This is understandable considering that the divine can *seem* invisible, unless we personally equate it to one or more *forms* (words, ideas, beliefs, etc.). In truth, the spirit transcends *all* of the forms of this universe, including our many objects, words, and ideas.

It is natural that we seek answers *within* the form, for we are indeed immersed in an experience of form. The experience of dualistic form is the very nature of the physical experience. And as experiencers of form, form is often very important to us – sometimes it even seems necessary – as we reach for the divine. For instance, revering a name, book, idea, or any set thereof can in fact be deeply meaningful and genuinely important to the individual along his or her spiritual walk. Yet eventually it can sometimes also benefit one to recognize that the form itself does not hold the answer, because form only exists within and is completely transcended by the realm of the spirit. Put another way: Conscious awareness itself exists, and the forms it entertains are secondary, so the forms will never truly hold the answer.

Regardless of the forms (or lack of forms) we utilize to pursue the divine, the spiritual walk of the individual is indeed very important and very real. *Your* relationship with the divine is real. *You* are real! You are more real than the forms that you are lost within. And that which stirs your soul, your truest self of selves, also dwells and exists beyond the ideas that you have temporarily adopted.

So how can we who are so bound to the experience of duality differentiate between the mythology of form and the true substance of spirit?

It is important to recognize that the realm of the spirit is not far away. In fact distance itself is not fundamental and exists as an experience only! Spirit is the most real thing you know: Your awareness is spirit. *You* are spirit. The awareness of being here now, reading this book with your intellectual mind of form, is an exercise ultimately being undertaken by spirit (your awareness). You may have gone very deeply into the dream of form, so deep that you don't remember how you got here – but you still have the ability right now to exercise your most inalienable spiritual power: your power to intend, your power to choose!

143

What can you intend or choose to help you separate the substance from the illusion? While the answer is complex and cannot truly be articulated with words, and while the path for every individual will most certainly be special and unique, we might say the following: *Be willing*. Your intent is your most fundamental, inalienable power. Point it towards *love*!

Humble yourself. Face your fears. Let go of your illusory ego-derived power and choose love. Rather than listening primarily to your rehearsed beliefs, admit to yourself all that you actually do not know. Intend to open yourself up to what the spirit is saying to you. Intend to let everything fall away that may wish to fall away, even if it causes you fear, even if it be your very life. Listen humbly to your intuition. Be willing to be wrong. Encounter what you feel. Feel what you feel. Feel what you are! Be willing to challenge anything, yet be gentle with yourself, for nothing can ever truly be wrong.

Humanity is ready to grow. We are ready to move away from fear-based dogma, self-righteousness, competition, anger, and the "survival of the fittest" mindset that has dominated much of our collective past for so long. We are ready for a more loving future!

It is time to stop fearing. In order to stop fearing, we need to be *individually* willing to actually face our pain and to process it. We need to take individual responsibility for all aspects of ourselves. We need to be willing to challenge and change our beliefs as our personal experience, reason, and intuition actually guide us. That path is a very personal path for each individual: It is sacred, and no one can walk it for us. But as you walk *your* unique path today, please know this: you are *loved*! You are full of light! You are free, and powerful, and good! And the power of our incomprehensibly loving Source is always with you, no matter what metaphor you may use to seek or serve it.

144

070

Creation Is Vast

Creation is very, very vast. It is so incredibly huge, so unbelievably complex, and so amazingly diverse that it is not possible for anyone to even remotely imagine its scope with the human mind. Our reality alone has over 100,000,000,000 galaxies (some now say twice that number), each possessing an average of approximately 100,000,000,000 stars. That's more than 10,000,000,000,000,000,000,000,000 star systems. The universe is so big that it takes light more than 13,800,000,000 years to cross it – while in that time, it expands even further! And yet, all of this scope is our universe only – our entire physical reality is in fact just one of a great many. Within that unimaginably vast context, how can any of us humans on Earth expect or believe that we truly grasp the nature of reality?

And yet many on Earth subscribe to simple human ideas passed down to them, enshrine those ideas as beliefs, and swiftly conclude that they more or less "have things figured out." Most humans believe they generally have a pretty accurate view of the world at any given time. We commonly claim knowledge where there is actually ignorance. Our basic assumptions about reality fade into the background, invisible to us, even though they color everything we are doing and experiencing in our daily lives.

One of those assumptions is that physical matter is what is most real. Many ponderers among us assume that materialism must be sound because we have been able to achieve certain physical accomplishments with our materialistic science. Many believe that our physical universe is all there is.

And yet, a true investigation yields a much, much vaster "Big Picture" reality than the cold basic experience of matter conveys. In fact, the experience of other reality systems can be more rich, more wonderful, more vibrant, and more absolutely astounding than any physical experience available to us! How can this be, when we remember nothing but the physical world in which we were raised? How can such an investigation be pursued?

145

In order to have your present physical experience, you had to accept a sort of "amnesia" for a while so that you could completely focus on being differentiated as a human. The entire you is so great, so vast, so connected to everything else, that functioning as a seemingly separate human would be quite impossible if it were not for the "amnesia." Nevertheless, you are still what you truly are: You are still spirit! You can't not be what you truly are. And thus if you truly wish to investigate reality, you need to be willing to fully look into what *you* are *beyond* the human mind. You can choose to spend time with and focus on your *awareness itself* – because that does always transcend the physical experience. Consciousness is the common denominator of *every* experience, so if you want to truly explore Creation, start by looking there! For indeed, within the realms of Creation there are realities far more immense and far more real than this illusory physical universe that we are so focused on – and your spirit is fundamentally connected to *all* of it!

(071)

Awareness Is Inherently Joyful

Awareness is inherently joyful! It can only experience pain as a temporary, nonfundamental experience. Resisting that experience tends to perpetuate it, because it is not allowing "what is" to be. True happiness and freedom are available in completely allowing "what is" to be, exactly as it is, without the judgments of the ego-mind. This is because by releasing the forms of the ego-mind, the consciousness naturally takes a step back towards its native state, which always fully transcends the forms that it is beholding. In relinquishing all resistance and simply being present with "what is," awareness naturally "sees past" the forms that were distracting it, and it is once again known that joy is always there!

Awareness is formless and unlimited! When awareness gets lost within the illusion of form and believes form is what it is, it temporarily believes something contrary to its true nature: It believes it is limited and separate when in fact it is unlimited and connected to everything. In so doing, it naturally experiences suffering. Suffering is a sign that awareness has bought into something that is not fundamentally true. Suffering is a sign that awareness has bought into an illusion, and thus has temporarily forgotten its true nature. When awareness knows its true nature, which is beyond form and totally free, suffering is not possible.

Existence Is More Than a Bunch of Relationships

People tend to define things in relationship to other things. Forms somehow gain apparent meaning because of how we relate them to other forms. In order to understand our reality, we "borrow" relationship after relationship, until we reach some subjective level of satisfaction that reality has been identified. In so doing, we automatically narrow reality down to the meaning that we have assigned it.

In fact, the Truth fully transcends all the relationships we have identified between its apparent parts. Reality is much, much bigger than the local meaning we have assigned.

As Rupert Spira says, "Objects do not have existence. Existence has objects." Existence may be equated with the word *consciousness*. Consciousness beholds objects; objects do not exist independent from awareness of them. Thus in order to truly understand things, we need to look primarily not at the things themselves but at the consciousness that is beholding them. That consciousness transcends all of the relationships between the forms that it is beholding, and is much more than all of them.

Beingness Is Not in the Intellect

As we consider spiritual ideas, we are in the intellect. Yet what we are –
Beingness! – is not an intellectual activity (though the intellect occurs within
Beingness). The name of the game – Love! – is also not an intellectual
activity. Love is a state of intention genuinely pointed toward the benefit of
another over one's self. Love is a state of intention genuinely pointed
towards inclusion, acceptance, freedom of being, and unity. Surrender is not
primarily an intellectual activity, either – it is also an intent. Love and
surrender can occur *through* an intellectual context, but they are not of the
intellect. The intellect and all of its knowledge and understanding of one's
current experience is but a tool and a *context*: The quality of the intent of the
individual who is using that tool and operating *within* that context is the
primary force that we are here to develop.

Our primary reason for being here is the growth of "what we are" toward
love. What survives bodily death then is our true self – our Beingness –
which retains its true nature. That is retained forever! Even as form falls
away, the quality of the consciousness which beheld the form and did
something with it, remains. To the soul, the development of that quality of
consciousness is well worth the price of being physical for a while.

Love and Fear in the Context of Unity

At the most fundamental level, all life is connected to all life. All life is a part of all other life. Everything is unified. Yet we choose to have the experience of the illusion of separation. Since being separate is not what is fundamentally actually true, we suffer when we *buy into* that perspective of separation. When our local perspective or belief does not align with the actual fundamental truth, we experience suffering. Our suffering is a sign that we have embraced the illusion and forgotten ourselves within it.

Beyond our forgetting, all remains connected. Unity is the underlying truth! This is why Love and Fear are the two great themes of spirituality: Love is inclusive, accepting, unifying; Fear is dividing, rejecting, separating. Love is the move towards What Actually Is; Fear is the move towards the illusion.

Addicted to Form

Being able to *be* something (while not "being something else") is an exciting and amazing opportunity for the spirit. "All That Is" can become even profoundly more when it – through you – can experience actually *being* "this and not that." Creation gains meaning in the process. Right now as you experience your own identity and circumstances, you are participating in that very valuable process.

As we participate in that process, we end up being deeply mired in the duality (being "this and not that"). We become so entrenched in the perception of duality, and we focus on it so much, that we become "lost" in it. We forget all else. We might even say that in a sense we are currently "addicted" to form. We are often addicted to thinking, to defining, to quantifying, to identifying. It is common to be addicted to these things when one is existing in a dualistic reality such as ours, as such stark dualism is a remarkably alluring and rich experience!

However, it is worthwhile to note that while we are here our larger state of being always transcends all of the form. Our awareness itself spans incredible distances of time and space – in fact *all* of the distances of time and space – as well as *all* of the "this or that" ideas that exist here on Earth. You may be completely focused on the form, but in fact you are fundamentally free! Those statements are not just ideas; they attempt to describe your very actual nature of being, even if you have forgotten it.

You *can* let go of the form. You are free enough to do that! You can let go of your judgments. You can let go of your needs. You can even let go of your thoughts themselves, and just allow yourself to be exactly with "what is," just for the moment. You do not need to quantify or qualify anything at all. In fact, you may find that when you finally let go, the peace and joy available to you far surpasses any of the wonders available in beholding the stimulating dream that is before you.

151

(076)

Breaking the Chain of Hurt

One of the "reasons" we are not condemned for our suboptimal choices is that God understands that we are often acting from a place where *we ourselves* have not received the love that *we* need. Others act unlovingly, and we become hurt, and we then make choices from the resulting "darkness" that end up hurting others. We buy into negative self-perceptions because others communicated them to us. Indeed, God has great compassion for the many ways in which we have not been loved. Yet often we do not practice compassion with ourselves.

When others hurt us, it is often not about us – it is about them. They are dealing with their own life situation, their own circumstances, their own constraints, their own beliefs, and perhaps most importantly, the pain of their own experience of lack of love. Those that hurt us are simply acting from their own place of lack of love. The pain gets passed along in a chain, often from one generation to the next. But all the pain, all the failings, all the fearful actions and judgements and hurtful words, are all arising from a place of lack of love.

We can break that chain! We can be brave enough to see hurtful actions for what they are: ignorance of love! Others hurt us because they hurt, and they hurt because they are temporarily blind to the love that is so nurturing to their soul. Rather than allowing ourselves to perpetuate the hurt, we can choose instead to see those hurtful actions for what they are – simple acts of ignorance to love – and put them aside! We can decide, rather than let them bring us down, to choose to respond with *love* instead! We can choose to love ourselves in the face of hurtful actions, and we can also even choose to love those who hurt us while *they* are acting from their place of lack of love. This is a truly powerful choice! For choosing to meet the hurtful actions of another with love meets the problem at its source: It meets the hurt by giving it what it actually needs – *love!* Doing so allows the powerful light of Source

152

to slip in to any situation. And when that happens, miracles can and do happen!

We can break the chain of hurt – and all it takes is our own choice to meet the ignorance of love, *with* love!

The Extremes of Duality as Expressions of Love

The rigorous cruelties of the world are not signs that reality is ultimately harsh and uncaring. Rather, they are demonstrations of the incredible lengths to which love will go in the name of creation and experience. As we lose ourselves in the experience of duality, including its many seemingly darker aspects, it is easy to see the extremes of our experience in form and subsequently reach some (form-based) nihilistic or existential conclusion about the nature of existence. We may correctly identify that form does not hold the answer, even as we forget the much, much deeper meaning of our experience here.

In fact, the extremes of this world have been created in a spirit of love, joy, and even play – not in a spirit of heaviness, necessity, and misery! We have become so lost in the duality, however, that we experience much of the latter. We have become so lost in the duality that we have forgotten ourselves, and when we do that, we suffer. And yet, consistently, the enduring nature of love never tires of standing firm. It waits for us – even silently – around every corner and every experience. We may see terror – but even the opportunity to see terror is ultimately a profound gift of love. The ability to add to Creation through the experience of deep contrast is a gift of love.

The ego rejects this. But it does not see the interconnectedness and purity of love that has given birth to the valuable experience of contrast that it operates within. Thus when you decide to step past your own ego, to stop fighting "what is," and to just be fully present with your experience without judgment or rejection, you permit yourself to take a step back towards being personally aware of the more fundamental loving nature of existence.

(078)

Spiritual Growth as a Change in the Being

Spiritual growth is not something that happens in the mind. It is not a correction of ideas, or even just a change in action. Spiritual growth is a change in one's very being, in "what one is."

This kind of change is not easily undertaken. In order to grow, one typically must be willing to undergo significant personal alteration. Spiritual growth is often a destructive or painful process, and when the moment comes, many are unwilling to actually experience and undergo the intense personal alteration that is necessary. It is far easier to tell oneself a story of what one is than it is to actually change.

Yet we are here to actually change. So much of the pain each of us experiences in our daily life remains with us because we are unwilling to fully accept responsibility for our own state of being, and we are unwilling to grow into the humility and selfless intent that our pain calls us to. By the "laws" of the greater divine reality, our own past intentions have brought us into exactly our experience of this present moment – and yet many of us resist that present moment and the lessons it has to offer.

Spirituality is about your relationship to the present moment. It is about your actual experience and what you do with it. If you meet that experience with willingness, openness, personal responsibility, fearlessness, humility, and selflessness, then you will allow the present moment to start actually shaping you the way it was intended. Willingness, openness, personal responsibility, fearlessness, humility, and selflessness all require a quality of intent – you must use your precious free will to *choose* the way your soul calls! Often that choice means walking *into* the discomfort, pain, insecurity, or danger. Often that choice means taking personal ownership for yourself, for your world, and for the well-being of those around you. Often that choice means allowing yourself to completely let go of all that you are not, of all of your stories and definitions, so that you may actually change and

155

become even more – no matter how dark or difficult that change may seem to the mind. Ultimately, you have absolutely nothing to fear – the Light is always with you and within you! And when you are willing to actually accept responsibility and grow, the universe itself actively responds to your willingness.

(079)

The Counter-Pressure of Circumstance

Physical life is a constraint set that offers the spirit the valuable counter-pressure necessary to participate in personal and collective expansion. To the unlimited powerful spirit, the opportunity to actually subject one's self to "participation within a firm and rigorous context" is an extremely precious opportunity. The circumstances of your life are the valuable counter-pressure that your soul uses to become more. It uses circumstances to expand its awareness of what reality can be, to identify what it wants and does not want, and to refine qualities of the self within a context. Your life is the context. You are the soul.

A couple very simple metaphors may be helpful. Physical life might very crudely be compared to getting on a roller coaster: Once you are strapped in, you are in for the ride and you can't get off. The ride may be terrifying while you are on it, but it's exhilarating to experience and creates a wonderful memory. Oftentimes those who get off of a roller coaster get back in line to get right back on! Others may decide they've had enough of roller coasters and not get back on. Another very crude analogy might be: Physical life is like lifting weights on a weight bench. The counter-pressure of the weights pushing against you is uncomfortable, but you utilize the counter-pressure to grow stronger and become capable of more. In our case, it is not physical muscle we are building but spiritual muscle: We are growing our capacity to successfully engage realities in a creative, loving, and fearless manner. We are growing our capacity to successfully engage our experience of the present moment.

The physical universe is a high-intensity, full-blown "experience context" wherein the soul (your awareness) can temporarily adopt a role within form, and use that role to better discover and refine itself. Your circumstances, then, are not curses, no matter how dire they may seem! Your circumstances are precious opportunities. At times those "opportunities" can seem

157

overwhelming, or perhaps even impossible to endure. There is no shame in becoming overpowered by circumstance.

Your true power does not lie in your ability to mold your circumstances to how you would prefer them to be. Your true power lies in your ability to choose *how* you will meet your circumstances. Sometimes, physically speaking, you can do nothing at all – and yet you *always* have the power to meet your experience with courage, humility, acceptance, and love. That power is the true power! For you have come here to do just that: to actually and personally meet your physical context with a high quality of intent. When you do that, you will be using the counter-pressure of the physical world as it was intended and will automatically begin to transcend the challenges of the physical experience.

(080)

Form Cannot Explain the Formless

You can't fully explain Reality by pointing to forms (including words or ideas). You can't explain the Whole by pointing at the part. Since the Whole is consciousness, the Whole can only be fully identified as it is experienced as consciousness. When one is experiencing form – that is, differentiation of any kind – one is not experiencing the Whole. Take care, then, when attempting to explain some things by using other things – any time you are doing that, you are not fully explaining Big Truth, or All That Is.

(081)

The Gift of Vulnerability

Being vulnerable with somebody is a gift to them. If you want to love someone, be vulnerable with them. Open yourself to fully expose your pain and weakness, show your tender heart, and allow them full room to show theirs. Be completely present with them, just as you are and just as they are, without any need for protection or judgment. That is in fact giving them something precious. But what's more, being vulnerable with somebody else also conveys a gift to yourself as well. For vulnerability is a wide road to love, and love is what you were born for.

082

Form Is Not the Answer

As we exist in this physical reality, we experience a universe of form. We live within a world of duality, where things seem separate and unique from one another: Cows are different than cats, hot is the opposite of cold, and the future happens after the past. We are almost totally engrossed in a life of beholding and manipulating form after form. Our minds are full of thoughts (which are forms), our eyes behold discrete colors and shapes (forms), and our days are spent manipulating objects (forms). This is our reality, and so we assume that *all* of reality is this way.

Thus when we seek to understand the "Big Picture," we naturally tend to do so using the forms that we know. Our form-based assumptions carry over into how we imagine the greater reality to be. Indeed, those very assumptions give definition to our experience of reality! Our beliefs (our deepest assumptions about reality) *form* the experience that we have. Once we have defined reality a certain way, the other ways become seemingly nonexistent to us. Indeed, that distinction to the exclusion of all other distinction is the very definition of form and the reason that form itself exists!

Yet *all* form exists within that which is formless. That formlessness cannot truly be named, for it is beyond any word that could attempt to describe it! But we might use the word *consciousness*. Consciousness – sometimes called "spirit" – is the fundamental "substrate" upon and through which all experience of form exists. Consciousness itself fundamentally transcends *all* of the forms it beholds. It can get "lost" in form for a while – indeed it is capable of doing even that! – but its true nature is transcendent. *Your* true nature is transcendent. And the unspeakable vastness, majesty, and total breadth of the Great Spirit that is the Source of All Things is most certainly transcendent! In other words, duality itself is not fundamental.

In the context of that incredible transcendence, how can any of us claim to have fit the truth into a form? How can any one earthly idea, name, person,

161

book, religion, or set thereof be "the truth"? It cannot. Many times a form may, through our own identification with it, help us to connect with our transcendent Source, but the form itself is not the answer. To believe otherwise is just that – a belief, which is a form itself. That belief can only have meaning as a consciousness assigns meaning to it.

We will never find the "true answer" within form. But fortunately, you are conscious, and therefore you are connected to the Source of all truth already, whether that truth presently seems obscured or not! Your human personality with all its form-based local understanding of reality may search under 10,000 rocks looking for the truth, and may hold on to certain assumptions about how reality is until the day of your physical death – and yet the Great Spirit *already and always* dwells within you as that which is transcendent!

Thus, when you are ready to fearlessly surrender your need for answers within form, to give up the power and control of your beliefs, and to simply meet your awareness of the present moment exactly as it is without any label whatsoever, know then that the true nature of your being will always be there waiting for you.

083

A Perspective on Suffering

As a human it can be difficult to understand suffering. But from the greater perspective of the spirit, the potential to suffer, and even actual suffering is greatly worth the trouble (though it's never technically a requirement to suffer). "What Is" can become more when it (through you!) can experience specific contrast – even when it can experience fully what it "doesn't like," which better defines the opposite. Creation utilizes definition; free will requires a context. The spirit in a fundamentally joyful state decides in all its eternal and invincible power to facilitate new experiences for itself so that it can *integrate* them – and in so doing become even more, expand the frontier of all experience, and add more to the *joy*!

Sometimes in that process the soul must seemingly be tried to its very limits. But so it is in a Creation that ever grows and becomes more. For if it did not, it would be stagnant; it would not become more. "What Is" is what it is and can't be anything else – so if it wishes to increase its scope it actually needs to also "be" things that are challenging, painful, and constraining, too. When even those challenges have been integrated, its "What Is-ness" expands in due measure, and the native love and joy of Creation grows with it.

Suffering is also meaningful in another way: It serves as the feedback and counter-pressure sometimes necessary to "drive" the individual consciousness to personally grow its quality of intent toward love. Many are driven to spiritual growth through suffering. While that may be incomprehensible to the human ego, to the spirit that exists in eternity, and to the one who sincerely wishes to grow in *eternal* love and fearlessness, such a price is actually accepted with gratitude!

There will come a time someday when you will be able to look back at your own suffering and see its greater context. Until then, let yourself feel what you feel, and let go of your judgments about it. Take heart, for your true nature always remains unharmed and invincible, no matter how much pain your local body may feel or how dark your human life may seem. The Source of all Creation is always, always with you! Be bountifully hopeful in your true invincible nature and in your inseverable unity with Source, for there is *always* hope available through what you *actually* are beneath this convincing physical experience.

(084)

Evil as "Ignorance to Love"

There is only love, though many of us are temporarily acting from the darkness of an experience of "lack of love." All beings at their core are the Light of Source! All beings are *of* love: All beings desire it, all beings are called to it, and it is the ultimate nature of the Light within us all. Sometimes the individual spirit experiences the darkness as a temporary sojourn: Even though the spirit's true loving nature remains unchanged, the spirit's local personality can, through its own experience of being "distant" from love, fall into a vibration that is experienced as "far from" its native light. From that place, the personality can make decisions which challenge others. That darkness is not some separate power or authority; it is merely the natural result of real consciousness exercising imperfect intent when experiencing "distance" from the native love. In that sense, there is no evil.

The human ego often rejects the idea that there is no evil, in part because our collective consciousness has grown within a history and environment in which it was meaningful to identify one's enemy. But at the most fundamental level, there is no enemy. Ultimately, you have no enemies!

Even the most heinous of crimes are acts committed from a place of a lack of love, rather than one of intrinsic evil. The evildoer needs love. Love is the answer.

This does not mean that we need to accept acts of cruelty or that we should stand by when intervention is required. It simply means that even as we do intervene, we can recognize that the one we intervene against is not a foe, but in fact is another embodiment of the Light making its way with free will through a very challenging world. Evil is "ignorance to love," or "perceived separation from love" – and having experienced that ourselves, can we not have understanding for those who seek to do us harm?

(085)

You Never Left Home

You never left Home. Your spirit is still there! *You* are still there. While you are there, you have committed a part of yourself into this local physical time-bound experience. In order to have this experience, the part of you that came here had to agree to temporarily forget the breadth of what you really are. That "veil" of forgetfulness was necessary for you to have the experience of being a human. After all, how could you experience being human if you fully knew you were the entire universe and that which created the universe? But your forgetting, and your highly specialized focus in this reality, do not change the fact that you already exist beyond it as well.

Spirit is not some substance that comes and goes. Spirit is the ever-present substrate through which all experience occurs. Spirit does not cease. It can take many shapes, and those shapes may change, but spirit itself is always present. You are spirit, and thus even as you entertain the life before you, your transcendent nature always remains.

For those of us who are so deep in the dream, this is an important fact to remember, because our believing in the separation of the spirit from the physical has helped to *keep* us in an experience of distance. As creative spirit, we form our own reality experience through what we believe about it. It is reality-changing, then, to wake up to the fact that we are *not* distant from our true nature or from the larger reality! In fact, we are there right now! Metaphorically speaking, we are dreaming the physical while asleep in the nonphysical. As each individual even gradually wakes up to his or her greater nature, a change occurs in consciousness space, which effects a change in our world. So be encouraged and be reminded that you transcend this rich reality experience before you, and even if you do not see it or feel it, you are already Home!

(086)

Focus Creates Momentum

What you practice being, you will be. This reality is a system in which you create momentum of interpretation, and over the long term the reality reinforces back to you a reflection of the momentum you have created. When you judge that reality is a certain way, it will then display itself back to you that way – not only in the sense that you interpret what you see in that light, but also in the sense that physical events actually tend to happen differently to reinforce your belief.

Put simply: You get what you expect!

Our momentum of interpretation is built up from moment to moment over the course of a lifetime. Each moment, then, is an opportunity to change the course! Each moment is an opportunity to redirect our focus to where we prefer! Our direction of focus is powerful. We often forget that, as we tend to believe that the external world occurs irrelevant of our interpretation of it. But indeed, we build creative momentum with each moment of our lives.

Right now is one of those moments. What momentum are you creating in your life right now?

087

Taking Change Beyond the Surface

The events that take place out in our world are far more than they appear to be on the surface. All things take place first in consciousness space and then in the world of matter. Thus in order to improve our world we must first make a change within consciousness. We cannot simply change our circumstances or our leaders. We cannot simply put new systems into place or enact new laws. The change must occur in *us*. The change must occur in *you*. There is no other way.

The change that is required is deeply personal. It is not a change just in the forms we work with – the specific ideas, the identifications, the beliefs, the human framework. It is not a change just in the contents of the mind. The change that is required is *of* ourselves, of what we are at the deepest level, beneath all the objects of the physical experience. The objects that we work with – the ideas, identities, beliefs, and systems – are just the "props" of our world, and they will come and go. What lasts is *us* – the consciousness of each individual who is actually wielding intent and making real choices every hour of every day. *That* is the real engine that drives what happens in our world. The physical details and the human systems will naturally work themselves out when we successfully change ourselves!

In order to do that, we must consistently work on the very nature of our *intent itself*, and consciously strive to exercise intent that is loving rather than fearful. We must bravely seek out our own egoic tendencies, challenge our own beliefs, and *feel*. We must be fully present. We must acknowledge our own weaknesses, take ownership, and do our very best to actually *be* a more loving presence in the world. We must actually put others before ourselves. The effects of such choices are far greater than they may appear to be on the surface.

In the face of all the tribulations of Earth, pursuing change can seem daunting. When we look inside ourselves and see all of our many imperfections, change can seem daunting there, too. And yet, in the scope of the Big Picture, every genuine step toward love is great progress! Every step forward that the soul takes towards actualizing love and overcoming fear is a genuine step forward for the entire universe! This is important to remember when we turn within ourselves in a common moment, and seek to be better. The real work is done in the common moment, in seeking to make the more loving, humble, freeing, fearless choice in any given situation, no matter how mundane it may seem on the surface and no matter the earthly objects involved.

(088)

Constraints as the Mechanism for Growth

A man I admire once said something to the effect that physical incarnation is like holding a pea between two fingers and squeezing down on it to force the pea's core out of the skin. It can't go up, it can't go down, but it's gotta go somewhere – so the pea just shoots out in some wild direction.

Being physical imposes all sorts of constraints upon us, in accordance with the rule-set of this physical reality. We experience the constraints of having to live, think, and function with a body of flesh. We experience social constraints as we are affected by others. We experience resource constraints and location constraints and time constraints.

Yet all of these constraints are meant to allow us to experience a truer and much more fundamental set of constraints: our inner constraints. The feelings and thoughts that arise in response to our physical constraints cause us to enter into a complex jungle of seemingly forced self-discovery. The world may seem to take our money – we feel powerless. The world may seem to thwart our relationships – we feel lonely. The world may seem to bring disease to our body – we feel pain. We typically perceive all these conditions as negative. And yet, hidden in them is the very meaning and power of the physical experience, for they allow us the opportunity to actually better our lasting selves.

In the near death experience of a woman named Amy Call, she recounts that a wise being who had mastered humility was gathered among many spirits who would also benefit from learning it. He telepathically said to her something to the effect of, "All I can do is plant a seed of interest for them to learn it for themselves. Without a physical body they cannot grow in that way. They need the contrast of the physical experience to learn it."

Let we who have bodies take a fresh look at the contrasts in our lives! Every pain, every challenge, every quandary holds a bountiful treasure – if we are

170

willing to fearlessly venture inward to discover what it is about ourselves that is being challenged by any given experience.

You are powerful enough to seek out your negative self-perceptions, and meet them. You are resilient enough to seek out your pains, and feel them. You are loving enough to seek out your demons, and hug them! You are brave enough to seek out your fears, and sit with them fully. For the power of that inward journey is great, and one of the primary reasons you have come to this place of apparent limitations is to have such a journey and to use it for all it can be!

Science and the Big Why

Science analyzes what is happening. It doesn't analyze why. Note that many people mistake causes for "whys." Determining a cause-effect relationship between two things is not the same as truly understanding why that cause-effect relationship exists.

As an example, scientists may ask, why did this ice melt? And their answer might be, because its temperature rose above 32 °F. They may then ask, why did its temperature rise above 32 °F? And they might determine an explanation for that too. They may further question that explanation, and so on, to perhaps even hundreds of degrees of questioning. In materialist science, every question asked must report an answer that is physical, as mainstream contemporary science and its language is only concerned about the content of this physical reality.

However, materialist science will never arrive at a real answer by speaking in physical terms. Why? Because the entire physical reality system is derived from a nonphysical source. There is nothing *within* the physical system that can explain *why* the entire system itself or any aspect of it is occurring. Science may go deeper and deeper into the rule-set of this reality, and may even identify universal physical laws and make certain wide-arching conclusions, but it will never be able to explain the entire system from within it. As an example, if science wishes to explain the origin of the universe as the Big Bang, it cannot do so without still being unable to explain why the Big Bang occurred. ("We don't know why; it just is that way" is not an answer.)

The nonphysical source of this physical reality is consciousness. Thus, it is only through consciousness that a comprehension of the "Big Why" can be attained. Fortunately, you are conscious – so you do have the ability to attain it.

172

Why Does 2 + 6 = 8?

Many who search for truth believe that it consists of some sort of knowledge, as they believe understanding relationships between forms brings one closer to understanding "what is." For instance: Knowing the equation for determining the area of a circle, or understanding how chemicals will consistently interact with one another, or learning the names of geographic locations on Earth, or even something subjective like understanding social phenomena, or something abstract like trying to understand if God is real – all tend to impart to one an ability to interact with "reality" (what the thinker perceives to be reality) with greater effectiveness. Such knowledge is therefore generally believed to move one closer toward "truth."

However, form cannot explain form, except *only* to the illusory extent that we identify our grasping of the *relationships* between forms to be satisfying to us, or not. Even "objective" (repeatable and verifiable) proof of effectiveness only demonstrates just that – effectiveness within the local known world – and not *why*. We can understand more and more effectively how form relates to other form per the rule-set of our local reality, but this is not true understanding.

The real question, then, is not whether we understand or don't understand that 2 + 6 = 8. The real question is, if we know *why* 2 + 6 = 8 even exists. Without that answer, there is not true knowledge.

Since all form, all differentiation, exists *within* and *by* something else, the answer cannot be known without that something else. That something else is always present, always existing, and always transcendent: It is consciousness itself.

Consciousness is inherently beyond form. It gives rise to the experience of form. It even sometimes seems to "lose" itself in the experience of form: in the experience of day and night, and brain chemistry and coffee and language

173

and pain. But it is, fundamentally speaking, completely formless, transcendent, omnipresent, eternal, and immortal. Its existence *gives rise* to the form that can be understood from a local, well-defined perspective in the first place.

This is why the truth can never be fully spoken or understood with the dualistic mind. Form and duality itself are transcended by that which gives rise to it all. That which transcends form, and fully contains and creates all of it, cannot then be named or explained *by* it. As the Daoist text *Dao De Qing* begins, "The Dao that can be spoken of is not the true Dao. The name that can be named is not the true name."

No one, then, can say with form (words, ideas, and explanations) the "why." No one will be able to articulate "that answer" to you. But you do not need them to. You are consciousness. You are awareness already. All you need to do then is completely let go of all the forms – all the understandings, beliefs, expectations, definitions, and identities that you have wrapped yourself in over your lifetime – and allow yourself to fall back into your transcendent formless nature which is already native to you. From that nature, all things are known just as they are.

And that is more than enough.

(091)

True Accomplishment

We often think that when we are not physically doing anything, we are not accomplishing anything. We also often think that when we are not doing anything, nothing is happening. Neither is true. Our very being exists on a level that transcends all elements of the physical experience. We can move around the physical props all we like, and in one sense we are doing little more than modifying pretend objects in a video game.

The real action takes place in consciousness. The real change occurs within consciousness. The real scene is the landscape of the spirit. And thus our accomplishment in this life is not measured in physical objects moved around on the stage of life, but rather in the lasting impact we have with others and within ourselves.

We are here to love! Loving another conscious being is a true accomplishment. Conquering one's own fear so that one may be more vulnerable and loving is a true accomplishment. As attested to by thousands who have seen the other side, the success of our life is in how much we have loved – not in what we have physically achieved. So take one moment today to do something truly loving for yourself or for another, for even if your act may seem small, it is the very reason the universe is here for you.

(092)

Separation Is an Illusion

There is actually no such thing as separation. The distance you experience is occurring *within* your conscious awareness of it – like a thick "sensory and thought cloak" passed over you that has deeply captivated your attention. Yet it is just an illusion. You are, in fact, everywhere.

If you're not actually experiencing that, such a claim may seem fanciful, if not totally absurd. Indeed, there are no words that can truly communicate many aspects of our greater nature, for words are meant to speak only to the dualistic forms of our local reality. This is especially true when consciousness – your consciousness? – has "lost itself" within the dualistic forms and temporarily forgotten what it truly is. In that case, the separation seems very real indeed.

Yet, in fact, everything you are experiencing is occurring within your awareness, and that awareness is irrevocably connected to the very same awareness that beholds all things. You do not need to *go* anywhere – you are already a part of everything!

While you are having this deep human experience of separation, allow yourself to fully embrace it for all it is meant to be. There is profound value in fully living the human experience. There is value in completely experiencing the separation.

Yet it is also important to remember that separation is an illusion, because you are actually connected to all those who seem external to you. Thus, what you do unto others, in a real sense, you do unto yourself. Love, then, is not merely an objective, it is a move back towards the *reality* of the unity that exists beneath the illusion of form.

176

(093)

There is Always Reason to Hope

There is always reason to hope! In fact, the things that "cause" us to *lose* hope are the dream. The more real and enduring reality is one of pure power, freedom, joy, and love! And thus encouraging someone to hope does not so much need to be an exercise in convincing them there is reason to hope, but rather it is reminding them of their true nature.

In truth, hope does not contend with hopelessness – because hopelessness is the illusion. Hopelessness can only exist as that which is irrevocably powerful and formless takes a sojourn into form and forgets itself there. What is far more fundamental than that dream is the ever-present nature of life itself. The truth of invincible hope is the presiding rock bed that is always just beneath our feet – it does not need to strive against that which is the illusion.

Being in the illusion, however, the physical personality portion of us often needs to be reminded. And so please be lovingly reminded now: remember! Remember what you are! Remember not just with your mind and with the learned ideas of this lifetime, but feel it with your ever present being! Dare to feel it with the life that flows through you itself! You are the light, you are hope and joy. You are freedom, and power, and love! You are so free and so powerful that you have allowed yourself to "get your hands dirty" by becoming "lost" in the human experience. Even with that being the case, no matter how dire the circumstances of the earthly play may seem, you cannot ever escape the pure hope of the immortal light that remains with you. The wonder, love, power, and hopefulness of that light is completely beyond earthly description – and even in the darkest times, it never, ever leaves you!

Allow yourself, then, to let go of all that troubles you and feel the precious presence of life that never abates. Surrender, and be reminded of that ever-present and completely unblemishable hope that always remains with you! For there is nothing you can possibly do that will ever remove you or those you love from its eternal care.

177

(094)

The Power of Small Choices

The real "playing field" is in the small, individual choices that we make. Your spiritual growth does not occur all at once. Healing the world does not occur all at once. Both are accomplished by making the choice in common moments to genuinely wield an intent that is operating from compassion and love rather than self-protection and fear.

Do not be distracted by the scope of healing that is required! Rather, bring your attention only to what *you* can do in any given moment and in any given choice, no matter how simple or mundane that moment or choice may be.

Every action we take is a choice. Every thought we buy into, even in the quiet of our minds, is a choice. Choices are constantly presented to us, both internally and externally. Yet so very many choices are not optimally utilized because we frequently make "routine" choices that are based in self-service, the avoidance of pain, or fear.

When the spiritually minded individual begins to get a real look at the self, it can be overwhelming to discover how much of what one does is actually motivated by ego or fear. It is too easy to then take yet another fearful step and say, "How can I possibly make a difference in such vast imperfection?" We often make a similar statement when we feel bewildered by trying to make a difference in our vastly imperfect external world.

Take heart! Contrary to how it may appear on the surface, you actually *do* have great power! At this very moment you have at your disposal the full power of the mightiest and most fundamental tool in existence: your intent. Do not underestimate it! Do not make the physical mind's mistake of believing that your nonphysical intent itself is inconsequential. Indeed, by making a conscious effort to shift your intent in any given common moment towards compassion, openness, courage, humility, joy, and love – even as

178

you genuinely do so in the quiet of your own heart – you are *already* making a move toward external and internal healing! The power of such choices may not be immediately apparent, but do not let that deter you: All change first occurs in consciousness space, and then only subsequently does it appear in the manifested world of form.

So recognize today the power of even the very small and common choices that you make. And have the courage to face your own imperfections and the imperfections of our world with hope, for the common moment is always available to you to actualize real, lasting change!

179

(095)

I Am, Therefore I Think

Descartes's famous conclusion "I think, therefore I am" is backwards. Thought does not precede being, being precedes thought. Thinking a thought does not create or even confirm beingness: Existing beingness thinks a thought. Or perhaps more accurately, existing unlimited beingness "becomes" the experience of being a perspective that thinks a thought.

While we are here in the physical, though, we often deeply "lose" ourselves in enticing yet shallow thought. We become almost completely wrapped up in the stimulating ideas of our minds: ideas of identity, ideas of responsibility, and beliefs. We think we are our identity, we think we are our responsibilities, and we think reality is just as we believe. None of that is fundamental.

That idea can sound frightening, because we are so wrapped up in the illusory identity, that when it is threatened we feel (incorrectly) that our very being is threatened. Ironically, it is *only* through being wrapped up in what is *not* ultimately real that we can even feel threatened! What we really are – that which we call spirit, or consciousness, or beingness – can never be threatened. Beingness is that which gives rise to all the ideas of the mind and to the entire physical experience. This allows it to engage in precious creation-expanding perspectives.

So next time you think that your thoughts or your beliefs make you *you*, or you feel fear or hopelessness as a result of them, remind yourself: Your thoughts exist *within you*; you do not exist within your thoughts!

180

(096)

Following the Signpost of Suffering

You are not fundamentally human. You are your "higher self" – the greater portion of you that transcends the physical experience and is ever connected to the Light. That higher self *knows* that it is powerful and unharmable and connected and loved.

And yet the human experience gives us the opportunity to actually experience something else. At times we believe – or even assume – that we are powerless, vulnerable, disconnected, or unloved. And when we do, we suffer. For some of us, much of our lives seem to be filled with these feelings.

We suffer precisely because these self-perceptions (perceiving one's self to be powerless, vulnerable, disconnected, or unloved) are not in alignment with the more fundamental *truths* of our greater nature! We suffer when we buy into a perception that is not in alignment with the greater truth. The higher self can't be (isn't) powerless, it is a powerful part of God – so when we adopt a self-perception of powerlessness, we suffer. The higher self can't be (isn't) vulnerable, it is unharmable and eternal – so when we adopt a self-perception of vulnerability, we suffer. The higher self can't be (isn't) disconnected – so when we adopt a self-perception of loneliness or distance, we suffer. The higher self can't be (isn't) unloved, it is profoundly celebrated and adored – so when we adopt a self-perception of shame or worthlessness, we suffer.

Discontentedness or suffering is a signpost to point towards the inaccurate self-perception we believe our circumstances are proving to us.

Yet the circumstances themselves do not automatically convey anything! No matter how rigorous or painful they may seem, they are neutral – they only give the experiencer the *opportunity* to place a meaning upon them, including one that is not in alignment with the more enduring truth.

181

When you suffer, then, follow the signpost! What negative self-perception are you buying into? What circumstance of your life is "proving" to you that negative self-perception is true? What fear are you avoiding? See if you can allow yourself to completely let go of all your stories, completely let go of all the meaning you are placing on the circumstance or sensation, and completely let go of even all the self-perception "buy-ins" you are entertaining. Beneath all of that, you are still *you* – the *real* you – and you are powerful, unharmable, connected, and always deeply and overwhelmingly loved! If you can follow the signposts bravely enough, they are pointing out your own negative self-perceptions and fears, so that by fully encountering them and seeing them for what they are, you can truly step past them and find your way back toward what *you* really are.

(097)

Finding the Sensitive You

Most of us are sensitive in ways that our ego won't admit. That sensitivity often leads toward the real you.

The ego is not a separate entity – it is the part of us that wishes to protect us. We wish to protect ourselves. And one of the most common ways to do so is to avoid feeling pain – especially the pain of negative emotions that result from the limiting perspectives we buy into and the negative beliefs we hold about ourselves and our world. We play all sorts of games with ourselves to avoid facing that which we do not want to face and to avoid feeling that which we do not want to feel. We effectively close ourselves off from our own actual experience.

But in so doing we temporarily segregate ourselves from our own true nature, which is unified and completely present with "what is." The ego creates a cage of ideas and beliefs to protect us, but as it does so, we are no longer free. We accept the illusion of the cage to avoid fear and pain, rather than being present with exactly "what is" and feeling exactly what we feel.

At the heart of the issue is our unwillingness to face our experience for exactly what it is because doing so may be terrifying or painful. The way to healing, then, is to choose to *fully allow* our own experience, no matter what it may be, *without* the protective beliefs, judgments, and stories of the mind. Leaving behind the cage can be absolutely terrifying, and can even feel like personal destruction! But in fact, *reality itself* is there to support you, because despite its appearances, reality is ultimately built upon love, not pain. In fact, the universe itself wants you to succeed in integrating your life experience and conquering your fear!

But such a journey is not one that can be taken abruptly: It is the small movements towards the courage to genuinely *feel* that help bring us closer to who we really are.

So when you are ready, make the choice to actually feel what you feel, no matter what you intellectually think it may mean *about* you. Feel your experience in your body, rather than listening to the age-old learned stories of your mind. Beneath all the scars, you are still sensitive – and when you find that genuine sensitivity, allow it, feel it, and embrace it, you will rediscover a piece of your true and ever-powerful self.

(098)

Seeking Truth Beyond Knowledge

Many who seek truth in knowledge believe that there is "some universe out there" and that our job as truth seekers is to go and figure out that universe. Ironically, the one who is looking at the external forms (sense data) and internal forms (ideas and dualistic understandings) to find the answers is often missing a constantly available clue: The forms one is evaluating only exist within one's own awareness of them.

All forms are contained *within* awareness; it is *not* that awareness only exists within form. That distinction is exactly what "the veil" allows the spirit to experience on Earth: It "clouds" the individual's awareness of his or her deeper transcendent nature so that he or she *can* get lost in the world of form. The individual then, having "forgotten" (lost sight of) what he or she really is for a time, goes out and seeks the answers to existence within the form itself, since form appears to be reality.

But looking in the world of form for the "Big Picture" answers is like a video game character looking for the answer to *everything* within the video game itself. There is not a single thing within the video game environment that will explain the nature of the physical computer server, or the building that server resides in, or the motivations behind the people that built the server building. In fact, since the video game character can only understand reality using video-game-world assumptions and concepts, it is not even possible for the character to understand the nature of the larger reality with his local video-game-knowledge-based intellectual mind alone.

You and I are similarly bound. *None* of the metaphors, ideas, or relationships of Earth can explain "The Answer." If one wishes to find truth, he or she must do so *beyond* knowledge.

How? There are no words that can truly communicate this deep and personal process, as it occurs beneath form and action itself; but for the

185

action-oriented mind we can say the following. One can seek truth beyond knowledge by consistently and genuinely moving one's focus towards that which *does* transcend the boundaries of realities: awareness itself! Or, if "awareness itself" is too vague and an object of attention is needed, we can say instead: "awareness of the present moment itself!"

In order to do so, one must be willing to consistently and genuinely direct one's attention *away* from the thought and the form, towards what one actually is. One must be ready to surrender, to completely let go of *all* the stories and understandings of the mind, and meet the present moment fully. This can take considerable patience and persistence, as we tend to build up a huge amount of "thought and idea momentum" over the course of a lifetime. In fact, one should be willing to let go even of the need to find the answer!

The benefits of such a practice may initially seem incomprehensible to the mind. Yet despite the challenge and the fact that the benefits may initially be hidden, such a pursuit is incredibly worthwhile. For indeed our greater nature never leaves us, and beneath all the illusion we have become so tied up within, the greater truth of our powerful formless being always remains available to us. The answers that are there far exceed the answers of the local human mind.

186

(099)

Awareness Has No Opposite

Awareness (here synonymous with *consciousness*) is not a thing that has an opposite. It just is. All opposites exist *within* awareness.

Have you ever had an experience that wasn't your awareness of it? Have you ever had a thought that wasn't your own awareness of it? Even the experience of waking and sleeping (which appears to be "gaining or losing consciousness"), or the experience of considering dualistic ideas like existence and nonexistence, are only known as you behold their forms and assign meaning to them. All of the content of your physical life, while deeply convincing in its apparent individuation and duality, has only ever taken place in your awareness of it.

Your awareness doesn't actually need a context to exist. It is That Which Is. It is that which has done those things, and had the experience of being these other things – but it always remains.

As such, *you* will always remain. All that your local personality is will not be lost when your body dies. You will not be lost. Rather, you will simply awaken to all that you truly are! And the walk in the physical that you just took will be recognized as yet another adventure that you have taken, another "form that you have been," in the great context of Creation.

(100)

Always Remember Your Light

You are a part of the Light! You are an unspeakably valuable and amazing fragment of That Which Is. You are spirit, brave and immortal spirit, now having the experience of a body. You cannot be harmed, you cannot be forgotten, and you cannot be replaced. You are never alone. You are adored, held up, and celebrated by countless thousands upon thousands of those who know and cherish you. You are a spark of the divine flame which shines bright in all things. You are a fire in the illusion of darkness. You are the presence of love, uniquely expressed as only you can. You are a powerful force, a mighty consciousness who has set out upon one of the greatest adventures thus far conceived, fully participating and yet fully transcendent. Your every thought and intent speaks to the galaxies, as they are your brothers and sisters. You are connected to every single thing that exists. You are so wonderful that you are beyond description! You are a universe unto yourself, and yet an ever-shimmering drop in the unspeakably brilliant ocean of the Light. You are loved, and you are love!

As you take your walk in the physical, set aside time to listen with your deepest being rather than your mind, and allow yourself to remember what you are.

(101)

The Importance of Your Worldview

Our physical reality is preceded by a nonphysical one in which we, both individually and collectively, help to "drive" what is physically manifested. One of the great "forces" that moves that process forward is expectation and belief. Thus what you believe – the nature of your worldview – is actually important for how our local experience will actualize.

As we "play the game," certain thoughts, ideas, and beliefs tend to gain or lose "momentum" within the collective consciousness. That momentum is a powerful force. It's important to recognize, however, that the collective momentum always starts and ends with individual momentum. The individual is important. What *you* believe – your worldview – is important!

You may not be consciously aware of it, but you are automatically communicating with all the many millions of other "players in the game" in consciousness space. Your beliefs, your expectations, and your intentions not only affect the "temperature of the water" in the collective consciousness, they also encourage others – and in a sense "give permission" to others, if necessary – to consider those same beliefs, expectations, and intentions, too. One person who shines bright with truly loving intent is like a beacon giving permission to many thousands of others to shine their light as well!

Take time, then, to look within and discover what beliefs and intentions *you* are sponsoring within the collective consciousness. What are you inspiring in our world today within your own mind and heart? Do not be discouraged by the apparent scope of change that may seem to be required on the "surface" of the physical world; but rather, recognize your power – for one person who is fully present and acting from a place of responsibility and genuine love can make a huge difference, and inspire many others to do the same.

189

(102)

Spirituality Transcends Earthly Ideas

As we live in a world of duality, we often approach understanding all of reality with the assumptions we've learned in duality. As one example, we believe distance is a fundamental property of reality, so we assume someone can only be in one place at a time. As another example, we believe reality is this one big shared objective place ("the world"), and that we all are seeing the same thing. Neither of those assumptions are correct.

An assumption we bring to spirituality is: We tend to believe that some ideas from our world – for instance religious conclusions or scientific conclusions – are themselves fundamental statements about all of reality, and that others are not. We assume this in part because we personally discover that some ideas end up proving to be verifiable and true in our local world, while others do not. We naturally establish beliefs to explain our life experience and how the external world seems to work. We then almost automatically extrapolate those beliefs into the "Big Picture."

Spirituality, though, is not fundamentally about a move towards one specific set of ideas, any more than it is about a person moving from one physical place to another. This is not to say that earthly ideas do not have an important place in spirituality – of course, they do! We are having the meaningful experience of duality, so the ideas of duality are important, useful, and meaningful to us. They are the forms with which we work. I wouldn't be writing these words, and you wouldn't be reading them, if there weren't some value in considering spiritual ideas.

But the spirit itself is something that fully transcends *all* the intellectual ideas and the many forms of Earth. The spirit in its actual nature transcends *all* the assumptions that we use to make intellectual judgments about reality. All intellectual judgments, and indeed all forms, occur *within* spirit.

190

Spirituality, then, is not just about ideas but, more fundamentally, about *what actually is*. Spirituality is about a "growth" of *what actually is* – an expansion in consciousness itself. That expansion transcends the forms with which we play, for it is not a growth strictly in the realm of ideas or actions. Rather, it goes far deeper – to a growth in *being*. Spirituality is about the way in which we, as consciousness, meet our experience, and how What Is becomes more as a result. It is about experientially learning how to wield our fundamental power: our intent. Spirituality is about actually growing towards – and becoming – creativity and love. It is not fundamentally about selecting the correct ideas, though ideas are an important part of what is occurring.

If we truly wish to walk the spiritual walk, we must go far deeper than working with ideas. We must do something that is far more difficult than selecting an understanding or belief: We must face ourselves. We must face our actual experience, meet it with full presence, bravery, humility and, most importantly, Love! We must be willing to allow ourselves to *change* towards – and actually *become* – more present, brave, humble, and loving. *We* are what continues after the physical world ends – so what we are here to work on, is *us*.

(103)

The Power of the Present Moment

The present moment is all that there ever is.

The "now" exists beyond the mind. It is not an idea of the mind. The "now" is your alert presence in the current moment, the silent witness that beholds and experiences all of the form (all of the thoughts, all of the feelings, all of the objects, and all of the contexts). The ideas of the mind can be temporarily experienced in the now, but the now is not the ideas. The now supersedes *all* ideas. You do not need to live your life lost in the dream that is the ideas of the mind, in thoughts about the future or the past. You do not need to surrender yourself to anxieties about the past or future – they too can only exist as they are recalled into the present moment.

Your power is always in the now. It does not exist in the past or in the future – it is always right now.

While you may have established great momentum in your life that may seem to bind you into a given circumstance-set or idea-set, you are not ever completely bound to the cumulative impacts of your past, because you *always* have the power in the now – right now – to change your momentum toward the direction that you choose. That direction can always be toward: brighter expectations for the future, new personal beliefs, greater awareness of your personal power and freedom, greater acceptance of the love that exists for you, increased prioritization of serving others over the self, or any other direction that you so choose. For as your consciousness moves in the present moment, so will your body – and even your reality itself – also move. Even if the effects may not always be immediately apparent, make no mistake that how you choose to use the present moment is always causing change. That which happens in consciousness space in the now *always* has an effect, even if you cannot see or understand it.

What momentum are you creating for yourself and your world today? If you are ready to do so, identify just one thing that has your attention, and choose to approach it with love, rather than fear. Even doing so with just one choice begins to move the momentum of your life in the direction of true freedom.

(104)

Using the Giant Mirror of Earth

The world is reflecting back to you the nature of your deepest beliefs. The physical universe is like a giant mirror provided to give you the opportunity to actually experience your beliefs, perceptions, and assumptions.

The physical world is not bad. It is a firm but neutral set of constraints engaged by consciousness for the purposes of self-realization and experience integration. The *quality* of your experience, then, contains precious clues as to whether or not you are utilizing that experience in a way that is in alignment with the more fundamental truth of love, or not.

How does your experience feel? What is life like for you? Where you feel negative emotions or fear, see if you can discover what negative self-perceptions or beliefs you have "bought into." When consciousness has bought into a self-perception or a perception about the world that is not in alignment with the truth, negative emotions result. Do you perceive yourself as – and then feel – powerless? Do you perceive yourself as – and then feel – unlovable, harmable, or trapped?

While these experiences are quite real, ultimately they are not fundamentally real or true. In that sense, they are illusions. Fundamentally you are powerful, you are loved, you are immortal, and you are free.

We buy into negative perceptions because we feel the evidence vouches for them. Our conclusions about reality become assumptions about reality, and they become invisible. Our conclusions about ourselves become assumptions about ourselves, and they become invisible. But the mirror keeps reflecting the appropriate experience of those assumptions back to us. Our experience remains a faithful gauge of the assumptions and beliefs that we are holding onto.

Your negative emotions can serve as guideposts to rediscover your assumptions. Seek out: "Why do I feel the way that I do?" When you find the belief that is giving rise to your feeling, do not assume it is true. Rather, use the discovery to help direct you towards the *fear itself, without* the story of the belief. Use the discovery to help direct you to the fear that you are – or were – too afraid to face and feel. What are you afraid of? Sit with the feeling, no matter how strong it is. Be with the feeling, no matter how strong it is. You can face your fears; you will not be destroyed. You can feel all your feelings; you will not be destroyed.

In fact, you may be set free! For underneath all the pain, confusion, and hardship, the true and ever-present nature of the spirit is always, always one of complete love, joy, and freedom! Your bedrock is one of love, joy, and freedom: It is always down there within you, beneath all the negative beliefs that you assume the physical world has proven to you. So where you don't feel love, joy, and freedom, allow the world to show back to you what you believe about yourself and the world that is causing you to no longer *know* it. That process of self-discovery, bravery, and feeling is exactly what the physical universe is meant for. And since the universe was built for that, it wants you to succeed and will work with you when you are ready.

(105)

Untying the Preciousness of Self from Form

Each of us intuitively senses the preciousness of our own being. However, the sense of preciousness we often assign to – or seem to find within – the forms of our lives actually transcends that form. But we often make the mistake of thinking that preciousness is a characteristic of form itself. We sense the preciousness of our being, and then because all we consciously remember is our human identity, we tie that sense of preciousness to aspects of our identity. For example we may feel innate preciousness when we consider our religious or national identity, behold the beauty of the human body, or as we take pride in learned behavior or personal human traits that we feel make us "who we are."

There is nothing wrong with sensing the preciousness of the spirit within the many wondrous forms of our lives! In fact, we come here in part to do just that. But as beings who have become somewhat "lost" in the forms of the physical universe, it can also be helpful to recognize that the preciousness that we are exists fully unto itself. We do not need the form to be, because we are ultimately not beings of form. We created form – it did not create us. We are *life* – which engages and entertains form and expands itself *through* the experience of form. Life does not need a religious identity, a national identity, a body, or human characteristics to exist. Rather, those things need *life* to exist.

The preciousness that you sense in your life is *you*; the preciousness that you sense in your life is your wonderful fellow spirits; the profound preciousness that you sense within everything in your life is God, by whatever name.

As you recognize this, you naturally begin to untie yourself from the form which seems to capture the preciousness of life. And as you allow yourself to rely less on form to find your sense of fulfillment, you return closer to the perfect freedom and joy that you truly are, beneath all the meaningful distractions of physical life.

196

You Are Not Fundamentally Human

On a fundamental level, you are not actually a human. You are having the experience of being human, which typically includes only remembering ever being human. In fact, you are *you*. You are the you that feels like "you" to you. That "you" transcends the experience of your local human character.

You also transcend the local human character's identity. You are not your job, you are not your responsibilities, you are not your nationality, you are not even your name.

What you really are is so amazing that it is completely beyond description! Yet we might simply say: You are immortal consciousness engaged in a well-defined and highly specialized reality experience, an important part of which includes forgetting all the rest of what you really are. You are participating in a very meaningful journey, a "rubber meets the road" attempt to actualize and expand your true loving nature within a rigorous context.

While you may not have conscious recollection of your greater self, it is *always* there within you. If you wish to take a step back toward it, let go of all the thoughts of your mind and listen deeply with your intuition. Listen with your being! The very life within you itself has more to tell you about what you really are than your intellectual human mind and its collection of local "facts."

(107)

Natural Joy

The spirit is *naturally* joyous! Thus the pursuit of happiness is not just about *pushing* towards brightness and joy, but rather is about fully *allowing what is* in the present moment. Through acceptance of *what is*, we naturally work past the many ego constructs that cause us to become stuck in unhappiness.

Ultimately, the experience of contrast allows that natural joy to deepen in measure with the degree of experience that is fully met and integrated.

However, whilst engaged in our local experience of contrast, consciousness tends to naturally "lose itself" in the form (thoughts, objects, ideas) and believe it is the form. This identification with something other than the whole brings unhappiness.

But returning to the natural joy is not an act of rejecting the form. Rather, we naturally release our association with the separate when we completely allow and accept it. Through surrender to form, we naturally "untie" ourselves from it and our intrinsically joyful nature effortlessly rises back to the surface.

(108)

Love Knows No Boundaries

Often when we think about loving others, we think about those close to us. We prioritize our family, our organizations, or our nation – but often at the expense of others. We tend to think of love as "protecting our own."

True love knows no boundaries! Love surpasses all labels, shatters all divisions, exceeds all limits. Love transcends all human distinction. Love accepts *all*.

We are to love *all* people! We are to love all beings, all expressions of life. We are to love regardless of identity, creed, or race. There is no identity label or condition that can preclude someone from deserving our love. If we believe otherwise, even if we do so in the name of some belief we think is moral, we are ultimately listening to our ego rather than the spirit.

When we (eventually) return to the Light after our walk in the physical, we will be deeply loved no matter what identity we adopted, no matter our preferences or affiliations. Even through our many imperfections, we will be profoundly and overwhelmingly loved! In fact, we *are* profoundly and overwhelmingly loved right now!

Everyone you meet is ultimately your brother or sister. They, too, seek the love from which we have all come. They, too, yearn for the love that knows no boundaries. And *you* have the profound opportunity to be the hand of compassion or kindness that meets them wherever they are! As you do so, even in small ways, you help the transcendent love of the spirit to shine forth and gradually transform our world.

(109)

Your Thoughts Are Powerful

Every thought has an effect, both in our local reality system and in others. You may not see the effect of your thoughts with your physical eyes, but in fact, every thought echoes throughout all space. Reality is affected by each and every intent that you hold! For instance, what you are intending and thinking right now is "happening" throughout all the Earth, and is affecting vibrations in other parts of the world.

How can this be? Consciousness is the fundamental fabric of reality. Since all consciousness is connected to all other consciousness, when consciousness "moves," all of reality is affected.

However, because we are largely not aware of this, we are "messy" with our thoughts. Because of the beliefs that we have collectively enshrined and perpetuated, we often don't know our own importance, or our own power.

It is time to remember! What is occurring within you is important! Your thoughts, beliefs, expectations, and intentions are important. Your personal experience is important. *You* are important!

The thoughts that arrive into your awareness started with you at some point. You receive sensory data and decide how to process it. After doing this for a lifetime, your beliefs and interpretations can be so firmly set that they seem like properties of reality itself. The beliefs and interpretations that you have bought into feed the nature of the thoughts that arrive.

Your primary power is intent; your point of power is the now. Using your intent in the current moment, you always have the ability to reframe your experience. This changes the world. Using your intent in the current moment, you always have the power to alter the momentum of your thoughts. You are not powerless before them; rather, they are expressions

200

of *your* power. They arrive to serve you, as you have requested. Modifying your relationship with your thoughts also changes the world.

(110)

Your Inherent Beauty

The flower does not try to be beautiful. You do not have to, either. The sunset does not strive to be red. Neither do you have to strive to shine with your own light. That light may seem to be obscured for a while as you take your walk in the physical, but it isn't truly. You shine because you are.

Being does not require effort. Only striving to be what you are not requires effort. You do not have to squeeze yourself to produce love; it is what you are, and flows from you as you Be.

You are ravishingly beautiful! *You* are an awe-inspiring expression of the divine fire that gives rise to All Things! The wondrousness of your being cannot be lost. The diamond can be no less precious if it is covered in mud.

Know this, let go of all that you are not, and shine!

(111)

Fear as a Sign of Potential Expansion

Fear is a reflection of the space in "experience space" that Beingness is expanding into. It reflects a "distance" that has not yet been experientially integrated. Fear is a sign that "That Which Is" is engaged in something (a form or perception) that challenges it and is giving it room – within itself – to expand into.

In part, our physical reality is what happens when unharmable consciousness decides to create a challenge for the purposes of actual experiential growth. Fear is not something that was created; it is simply what happens when existing consciousness engages a new constraint-set that it is not yet optimally developed to handle, and buys into perspectives that are not in alignment with its true nature. Fear is only possible when the spirit is engaged in challenge, which means it is working with a yet unintegrated experience. That is, fear is only possible when the spirit is engaging sense data or form that it does not yet recognize for what it truly is, or when spirit is buying into a belief that is not in alignment with the truth. Fear is a growing pain that happens when "That Which Already Is" engages in a real process of perspective integration to expand and become even more! In that sense, fear ultimately serves love's purpose of joy and expansion.

Ultimately there is nothing at all to fear! Fear is completely subservient to the greater and perfectly enduring truth of love. When the "game" of growth and expansion is won or departed, there can be no fear. Fear is an illusion – an artifact of "perceived distance" from true love and unity, where no distance can actually occur. Fear is not native to the soul, for our native being is one of total power, freedom, and love – and in the brightness of that Light, every shadow of fear is completely dissolved.

(112)

Are We Growing or Are We Whole?

Some say we are here in the physical to learn and grow, and others say we are already complete and whole. Which one is it?

Both are true, and there is no contradiction.

Our true being is always complete and whole. Even as our completeness and wholeness is maintained, we choose to express our incredibly creative nature by participating in reality systems like our own. As we integrate specific experience, we grow in our capacity to know and actualize our true being. Adopting unique and well defined perspectives – for instance, the human perspective that feels separate from everyone else – allows for a great deal of experiential growth.

The only way to adopt the highly specialized human perspective is to forget all of what we really are. If we remembered all of what we really are, we would constantly know that there is nothing ever to fear. But, the capacity for challenge is commensurate to the opportunity for experiential growth: it is precisely the "apparent distance" from our true nature that is the "frontier" of new perspective creation. We love to see "what we can do with" that highly specialized perspective! We rejoice at the opportunity to see how well we can express love even through the challenging constraints of the human experience, and even through forgetting!

While we are already whole, that which is already whole "increases" as we grow experientially towards love. The possibilities grow when consciousness – life itself – deeply engages in and integrates specific experiences, including experiences of incompleteness.

(113)

The Playground and the Classroom

Our experience here is born in the spirit of play! Our true nature is one that is completely free, unlimited, creative, and powerful. It is from that true state that we decide to ultimately express ourselves here in the physical experience.

And yet, here on Earth we often go through experiences that seem far from playful. We are engaged by what seem to be the "hard constraints" or "hard rules" of our world: A knife will always cut, resources will always be finite, and the body will always die. Indeed, there is profound growth opportunity available to the spirit when it is "forced" (*apparently* forced) to face these "hard constraints." Such experiences help us experientially "learn": We learn how to deal with circumstances, we learn how to make choices, we even learn more about who we are. Even through and beyond our local reality, there are "spiritual laws" in place that help guide us through growth that is beneficial for us – and sometimes that process can be extremely painful.

So is life more like a playground, or a classroom?

The following two statements are both true and do not contradict:

1. Nothing is required of us. The universe is born out of a desire to play, to exercise our great creative natures in a unique way, just for the sake of doing so.
2. There is meaning and value in integrating challenging experiences and adding to Creation. Sometimes the "spiritual laws" in place end up guiding us through what seem to be very difficult experiences for the sake of growth.

The classroom is in the playground.

Even when you are in class, you can play! No matter what circumstance you find yourself in, your true nature remains unharmed and shining and joyful!

205

And when you can fully let go of the burden you have assigned to your assignment, and get in touch with and express that ever-abiding true nature, often the lesson is ended – and you can now be full of even more joy than you were before you playfully went to class.

(114)

Trying to Name the Attributes of God

Attributes aren't fundamental, Spirit is fundamental. Attributes occur within and by and through Spirit. Said another way: Forms and objects aren't fundamental, life itself is fundamental. Forms and objects occur within and by and through life.

So it is not correct to ask, "What form is God? What attributes belong to Him, and which do not?" That question incorrectly imposes attributes with the fundamental quality. That which is fundamental expresses form; it is not that form has fundamental existence. As Rupert Spira says, "Objects do not have existence, existence has objects."

Does this mean that God is not kind, or compassionate, or loving? No, it does not mean that. It is quite accurate to say that God is absolutely and unconditionally loving, understanding, and compassionate. And indeed, the sojourn of the Spirit into duality ultimately expands the real depths of kindness, compassion, and love. What it means, though, is that we cannot successfully impose local qualities on that which gives rise to them. As we ponder the nature of God, then, we are wise to turn from the thinking mind to the depths of being within us, which itself transcends the distinctions that abound in our physical experience, and already knows the truth that cannot be named.

207

Loving Intent Transcends All Axes

Our walk in the physical is a journey of experiential growth. A fundamental part of that growth is improving what Tom Campbell calls our "quality of intent": that is, evolving our deepest "why" towards love, and past fear. This movement does not occur on one axis. We are multidimensional beings, so our expansion towards love is also multidimensional.

Yet since all we remember is our experience in a universe of duality, as we explore how best to respond to questions of spirituality or morality we sometimes assume that we should be "moving in one direction and not the other." We sometimes imagine that there is one "axis" for any given spiritual or moral choice; and as spiritual people, we wonder if we should be moving in "one direction" along that axis. For example, we ask: Should we always be peaceful, or is it sometimes acceptable to harm others? Should we strive and exert will to accomplish things, or relinquish effort and surrender? Should we always give when another has need, or cut them off if we feel it is best for them? We might even include: Should we believe in religious teachings, or let them go?

In all these deliberations, the paramount question we should be asking ourselves is: *Why* are we making the choice that we are? Are we truly motivated by the best interests of the other and of the whole, or are we actually motivated to protect or serve ourselves?

As we genuinely explore that question, we find that even in love, different circumstances may demand different answers.

It may be meaningful, then, to recognize that as we refine the quality of our intent towards love, when it comes to making spiritual or moral choices there are two important ways that we spiritually grow.

208

The first is that we grow strong in being able to perform in any given direction. Put another way: We "strengthen" a given virtue. We see "how far" and "how deep" we can go in making any given choice, even when the circumstance is difficult. So in response to the above examples, we learn how to be peaceful, even in the face of conflict; and we learn how to be courageous and to intervene when necessary, even in the face of danger. We learn how to strive and exert great effort; and we learn how to release control and surrender. We learn how to be selfless and give all that we can, even at the expense of the self; and we learn how to refuse. We learn when and how deeply to put our faith in the ideas of our world; and when to go our own way. Any one of these or many thousands of other aspects of experiential learning can be its own lesson: Sometimes we can spend an entire lifetime or more just experientially "learning" one type of strength. But each of these qualities, and a great many more, have their meaningful place in consciousness-based Creation.

The second way we grow is that we refine our ability to best discern *which* choice – which "force" – to employ in any given circumstance. We grow in wisdom. As we learn from our experiences and repeatedly live the results of our own intentions, we experientially develop discernment that is unobscured by ego. We develop clarity of awareness when appraising both external and internal environments, such that we can appropriately identify and acknowledge what will best serve the whole. We grow in our ability to make the best choice for the betterment of others, and we refine our ability to identify and select that choice even when the circumstances are complex and even when the personal costs may be great.

Both of these types of growth are precious to the spirit! The spirit seeks to mightily develop both as it journeys through lifetimes.

Both of these types of growth contribute towards the expansion of Love! Love is not on one axis – it encompasses them all! Love encompasses many virtues: peace, and bravery; will, and release; charity, and discipline; faith, and self-reliance; rest, and service; self-love, and love for others; confidence, and humility; prudence, and sacrifice; and many, many more.

209

In truth, the two "ways we grow" that are described above are not separate, and these dualistic ideas are very crude representations of the complex evolution of intent. But for we who are rooted in duality, it can be helpful to recognize that there is not one teaching or behavior that can fully communicate what it means to grow spiritually. Rather, each of us should do our best to meet our experience fully, genuinely, and selflessly, wherever we are, without necessarily leaning on a given belief or axis. This open approach helps us to use the human experience for all it is meant to be and facilitates growth towards Love in *all* the many ways that are possible.

(116)

We Will Get There

Near death experiencers often describe that they sense everything being in perfect order. One may ask, how can this be, given all the apparent destruction and suffering in the world?

"Everything being in perfect order" does not mean that we are expressing love in the most optimal way, yet. We knowingly came into a very difficult constraint-set (the physical universe) to refine our ability to make love-based (rather than fear-based) choices within a challenging environment. We have a long way to go: Each of us still often makes choices based out of fear rather than love. But, because of the "divine law" that Source has in place, we *will* get there, whether quickly or slowly (depending on our choices)! The process is unfolding successfully! But it's a real system – real beings are making real free-will choices – and that can get apparently messy. That messiness is a price that we were all willing to pay to participate in such an amazing endeavor of creative expansion!

To put it in religious language: God's plan cannot fail. We all choose every day how readily we will work with it, or not – but it cannot fail. The spiritual systems that are in place do, over time, encourage each of us to actually grow up towards love, to integrate our fears, and to fully express ourselves in a huge variety of conditions. As we do that, the plan of God is fulfilled. And, despite how circumstances may appear on the surface, we are doing that right now!

So take heart, have hope, and be encouraged! There is great opportunity and power in any given moment to choose love and compassion, even in the simplest of ways. As you do so, as a part of the One yourself, *you* actually facilitate the successful fulfillment of the great plan for this universe!

(117)

Goodness Can't Help but Win

No matter what happens, life ends up using it for the good. There is no loss that is not eventually followed by the victory of life, which becomes more through that loss. No matter the loss, failure, or destruction, there is always some good that comes into being afterward as a result. This is the nature of permanent life versus impermanent change.

Everything that happens within Beingness occurs for Beingness' sake. There is no circumstance that can overcome Beingness, nor escape use in its evolution.

So while the churning of changing circumstance may seem to burn us, we can never be lost, and we can never truly fail. This means that we do not ever have to surrender to the feeling of defeat.

(118)

The Spiritual Message of Empowerment

The spiritual message is one of empowerment. This is because powerlessness is just a nonfundamental experience, while freedom and power are the enduring truths.

Spirituality is about moving towards *what actually is*. Since freedom and power are our true inalienable nature, true spirituality naturally moves towards them. But because we have fear, we resist our experience in a myriad of ways. We use our ideas and our will to set up many boundaries and to block our own experience. We even use ideas about spirituality to do this. We (seem to) lose the powerful truth as we assign it to the powerless form.

Can life itself be repressed? It can choose to express itself through a great variety of conditions and within a great variety of constraints, and those conditions and constraints can change, but life itself is totally free. Spirituality is about that true nature of life, about allowing it, and knowing it, and becoming it – not just about the nature of the forms or constraints that life expresses through.

Spirit transcends form. Thus no form can truly convey its breadth. And yet, as life seeks to express itself through its creations, it can strive to reflect its ineffable and inalienable qualities through them. Those qualities, among many others, are ultimate love, joy, peace, power, and freedom! And thus, the spiritual message is one of ultimate love, joy, peace, power, and freedom!

(119)

You Are Worthy

You are worthy of love! You are not only worthy of it, it is native to what you truly are! You – specifically *you* – are cherished, adored, and celebrated! And, despite what you may believe or what you may think about yourself, you are deserving of that love!

Religious ideology often teaches that we must earn God's favor or acceptance ("God" by whatever term) through action or belief. This is untrue. Unconditional love is just that: unconditional. But God's love is not just unconditional in a general way, God is unconditionally loving *even* with *full* knowledge of all your personal failings and imperfections. Imagine the depths of love necessary to completely and fully love you even as you perform your darkest act – and only then would you even begin to just barely touch the understanding of the fullness of God's love.

No matter what you have suffered, what you have endured, or what you have done – you personally are loved, cherished, adored, celebrated, and upheld. You are celebrated for being *you*!

Allow yourself to feel this, right now! Let go of all your self-judgments, all your preconceptions, all your stresses – and feel it, deep down within you. Let go, and allow yourself to feel and remember that you are profoundly, deeply loved! Though the human journey is long and filled with the obfuscation of physical life, your deepest being remembers. Your deepest being yearns for the love that you have never lost. Can you feel it, even if but as a precious glimmer?

When we *know* this about ourselves, when we *know* with confidence that we are loved and celebrated – really know it – how much better can we then express love in our world? How much better can we shine the light to each other when we know that the Source of all Life completely *loves* us, personally?

214

For indeed often as we seem to get lost in the fog of circumstance, it is by shining *our* light that the other person may remember the love that exists for *them*! It is by *our* kindness and compassion that the other person may be reminded of *the* kindness and compassion that never ceases. We have the profound honor of having the opportunity to shine the light of love to each other in a place where we seem to have forgotten it. Many millions of beings yearn for this opportunity – you and I have it today.

So remember today, this very day, that *you* are worthy of the love of the Source of all Creation – and as you do so, shine it to those around you! Remind them that they, too, are worthy, no matter how messy life may seem! For as you shine the light of love to others and remind them of who they really are, you help facilitate the great plan of bringing the foundational Love of Being into *this* reality.

You Are Free to Choose Your Beliefs

You are completely free to choose what to believe. The only way this can seem untrue is if you believe it is untrue.

Your beliefs act as a filter through which you experience reality. Our physical reality is a place where you are able to buy into some set of ideas, including ideas about yourself and the world, and then experience exactly what it is like to have that perspective.

Does that mean there is no absolute truth? No. Absolute truth exists within Beingness, but Beingness transcends all form (all "this and not that" distinctions as we perceive them). That which we call God is the living conscious source of "Big Picture" Truth. But God is not a "thing," not just one thing among many, but rather God is in fact beyond all form and gives rise to it all. Beingness is not beholden to perceived objects or ideas, which exist only because of Beingness and within Beingness – so no objects or ideas can fully speak to What Is Happening.

Meanwhile as our consciousness is engaged in a form-based reality like ours, of course we use form to understand and engage this physical experience. Our reality experience takes place within a consistent rule-set (the physical rule-set) and within a rigorous context, so we intently look to that context for answers. In other words, we understand and engage our experience through the ideas, objects, symbols, sights, sounds, and all the other many forms of our physical lives. That is good and natural, and the divine can and does work through those forms to engage with us! But ultimately, "Big Picture" Truth is beyond naming. There is no way to even attempt to utter the depths and vastness of "Big Picture" Truth with physical language. As we strive in vain to do so, we might, however, say that the Truth is absolute and total love, limitlessness, and transcendent Beingness!

And *that* is what you really are.

216

As transcendent Beingness yourself, you are absolutely free, then, to decide how you will frame this reality experience you are having. You have that power. If you don't believe you have that power, it is because *you* bought into that belief. Perhaps you did so long ago, in your present earthly childhood. But the power is still yours. You cannot not be what you really are. Your true being transcends the forms of your life – and thus, *you* always get to choose how you will interpret and what you will believe about those forms.

(121)

You Can Trust Reality

If you trust God, you trust reality. If you trust reality, you are trusting God. An experience of form is not the experience of the full reality of God, but physical reality does not occur apart from God. All occurs within the One, and in accordance with the divine laws of the One. Since those divine laws arise from unconditional love and unfathomable wisdom, all of our experiences ultimately take place within and for the purposes of unconditional love and unfathomable wisdom!

Our reality system is one in which experiences of tremendous difficulty are possible. From this side of the veil, beset by so many difficulties and even burdened by the requirements of physical survival itself, we tend to see reality as an adversary to strive against. We "fight to survive" in many ways every day. But what we are truly working to overcome is the difficulty we perceive from our relationship with the content of the present moment; what we are truly striving against is our own imperfection.

Our rigorous universe with its high potential for challenge has been established purposefully. It has been established so that we may expand the very nature of Being. It has been established so that we may more deeply understand and apply the power of our own beliefs and interpretations. It has been established so that we may truly learn what it means to grow in love and compassion, even in this rich context.

No matter what happens, no matter how much pain you may be in or how dire the world may seem, your experience does not escape the bounds of God's perfect love and wisdom. Even if you rage in response, you are loved. Even if you denounce the world as terrible and unjust, the divine laws of God are working to fulfill plans of love and joy that are far beyond our comprehension!

And we can trust those plans. We can trust the love and wisdom of God!

218

Reality is not your enemy. Your only enemy is your own fear and your own resistance. Your obstacle is your own unwillingness to fully find and then meet your reality for exactly what it is any given moment, beneath the story. That is not easy – our own imperfection is vast, our fears are many, our wounds are deep – and our stories and identities protect us. But our reality is here for us so that we have the real opportunity to resolve that imperfection, to face those fears, to heal those wounds! And when we are genuinely ready to do that, when we trust reality enough to really take ownership of our experience and surrender to the fullness of the present moment, the spirit can then flow through us and once again reveal the truth of the ever-present love and joy that is the enduring foundation of even our earthly existence.

219

(122)

Beingness Has No Lack

There is no lack in your being. Lack is a perspective voluntarily entertained to help That Which Is truly know the abundance of its own nature.

Beingness is already perfect. It does not have error or flaw. And yet, Beingness also works to create and to expand within manifestation; and through that, much growth in actualized joy and love is possible!

That is true of you, too, because you are Beingness. Even though your experience may have many apparent shortcomings, your perfect true nature transcends them all! That transcendent nature is not abstract, it is the real abiding truth that forms the foundation of your experience of form, including any given perception of lack.

Know, then, that beneath the noise you are the fullness that surpasses all things! That is true no matter how your local reality experience may appear.

(123)

The One and the Many

We are One, and yet we are Individual. This is a great truth. From our local perspective, those two statements may seem like a paradox, but they are not. In other systems you are aware of your oneness with All, and yet also your individuality, which is precious and preserved.

You have likely forgotten that you are connected to everything else because you agreed to adopt that restriction (in appearance only) in order to have the human experience. Even though that is true, you are still what you are. You cannot ever be separate from All That Is! You can only agree to have an *apparent* experience of separation so that you can participate in experiential expansion!

When physical life ends, you become aware of all the ways you affected everyone else in your entire life. Near death experiencers often describe this "life review" process as being "first-hand": You experience exactly what you caused others to experience. You know because what you have done to another, you have done to yourself, for the other is a part of you.

And this is why love is such an important theme: Love is reflective of the unity that is native to our being. Love is reflective of what we really are! Love is the body of the One Being working in concert. Treat the other as yourself, for the other *is* yourself!

Your Body Is an Experience

Your body is an experience, not a fundamentally real object. Your body is a set of constraints that your consciousness is experiencing per a defined physical rule-set in consciousness space. There is not a fundamentally real piece of flesh that you are inhabiting. Rather, your body exists as an experience that is occurring within *you*!

You already existed before you engaged in the experience of a physical body, and you will exist after that bodily experience ends. Just as a movie screen exists before and after an image is projected upon it, your awareness exists before and after the experience of the body appears within it.

However, many of us do not remember existing before the body. That is because the veil of forgetfulness is tied to our acceptance of the bodily constraint-set. It feels to us like the body is all we have ever been, because that is the nature of such a highly specialized experience as being human.

Regardless of the veiling that occurred so that you could have the focused human experience and remember nothing beyond it, your true nature stands firm. Your true loving nature does not give way; its existence is sure and ever-present! It is only within that sure and ever-present true nature that the experience of the body with its limited perceptions and recollections exists.

(125)

Beingness Transcends Religion

God has no religion, except that we do.

As we exist in a world of form, we come to understand reality within the context of that form. We impose meaning upon the form we have experienced. We formalize and institutionalize our interpretations, and we are often happy to buy into the interpretations that are passed to us, and to pass them along ourselves. In spiritual matters, we tend to attribute the very real internal experience of the divine to the forms themselves. But the forms – the ideas, the objects, the traditions – do not have fundamental existence. They are but shadows arising within the One, as are all forms. They are fragments and not the Whole. No fragment can fully satisfy, because our true nature is not fragmented at all.

Beingness needs no name. Beingness transcends all names. Beingness can arise into the experience of limited perspective and temporarily assign the power to the shadowy forms occurring within it, but such forms are not truly reflective of the perfect unity and limitlessness of What Truly Is.

The true path is Love! Love transcends all restrictions, all requirements, all definitions. Love cannot be contained within a given set of ideas or practices – it can operate through them all. Love can mean both structure or lack of structure; beliefs or lack of beliefs. The living power of love thrives both within and beyond *all* the forms of our entire universe! May our human practices align with that living power! May our religion be the religion of compassion, kindness, humility, personal ownership, bravery, and selfless love – whether outside of any named structure, or within whatever structure or form we genuinely feel called to express it.

223

Love Is the Absolute Foundation

Love is always the foundation upon which all is built. There is not one process that did not begin in love and will not end in love.

The truth is not hard or cold, ever. The truth always falls back to love. If something appears hard or cold, that is an appearance. Appearances can last a long time; appearances can seem very real as we buy into them and believe our own interpretations about them. We only have the power to do so because we are a part of the One sovereign consciousness, and we can even choose to deeply experience temporary, limited interpretations for a while. But the greater truth, the ever-lasting unshakable bedrock of all of existence, is love! Freedom, joy, and love are the true root of all creation.

Every single thing always, always occurs as a result of the unfathomable depths of unconditional love giving rise to it. Reality systems come and go, complex patterns in the tapestry spun out of love, and spun because of love. The tapestry may contain horrifying images; but no more than the greatness of love that gave rise to them and that expands its own creative depths even through them.

We are free to buy into our interpretations of less-than-love. We are so free we can do even that. But we cannot ever truly escape the truth of the freedom, joy, and love of our own being. Even as we take temporary experiential sojourns seemingly far away from that freedom and joy, we are still within it. Love cannot be overcome, and we are love – so what shall we fear?

(127)

Your Soul's "JOB"

The soul's JOB is the Joy Of Being! There is nothing else required of the soul – it only needs to exist, and then flourish the beauty and bliss of that existence in a multitude of ways!

We are bold in how we create. We are so bold that we have embarked upon this great journey of the human condition. We are so free, and so powerful, and so loved, that we have decided to exercise our Beingness to new depths by experiencing almost complete separation from Source and from each other. And now that we are here, most of us have come to take this experience quite seriously.

But beneath the seriousness and the pain, the soul has no restrictions, no requirements, and no hardship. The soul is free in love! The soul ever-burns with the joy and bliss of Being!

You are soul – so that is true of you, too. You do not need to fret or fear: You only need to be. Your only job is to exist in the radiant joy of what you are, and to share that joy richly with all other parts of the One!

Your job then is to exist, to experience joy, and to love! There are no other true requirements of you. And when your mind says otherwise, be brave and bold enough to find the beliefs you are holding that "prove" that to you. Those beliefs are, in an ultimate sense, untrue. Yes, we must strive to do our part in our local world in a practical way, to care for those who need us and to perform the many daily actions of life. But that can be done through the freedom of being that is already ours, and not only as a struggle against the weight of responsibility. Any belief in shame, or fear, or powerlessness is ultimately untrue. It is only when we buy into the illusions of those perceptions – when we wrap our true selves up in those negative beliefs and self-perceptions – that we, because of those beliefs, feel something is required of us to return to wholeness.

We never left; our true job never changed. The Joy Of Being is all that we must do, and even as we perform our many meaningful roles in the human drama, the Isness that we are dwells firmly in joy beneath all the requirements that our local self may have put upon it.

128

Not One Ounce of Pain Is Wasted

Reality is efficient. All things occur within "divine laws" that have been established from inconceivable wisdom and love! That includes experiences of hardship and pain. As difficult as it can be for us to understand, pain too is meaningful, and ultimately has an important role that serves lasting love and joy.

How can this be? How can terrible pain and misery exist within love? What purpose can it possibly serve? While this is very difficult to speak to from the human perspective, there are three important points we may consider.

First, the experience of contrast creates a distance into which the fullness of the Joy of Being may expand. Everything "negative" serves as a point of contrast to help establish the experientially known depths of what is "positive." In other words, love can be better known, forever, when the spirit has actually known and understood separation from love.

Second, "negative" experience, even when unanticipated, offers a "counter pressure opportunity" for the spirit to exercise loving or brave choice-making through. Put as a very crude metaphor, if you can play the video game on a harder difficulty level, you develop mastery very quickly and can then later apply that mastery in other games (other realities) in other ways. The counter pressure of challenge enables us to expand our capacity for expressing and actualizing love.

Third, by experiencing challenge, the whole system ends up "discovering novelty" within itself and adding potential. Creative manifestation begets more creative manifestation. Put another way, even in apparent destruction, more things become possible than may otherwise have been possible.

All three of these ultimately serve lasting love and joy! Indeed, in the perfect balance of What Is, not one ounce of pain is wasted – for even when we

227

cannot see it, every element of our experience, including our pain, is a precious and meaningful part of the great love-threaded tapestry of Creation.

129

Tearing Down the "Wall of Belief"

We commonly turn to beliefs for answers when the world "does things" to us that cause us to feel personal fears. Beliefs give the illusion of control, which makes us feel better. Thousands of times over a lifetime we turn to our beliefs for comfort. We justify, bury, or avoid certain pains or fears by buying into the stories of our beliefs. If and when we eventually want to truly question our beliefs, we often find that we cannot, because questioning them would mean tearing down the wall we built to protect ourselves from what we didn't want to feel in the first place. It can be difficult – and even completely terrifying – to finally face the fear that we originally needed the help of beliefs to avoid fully feeling.

Two brief examples: If you are afraid of being (feeling) worthless, perhaps you have adopted a belief that your actions or affiliations give you worth. If you are afraid of dying, perhaps you have embraced a belief in a prescribed afterlife. Typically, we each have many examples of such beliefs that we have erected over a lifetime. In fact, over time our core beliefs end up becoming so deeply rooted that they do not appear to us to be beliefs anymore, but rather they appear to be fundamental characteristics of reality itself!

Yet in fact, the "Big Picture" reality exists firmly beyond personal beliefs. As stark and unforgiving as this current constraint-set of physical reality may seem at times, truly it is subordinate to the greater reality of love, peace, and bliss! That is true even if we don't see it in our current level of awareness. Thus, if we are willing to leave the comfort of our beliefs and walk through the opaque hellfire of our fears to experience exactly "*What Is*," we have the opportunity to reach true relief and joy. It may take incredible personal courage and humility to do so, but such are some of the most exciting and rewarding challenges to the spirit!

So be brave, and be hopeful, and when you feel you are ready, know that you are free to tear down those walls where you find them. For you exist firmly

229

beyond the concepts of your local identity, and ultimately you have nothing to fear by challenging your beliefs.

(130)

You Are a Creator

You are a powerful creative being! You are capable of creating realities. You do so individually, and you also do so collectively. Source is immeasurably creative – and you are a part of Source.

Our world is a place where we learn how to manage the contents of our own nature. We experientially learn how to wield our intent. We experientially learn to actualize our deeper creative and loving Beingness within a rigorous context. We experientially master the power of contrast! As we do that here, we are better able to do so in contexts that are beyond our human comprehension. No matter the type of experience we entertain, no matter how deep and dark it may seem, we are always beings of love and creative power. Indeed, as immortal spirits we are bold in the depths to which we are willing to go in the name of creativity and love.

Compared to other reality systems, ours is dense and firm. But even here, our creative nature always operates. Even here, we alter the contents of our personal experience, our collective experience, and our apparently shared external material world, by the nature of our own thoughts, beliefs, and intentions.

So be reminded of your power today! Reality is listening to you. What are you saying to it?

(131)

The Playing Field of the Small Stuff

The name of the game is to perform even the simplest actions from kindness, compassion, or love! We do not necessarily need to aspire to achieve some great physical accomplishment. We only need to meet any given moment or interaction with a right state of being.

From the perspective of the spirit, success is when kindness, compassion, or love is genuinely brought forth in even the smallest way. Even the whisper in the quiet of your own heart is important. Success is not measured in moving mountains, because the mountains of Earth are not fundamentally real anyway. What is real is you – your consciousness itself – and when that you chooses to meet any given moment with love, the heavens themselves rejoice!

The goal, then, is not to achieve a given physical configuration in how the contents of Earth look. The playing field is the moving of your own spirit, the wielding of your own precious intent. And the wielding of intent is done within all scales of physical activity, whether large or small, and whether by thought, word, or deed. All choices, no matter their scope, are grounds for the real opportunity – which is how we bring our being to bear within the physical context. Our simplest and most noble power is in how we choose to meet our experience.

And when genuine love is the motivation behind even the small choices, the contents of Earth work themselves out on their own!

Let us focus, then, not on the scope and size, not on the forms and systems, but on who we really are and on how we may be there for each other. Let our choice be a kind gesture, a supportive smile, a gentle hand on the bark of an old tree. For though those choices may appear small, when motivated by genuine love, the smallest choice is the greatest accomplishment.

232

(132)

Working Past the Assumption of the Objective Material World

We live in a world that appears to be a shared objective reality. In our world, if someone goes to some place and sees something, they can report that something to you and you can gain knowledge about it secondhand. We often assume that the same is true for the larger reality.

Reality is ultimately consciousness-based, not objective material world-based. So the nature of the experience of any given individual can be significantly different than that of another – in fact they are two different experiences entirely. This is true even in our local world, where two people experience the same physical event in their own unique ways, and often quite differently. But that truth is even more apparent in other reality systems, many of which are instantaneously responsive to the personal nature and intent of the individual. The "objects" reported from those environments then are often more a reflection of the individual and their beliefs than they are of the "reality itself."

In order to pursue understanding of the larger reality, then, we need to be willing to let go of many of the physical assumptions that we hold so dear. One of those assumptions is the belief in an objective material world. The world of matter is a consistent, shared experience, not a fundamental place. What is truly present is not the matter but consciousness itself, which is having the deep dream of matter. While the veil of the dream remains thick for many on Earth, the spirit is not fundamentally constrained by distance, or matter, or certain methods of perception, or even linear time. Thus as we seek to understand the Big Picture from the human perspective, it behooves us to release those assumptions. For even though we naturally associate with the context of the physical dream, our true nature is far more wonderful and unlimited than any part of the dream's structure.

233

(133)

People Are Good

People are good! Or more accurately, the spirit is good; but when engaged in very real constraint sets, each spirit is only "so adept" at optimally expressing its true loving nature in its local context. Each spirit is only "so good" at operating from love-based intent rather than fear-based intent in any given context – and the journey to actually grow from fear to love can be a painful one. Regardless of how well the spirit executes choice making, it is still fundamentally good. Some individuals are more adept than others at operating lovingly within a given physical and biological context – but at their core, all spirits are fundamentally beings of love and joy. This is true from the "best" to the "worst" of us.

Our society does not currently teach this: We habitually wish to identify enemies. Just as the wind has no enemies, even as a wall set before it is not the wind's enemy, you also do not have any enemies. Those labelled as enemies are other loving spirits playing other roles in our limited local system, making imperfect choices while in a rigorous state of artificial separation, just as we are. It is beneficial to see them for the love and joy that they really are, even as they, like us, may be befuddled by the rigors of being human.

(134)

The Search for Wholeness

We seek pleasure not just as a biological impulse but also because, spiritually, we always seek Source. We yearn for the unity with Source and each other – the unity which is native to our true spiritual state. As humans in a universe of form, we tend to constantly look for that unity and joy in form – in objects, people, ideas, beliefs, sights, sounds, substances, sensations – and while we may temporarily enjoy such unique form experiences, they never fully satisfy us, because they are not what we are looking for. They are not what makes us complete. Our true joy is in our true nature – not in the stimulating illusion of separate things. One of the reasons we come to be human is to discover that experientially.

Eventually, when the allure of form has failed us enough times, we have little choice but to turn inward. When we finally drop our frantic search and surrender, we find – spontaneously – that the wholeness we seek never left us at all! The wholeness is what we are! We only experience separation because we are focused on, believe in, and (seem to) depend on the form. So when we finally fully let go of form, wholeness naturally rises back to us, all on its own.

This surrender can be very difficult, however, because the truth of our being seems to get "wrapped up" in the forms of our lives; and as that happens, our true nature seems to become invisible. We really believe we are human! We really believe we are our occupations, our relationships, our affiliations, our ideas, and our bodies.

Letting go of the form is not an act of pitting yourself against the form. Rather, letting go of the form is a process of allowing "What Is" to be. All the form exists within you; it is not that you exist within form (like a spirit inhabiting a body in a material universe, for instance). Your awareness is always present for all aspects of your reality to exist. As you move towards

235

that awareness itself, exactly as it is in the present moment, you automatically open the door for the wholeness that you seek to rise back up to you!

When we finally re-sense it, we discover that the wholeness is *always* there! Indeed, our unified true nature is always present; and despite the rich and convincing experience of separation, our Being through which the experience of form occurs cannot ever truly be anything other than free, blissful, and whole.

(135)

The Deepening of Experience Through Focus

Because consciousness is fundamental, there is always a result when it directs itself towards something. The focus of consciousness itself has an effect. Focus tends to deepen that which is being focused on.

The more we focus on the physical, the deeper we go into the experience of it. The more we focus on one way of thinking, the more real it becomes. The more we repeat a belief to ourselves, the more real it becomes. The more we spend time in a culture, the more it tends to become normalized. Through our focus we wear pathways into the fresh wilderness of conscious experience, and then we experience reality as just those pathways.

It is important at times, then, to pause and appraise what we are focused on, so we can make a conscious decision to shift our focus. Practicing this allows us to gain control of what we are experiencing!

Often, though, we must do so from a place of significant previously established momentum. Sometimes the pathways of our identity, thoughts, and beliefs are so worn into our experience that we lose sight of them completely. So as we work to more consciously reclaim our focus and forge new paths in the grass, it is important to give ourselves permission to release all assumptions and all requirements. Our deepest beliefs about reality may not be true – and even if that's so, they will often appear as facts. We need to give ourselves permission to relinquish even those.

The truth of our being is perfect love, joy, creativity, and freedom! So as we more consciously choose where to place our focus, we benefit mightily from choosing new paths of love, joy, creativity, and freedom! Do you know that you are worthy of doing so? If not, please be reminded now: You are deeply, profoundly worthy! Do you know that you are permitted to consciously choose where to focus and what to believe? You are completely allowed to choose where to focus and what to believe! No matter your circumstances,

237

you are allowed to focus on that which you deem to be full of love, joy, creativity, and freedom.

This is not a process of avoidance or escape from some "reality of suffering." Rather, even as we choose our focus, we can simultaneously fully accept all that we have previously rejected! We can do this because all experience is ultimately rooted in love and joy. Put another way: While perspectives of suffering are valid, ultimately they are incomplete in that they actually fall short of the broader enduring foundation of love and joy that is native to all experience.

Whether we are consciously aware of that or not, we can benefit from utilizing the power that is available to us to choose a focus that is more in alignment with that enduring foundation of love and joy. And as we do so, our new focus will begin to wear new paths, and our actual experience will gradually brighten to match our new focus.

(136)

Spirituality Is Beyond One Direction

The pursuit of the transcendent and formless does not mean rejecting the world of form for the sake of the transcendent. Rather, form is a part of that which is transcendent. The formlessness and unity of our being is in all things; it is *not* "over there and not over here."

This is important because, as beings who are currently focused in an experience of duality, we often believe that pursuing spirituality is about pursuing some thing or things to the exclusion of other things. We often believe spirituality is about moving in one "direction"; we confuse that which we seek with the things themselves. To the duality-conditioned intellect, of course it can often be beneficial to select some form (some belief or behavior) to move towards at the expense of others. But ultimately the move towards the unity of our being cannot be a move of division. We cannot pit form against form and find unity.

All forms that exist do so within the context of the much broader fundamental reality of love, wisdom, freedom, and joy!

As we search for that joy, it is not the forms we seek, not some destination, not some "this or that." Rather, we seek that which is already fundamental and always present! We seek that which seems to have vanished before us as we've bought into the dense world of form and our many interpretations about it.

What we seek is not in "one thing and not another." What we seek is the fabric of our native Beingness itself, the living essence of our awareness that beholds all things, which is the same living essence in all things everywhere!

And that awareness is always close! It cannot go anywhere. It "follows" you wherever you go – nay, it is you, and you are it! It is with you in all the directions that you choose, all the efforts that you make, all the experience

239

and pain and pleasure. And your search for that is not a search of choosing the right forms, or of division or striving – but a move towards complete and total personal genuineness in meeting the present moment. Whatever directions you have chosen before, allow yourself to meet the Now deeply. In the naked truth of the real present moment, the light of Being always shines!

(137)

To Know It You Must Be It

The only way for spirit to know what it is like to be a human is to be a human. The only way for the spirit to experientially learn how to successfully express its true nature in a world of flesh, is to be flesh.

You cannot truly learn how to do something by watching someone else do it – you must do it yourself. You cannot truly know what it is like to *be* something unless you *are* that thing.

This is why the human experience is so real. Spirit chooses to do its best to "actually become" that which it wishes to truly experience. The veil serves that purpose.

If you do not remember your higher nature while you are human, that is OK – and not only OK, it is wonderful! It means you have successfully arrived at an experience of *being* whoever and whatever you think you are right now. That experience is a gift!

Simultaneously, if you wish to, it is also your birthright to wake up to who you really are. You have committed to your walk in the physical beneath the veil, and the veil is effective, but that doesn't mean you aren't still far more than your physical life, too. Indeed, even right now, what you really are vastly exceeds the confines of your human experience! So while you have come to experience all that being human entails, you are not required to lose yourself completely within the forms of human life. No matter the nature of the forms you are currently associating with, you are actually far, far more than that which you have chosen to be in this life on Earth! Your true identity remains.

In the meantime, while the human experience remains thick and firm, honor yourself for your choice – even a choice that you may not remember! For to know what it is like to be human, you had to actually *be* human – and that is a most celebrated and awe-inspiring choice indeed!

(138)

Your Destination Is Joy

No matter a given experience of physicality, ultimately all consciousness returns to joy. Joy is the spirit's true nature, its fabric, its native state. Your destiny is joy beyond physical imagining! That is where you are inevitably headed, no matter how the forms of reality may have bunched up around you at the moment. Those forms are made of the same fabric, even if they do not appear to be.

The present moment itself is beautiful and gentle. It is willing to touch you when you are willing to let go of your stories about it.

The ability to experience strong sensory data (for example pain), or the ability to experience the interpretations that you have put upon your circumstances, do not reduce the fidelity of the native joy that gives rise to such experiences. The experiences of form – including sensory experiences or given interpretations of the mind – will pass. But the truth of being cannot. Since that truth of being is untold joy, peace, freedom, and love, you cannot help but return to that joy, peace, freedom, and love as the forms that you are associating with pass.

Your destination is joy! So while you are on your walk in the world of form, take heart and allow your native joy to rise up and shine through you! For your true Being is ever-present, even when the forms may seem on the surface to be opaque or insurmountable!

(139)

The Unrealness of Paradox

Paradox happens when perspective is incomplete. Paradox only happens from the limited human perspective within form. In truth there is no paradox, and there can be no paradox. All things occur in accordance with the purposeful and fully coherent movement of Life.

The "laws" of God, including the laws that govern the operation of realities, work perfectly and inexorably. There is never a moment that is not governed by their perfect execution, even within many levels of complexity, and even within many different reality systems. When viewed from a "local" vantage point, however, it can appear to the philosophical form-based and duality-conditioned mind that two forms contradict. This is only an error of belief in form as fundamental, when in fact the experience of apparently discrete form is birthed by "something greater."

Beneath the thinking mind, the deeper parts of you are always connected to that "something greater." When you are willing to let go of the local human content and truly look within the depths of your consciousness itself, the intellectual contradictions have a chance to fall away into the vastness of Being – the same Being within which they seem to arise.

(140)

Honoring the Constraints of Being Physical

The veil holds you fast so that you must face that which you otherwise would have simply escaped. You knew ahead of time that being held to the human experience had great value, so you agreed to that commitment.

Honor your willingness to sign up for the constraints of the world by surrendering to them and allowing them to work with you in the way they were intended.

The world is not your enemy. The world is an "in your face" rigorous context that provides an opportunity for you. That is true even when, and especially when, you don't want that context. Even if you do not remember it, you agreed to be bound in this way, because you knew beforehand that this type of apparently inescapable context would provide incredible experiential opportunity for the growth of what you are, and what everything is. Now that you are here, you have the valuable opportunity to consciously intend to use that opportunity!

Each of us is called by Love to meet our given present moment in any number of a myriad of ways, so there is not just one action or response that such an intent might potentially prompt. That being said, here are three general suggestions for consideration.

First, we can choose to say "yes" to any given experience. We can choose to not resist. We can follow where the circumstances lead, rather than fight them. We can allow ourselves to fully experience everything, including pain. We can surrender to what is happening rather than fight it. We can give up our small-picture control, which isn't real power anyway.

Second, we can let life be our teacher. That is, we can intend to cooperate with the feedback of our own life experience – to listen to and take full personal ownership of both the pain and the joy of our lives. We can choose

245

to be willing to be wrong, or weak, or powerless. We can choose to swallow our pride and accept our failings. We can let joy lead us where it wants to! We can let ourselves "grow up!" The actual nature of our own life experience is a teacher of great fidelity. We can choose to actually cooperate with the process of learning the lessons that our life is working to teach us by listening to the feedback and taking ownership of our life experience exactly as it is.

Third, we can study how our own meanings and interpretations, and our own story, are affecting both ourselves and others. We are assigning the meaning to the physical content in our lives. We can choose to pay close attention to how that meaning is playing out. In other words, we can take ownership of our own beliefs about ourselves and our world, and we can take ownership of the effects we are having on others because of those beliefs. We are far more powerful than we generally understand – our power for interpretation is great, and far less limited than we might believe. And part of the way we can honor the physical experience is by having the courage to actually acknowledge that experience for exactly what it is, just as it exists, *before* any interpretation is applied – and then by taking ownership for all of the many interpretations that we have subsequently placed upon it, and the effects of those interpretations.

Being physical is not always easy. But it is purposeful. When we choose to honor the physical experience by working with it, we allow it to fulfill that purpose. And that is a wonderful thing! Because despite all the apparent trauma and destruction, our universe is born from purposes of deep joy and love! And so when we work with it, we actually facilitate both our own joy and the fulfillment of great "love plans" that are beyond our personal comprehension.

(141)

The In-Breath and Out-Breath of Life

Consciousness sojourns from the unlimited and formless, into form, and back again.

After great journeys into the worlds of form, we often long to return Home. We yearn to reconnect (though that connection can never be truly lost) with the total limitlessness, wonder, love, and freedom of Source!

Then, as the unlimited, we may choose to follow our interest in expanding joy, creativity, and love by once again "being something" and having certain experiences. Our journey into discrete perspective is ultimately additive, even when – and often especially when – a given journey is temporarily challenging.

All That Is thrives and expands through the processes of Creation! All That Is rejoices in the capacity to experience things, to *be* things, to be ever more, to ever add to What Is Possible. You and I are that, too! You and I, including you and I as human personalities, are precious and deeply adored participants in this process.

There is not an "end point." The system of Creation is an ever-expanding movement towards greater joy and love! That is ultimately not an arduous process but a joyful one!

Hardship Is a Gift

A challenge is a gift! When the individual is challenged by circumstance, the opportunity for the spirit to apply itself and expand through that experience is a gift. It is not that hardship itself is good, but rather, it is a neutral (even if painful) catalyst that can be useful.

The ego may reject this. The ego may see hardship as simply terrible and negative. But nothing terrible and negative arises that the spirit cannot ultimately use. There is nothing greater than All That Is – nothing can arise within it that is not of meaning. Even hardship – and often especially hardship – ultimately has great value in the churning processes of manifest creation, which ultimately serve the expansion of everlasting joy!

To the immortal and all-powerful spirit, challenge is a precious opportunity to bring virtue to bear – to expand and actualize the depths of one's own love and light in a real, lasting way. We are spirit first and human second. The challenges of the secondary human experience are often worth the temporary price to the bold spirit who knows the truth of immortality and wishes to expand itself and the joy of All, forever!

In what ways is the world pushing you, painfully, to let go of your fear and ego? In what ways is the world compelling you to embrace your joy, live your truth, and share your love? What is the hardship of your life teaching you? What is the pain of your story saying? If you listen deeply, beneath all the labels, your deeper spirit is always there ready to help you utilize this current circumstance for lasting purposes that may far exceed what your human mind can imagine.

(143)

The Falseness of Fear

Fear arises when we think we are lacking something that is actually intrinsic to our being, like power, or freedom, or love. Fear encourages us to think further that we are so lacking: In fear we tend to travel down the rabbit hole of further believing we are lacking power, or freedom, or love. But the underlying truth of our being is that we lack nothing. In that sense, fear is a lie. Fear is a lie because separation itself – and the apparent lack of freedom, power, or love that we may experience with it – is ultimately an illusion! The experience of separation is a real experience, but it is also not fundamental: It is transcended by something far more enduring.

We know that we are "buying into" the illusion of separation when we are suffering. When we act from fear or selfishness, ultimately, we suffer. And when we act from fear, others often end up suffering, too. Our ego may play all sorts of games to try to justify and protect us, but we can't fool reality – when we are acting from fear or selfishness, painful experiences naturally result.

This process is not an act of punishment by Source. It is the natural result of choosing non-native separation over native unity and love. Love doesn't even require love in return; yet where we choose not love, we do suffer. It is our choice.

Fear can be very convincing. But you always, always have the power to choose how you will meet it. Do not be daunted by the scope or by the circumstances. Rather, simply choose: How will you meet this moment? Allow your heart and soul to guide you! The circumstances are not of primary importance – what is important is *you*: your simple but powerful intention, your state of being. Be willing, and open, and vulnerable, and genuine, and brave. Do so even when it is difficult – especially when it is difficult.

249

And as you do so, allow yourself to remember: Whatever perception you are buying into that is giving rise to the fear is not greater than the truth. The deepest truth is never, ever one of fear. Fear is ultimately false – and the power of Love and Life within you is true.

(144)

The Never-Ending Abundance of Life

Life itself is abundant beyond measure! Life itself is so rich that no physical form can possibly express the depths of its native bounty. You are Life, having the experience of being a person.

Thus the depths of abundance exist within you! You do not need to turn to the things of the world to find your richness. You do not need to turn to objects, ideas, beliefs, actions, substances, sensations, or relationships to find your worth. Worth already belongs to you, because you Are. That is not a statement of ego, it is a statement about Being.

There is never truly a reason to give up your hope, joy, or peace: Life is always there with you, because Life is what you are. The incredible depths of the bounty of that truth can never, ever leave you. Listen to the richness of your Being beneath all the earthly conditioning, and allow yourself to know this while you are human, that your physical experience can that much more be one of joy!

(145)

The Importance of Action

We must take action. Spirituality without physical action is not true spirituality – because spirituality is about our real relationship with the present moment and the intent we wield in that present moment. Intention without action is not true intention. Intent equals action. When you intend to lift your hand, your hand lifts. When you intend to care for the other, you physically care for the other.

It is all too easy for the ego to justify inaction as the right thing to do. True loving intent questions even that, and sacrifices one's comfort and certainty in the name of the whole whenever necessary.

We must take personal responsibility for our place in the world! In fact, we must take personal responsibility for the whole world!

Simultaneously, we do not need to be overwhelmed by the scope of the change required. We simply need to act where we are.

As the saying goes, *you* must be the change that you wish to see in the world. But this does not mean that you need to lose your peace. Your true nature transcends the rigorous "external" context. Your true nature is far greater than the ample opportunity around you to actualize that nature into our world. You are peace, and love, and freedom, and joy! And as you know that, you are able to then bring that to those around you in important physical and tangible ways. As you actualize both that physical change and also that change in your own consciousness, you help fulfill your extremely important role in the great expansion of being that is happening through this place.

(146)

A Change in Consciousness Precedes a Change in the World

The great challenge of our world situation today is ultimately an issue of consciousness. The situation will not be solved by any given political party, nation, or religion, because the problem is us: in our making decisions every day from fear, rather than love. Until we all both individually and collectively "grow up," face our fears, and become living conduits of the love and unity that is native to our being, we will suffer.

The changes in the physical Earth situation are very important. But they are not primary. Consciousness is first; the physical is subsequent. Consciousness must change first; and then as it changes, we will naturally change the Earth situation.

Every time any one of us faces and integrates fear, we are making real progress. Every time any one of us chooses to selflessly support the person near us, even when it is difficult, we are making real progress. Every time any one of us finds joy and freedom even when the constraints of physical life are extreme, we are making real progress. Every time in the quiet of your own heart that you choose love over fear, that you choose freedom rather than the restrictive conditioning of your past, that you listen to the deeper parts of yourself even when the local story's terrors seem so convincing, we are making real progress! Many times, real progress is made even when a physical finger has not yet been lifted.

You are important! Your journey, your choices, your intent is important. Your well-being is important. That is true regarding you *personally* – not just you generally. You are very important indeed! And you are powerful. What you choose to do with that power as you engage this experience of the physical has a far-reaching effect. That effect may not be perceivable with the physical senses, but it does not make it any less real. You are affecting our reality, and other realities, in profound ways every day. *How* you choose to

253

meet your daily experience – indeed, how you choose to meet each precious moment – is important!

So be encouraged! You have power over everything that you need to in order to effect real, lasting change for the better. Because *you* – your consciousness and spirit – are a part of this great unfolding. And as you change, so does the world!

(147)

The Answers Transcend the Local Intellect

The local intellect, which deals exclusively with forms (discrete thoughts and ideas), cannot understand higher truth. In other words, you cannot find the "Big Picture" answers by thinking. But that doesn't mean that you can't find them at all. The answers are there, always available as what is real within the powerful reservoir of Being.

We believe thoughts have power, because we see the power they have in this local world every day. Through thinking we establish models by which we understand our environment and successfully interact with it. We have come to believe that the apparently objective "outside" world is what is most real, and through thinking we are able to learn about that world and effect change in it – so we believe that thinking holds the power. But in general we have lost sight of the real larger context. In focusing so deeply on the physical, we have become so single-sighted that we believe *all* truth must fit within our physical understandings. That is an erroneous assumption, because the "outside" physical world is not what is most real. *You* are real; your awareness and Being, which is a part of *all* awareness and Being, is what is most real! And that Being contains far, far more than this local character and this physical world.

Your Being is here, now! Your Being is the wonderful presence of life itself – that same life which has become "wrapped up" within the identity of this local character, and within that character's many thoughts. You are more than that; the truth is more than that. So if you truly wish to know that, you must be willing to find the answers outside of thoughts.

255

(148)

The Body as a Vessel for Experience Integration

The wearing of bodily constraints enables consciousness to know and integrate a very unique type of experience. Much is possible in the body that is otherwise not possible.

For the spirit, the body is metaphorically like wearing a space suit that enables the spirit to enter a hostile environment. But unlike a space suit, the body is living: It adapts, changes, and biologically remembers everything that the spirit has experienced in this local journey.

If we want to fully use this physical life for all it can be, we must fully experience the body. The sensations, limitations, and memory of the body are all valuable elements of the physical experience. So rather than resisting the often highly constraining and challenging experience of being bodily, we should embrace it! For doing so facilitates the integration of this experience by immortal consciousness, and allows us to spiritually grow in important ways that will remain with us long after the body is gone.

149

The Two Great Themes of Love and Fear

All things are connected: You, I, the seat you are sitting in, the sky outside, the screen or page you are looking at right now, and even the thoughts of the person next to you are all connected to each other. All things are connected because at their deepest root all things are Source. There are no exceptions. "Source," or "God," is just a word – but truly, it is beyond any name and definition, because all form itself exists within it. Source is conscious and alive, the great and loving I Am – and you and I are part of that, precious individuations of The One. We are forever a part of its Light, even as we exercise our individuation through experiences of separation. And there are few places in Creation where separation can be more starkly experienced than right here on Earth.

The world we live in is a real experience of the *illusion* of separation. We are not actually separate. But we have adopted the illusion of separation for purposes that are often beyond our human understanding. We have committed to all the definition that goes along with the human condition: We have committed to being biological, temporally constrained (bound to time), and subject to the laws of physics and discrete location (distance). None of those things are fundamental. Distance is not fundamental, linear time is not fundamental, biology is not fundamental. What is fundamental is our awareness, our spirit, our living consciousness itself! Because consciousness is a part of every experience everywhere, and because we are consciousness, we are connected to every single other thing in all of Creation!

But the multiverse of form is not "perfect." We as spirits, who seek to engage in the integration of experience and to participate in all that is occurring, are not necessarily optimized for any given context or set of constraints. In all the many varied experiences we find ourselves, no matter the reality system or lifetime, there is one "primary action" that remains constant: our intent. We always have the power to choose things, in accordance with the "rules" and context of whatever reality we are participating in. The decisions

257

available to us may change drastically depending on a myriad of factors, but the action of consciousness itself to choose something always remains.

When intent operates in a way that is supportive of the whole and in alignment with the unity that exists at the foundation of all things, we call that love. When intent operates in a way that is divisive or that promotes the illusion of separation by prioritizing the self over others, we call that fear. Every intent exercised in our world is either a movement towards a more integrated, expansive, and mutually supporting state of manifestation (one that is more in alignment with our native fundamental unity) or away from it.

This is why love and fear are the two great themes in spirituality. Love reflects the power and perfect unity of our true nature; fear reflects the incomplete, nonfundamental, and ultimately powerless illusion of separation. Loving intent supports the other, and is unity-promoting; fearful intent supports the illusory separate self, and is separation-promoting. Since separation is not fundamental and not reflective of what we truly are, we suffer when we act from fear. Our experience on Earth currently includes a great churning cacophony of suffering because, on the whole, most of us exercise fearful intent, rather than loving intent, every day.

Exercising loving intent is about honestly choosing what is best for the being next to you, and best for the world. Exercising loving intent is about, among a great many other things: being willing to act on the behalf of another even when it is difficult, being willing to actually feel the pain of being wrong, being willing to feel the humility of being imperfect, and being willing to face the fear of not knowing all the answers or even not having much physical power at all. The true playing field for this great endeavor is not primarily out in the objects of the world – it is within yourself! The true playing field is in your heart and mind. Some of the most important work you will ever do will be in the quiet moments of your heart. *That* is where the truly meaningful actions of Creation are occurring – and *you* are an incredibly important part of that process!

You have the power to choose! Your heart and spirit will always speak to you: If you are willing to relinquish the stories of the ego, you will always be guided where love is leading. You can be brave, for you are a powerful part of the Source of All Things. What will you choose then in this powerful moment, now?

150

The Rich Realness of the Formless

Since we believe in and associate so strongly with form, when we learn that form is not fundamental and awareness itself is primary, we may make the mistake of thinking that spirit is something abstract or ephemeral. We may make the mistake of thinking that "no form" or "beyond form" means "nothing" or "not very real." In fact, formless aliveness is the completely, tangibly rich wellspring of Being from which all realities of form spring! Some of those realities are clearly perceived as being far more real than the earthly experience. And even those realities are ultimately transcended by the rich realness of Beingness itself.

While this may sound abstract now, your whole Being is full of far, far more than you may be able to conceive of with earthly ideas. And that fullness is rich and alive!

When you attempt to let go of earthly ideas and associations, do not be discouraged by the initial apparent emptiness of the silence. Often, one must first be surrendered to silence before the extremely, tangibly real wellspring that dwells beneath and within it can arise on its own. That process is done not as a search for more form (more thoughts, or feelings, or objects) but as a search for what is actually real in the alert present moment. It is an investigation of the present moment for exactly what it is; it is a conscious exploration of the aliveness itself that is always present, bearing silent witness to every experience. That aliveness is real – and rather than being nothing, or some things, it is full of everything!

(151)

Fear and Ignorance Are the Obstacles

Fear and ignorance are the only real obstacles to being able to fully actualize our true loving nature on Earth.

When we wield an intent based in fear, we are acting in alignment with the illusion of separation, and we perpetuate suffering. When we act from fear, we are promoting a temporary contraction away from the full vibrance, power, and peace that is inherent to Life, towards the much smaller and inherently limiting protection of the self. Acting from fear is painful.

When we are unaware of the truth and are ignorant of our true nature, we try to take shelter in all forms of illusion. We pour tremendous energy into erecting and defending the structures of the ego: beliefs, self-justifications, and identity. We would rather protect ourselves in stick shelters made of paltry ego beliefs than expose ourselves to the ego-burning and identity-searing truth of who we really are. When we know our true nature, the painful trappings of separation evaporate.

Both fear and ignorance can be – and will be – overcome! They can only exist within the illusion of separation – and while you are here in the illusion, confronting them and healing them is an extremely powerful act. *You* are incredibly important! Your choice to confront your own fear, and your willingness to surrender what no longer fits and to dispel your own ignorance, is powerful indeed. Fear and ignorance are the only real obstacles; so when you work through those, even in yourself, or when you help another to do so, you are working directly to address the heart of Earth's problems.

Humbly Acknowledging Your Divine Identity

"You are not just a part of God. You are altogether God, and God is altogether you. This is not blasphemy. This is your identity." – *Wayne Dyer*

Even in deep humility, you can simultaneously recognize that you are a part of Source. You contain the potential and power of the Whole.

That which is perfect and unlimited, when divided into parts, is no less so. As an individuation of the One, you are simultaneously not God, and yet you are God. You are just a drop in the ocean, and yet in the words of Rumi, *"You are not just a drop in the ocean, you are the mighty ocean in the drop."*

While the ego can easily try to claim this idea, the truth of it far surpasses the limitations of the separate self and its ego's fierce quest for identity.

Yet, even as we feel separate, there is power in acknowledging what we are. For in the truth of what we are there is nothing to fear! In what we truly are, there is no lack and there is no limitation. In what we truly are, there is no death, or captivity, or disease. Acknowledging that helps to liberate us from the fear of the lack and limitation that we have bought into while lost in the dream of being human. The truth of what we are is freeing!

The power of the Whole that belongs to us is the same power that gives rise to universes, the same power that is the root of all beautiful or ugly expressions of form! As creative beings, we are responsible for how we use that power. For where you go, and where we go, reality ultimately follows. Acknowledging who we really are, then, can be the first step to more deliberately using our power and intentionally carving a path in the world of form that is more reflective of our true nature of love and joy!

(153)

Form As an Expression of the Joy of Being

The joy of Being expresses through form. Form is of Being, even as Being transcends it, and so Being revels in the forms that it loves and that are expressions of its native Love. The love of a sunset, the love of the beauty of a child's laughter, the love of color and song – these and more are Beingness being what it is, even as it rejoices in the forms that exist within it and of it.

Beingness revels in manifest creation! Beingness revels in creating sunsets and laughter and color and song. Consciousness loves sensation. Consciousness loves experience.

This love is at the root of all manifest experience – even experience that can, for a time, have a most severe edge in the world of duality. The soul is so churning with this love that it may even seek to test the very boundaries of manifest expression – to test the farthest extremes of duality, to know them. Our world is one of many that fulfill such powerful love-based creative ambition.

Even though here on Earth we have accomplished a daringly deep dive into the world of the discrete, that love is still what we are! Every single experience is, ultimately, underlined by this love. And thus any form – no matter what it is – has the potential to be known in joy. We may feel constantly experientially distanced from this joy by the boundaries of the separate self: by our addiction to thinking, by our thick association with our labels, by our resistance to truly feeling what we feel, and by our fierce and constant grasping for human identity – but even those experiences are made of the same substance. Even the separate self arises in love and from the joy of Being as that joy of Being actualizes its powerful adoration of manifest experience! And that joy of Being, rather than separate humans, is what we really are.

263

(154)

Operating Creatively from Within Human Conditioning

The belief in an objective external physical world can inhibit us from understanding the larger context in which we exist. Reality is ultimately consciousness-based, not based on our shared physical environment or the activities that we can mutually validate here. The content of our shared physical environment is of course valid and worthwhile, but it is not fundamental. And indeed, in the Big Picture, our physical experience of Earth is actually quite a specific and unique form of experience!

In thought-responsive systems our personal nature gives rise to reality experiences of incredible richness and depth. Our thoughts, beliefs, expectations, and intent all have profound power to shape what we and others experience. Our innate creative power becomes immediately evident.

Since our thoughts, beliefs, and expectations are currently based on what we've learned during our time on Earth, when we (as human personalities) encounter thought-responsive systems, we often engage with them in ways that are very human. We see human environments, we interact with human objects, we perform human activities, and we encounter very real forms that arise from the rich and varied content of the human collective consciousness – including religious, mythological, and symbolic forms. The symbols become alive, and we may forget that they arose from us.

But you and I are far more than human! We are far more than the patterns, sights, sounds, teachings, ideas, thoughts, and beliefs that we have become so wrapped up within while we have been veiled in the human experience on Earth. In large part, our limitations are something we learned while on Earth. You and I are not so limited as it may seem!

Here and elsewhere, be aware of your power! You are not powerless – except that you believe that you are. You are not trapped – except that you believe that you are. You are not the forms and restrictions. You are not even your

264

body. Rather, you are a powerful spark of the creative Source of all things! And whether you are consciously aware of that or not, you will be wielding your creative power: You *can* choose to do so consciously.

Be aware of who you are! The "content" that you are holding within you is the fuel of your current experience. Face that content, process it, integrate it, overcome it – and find who you really are! Face yourself, your motivations, your intent. Face your fear! You always hold the keys within you to what you see around you, both in this system and in others.

(155)

The Ubiquitous Presence of Life

Life is always present in everything, because Life (which is synonymous with awareness, or spirit, or consciousness) is always present in every experience. An experience cannot occur without awareness of it. Life is present for everything ever experienced. You are living awareness, too – and as your awareness is a part of the "sea of awareness," you are connected to everything, everywhere.

How can you be alone, when everywhere you go, everything you see, and everyone you meet, is Life? How can you be alone when the you that sees is the same you that is all things?

There is no content that can occur within Life that can separate you from Life. There is no experience of distance, no experience of pain, no experience of loss that can truly separate you from what you really are. All things are made of Life, and you are Life – so how can you ever be absent from its care?

(156)

Becoming Comfortable with Uncertainty

"Become at ease with the state of 'not knowing.' This takes you beyond mind because the mind is always trying to conclude and interpret. It is afraid of not knowing. So, when you can be at ease with not knowing, you have already gone beyond the mind. A deeper knowing that is non-conceptual then arises out of that state." –Eckhart Tolle

In its desperate striving for control, the ego hates uncertainty. Because we have fear and ego, we hate uncertainty. But the uncertainty that can occur within this veiled experience of this rigorous physical universe is actually taking place within the larger context of spirit, which is built on the law of love. Therefore, even when great uncertainty arises, we need not fear it. We are always in love's care.

Uncertainty is an opportunity. As it arises, it provides valuable counterpressure that can allow one to face and feel the real fear that is within. There is no shame in feeling fear when our physical life or stability is threatened: Even acknowledging that we feel it, and allowing it to arise clearly, is a step toward integrating it and healing it forever.

While uncertainty may evoke the fear of lack of control (the perception of powerlessness), that perceived lack of control is actually an opportunity. Power lies in accepting powerlessness. When that acceptance is not just an idea but a deep personal surrender, true power is regained.

The process of becoming comfortable with uncertainty may not be a swift one, but that is OK – every step toward conquering fear is accomplishing real work! It can potentially take many moments or many lifetimes to face and heal our deeper fears. Yet we need not be daunted by the scope, for there is immeasurable power in this present moment!

What uncertainty is arising in this present moment for you? Whatever it is, be here. Listen to your deepest heart, and meet it as truly as you can. Do not fear – it is how the "play" on the earthly stage is arising for you at this time. Your inalienable power to choose has not been removed, and it never will be. Make a choice from love, courage, honesty, and nonresistance, rather than from fear. The circumstances do not have to land a certain way for you to be free, for you to be you. Spirit is with you, indeed the very Source of All Things is with you right now! In that, truly, what is there to fear?

The Absolute vs. the Manifest

Consciousness itself transcends manifest experience entirely. And, simultaneously and without contradiction, manifest experience happens and is real. The absolute and the manifest co-exist, without contradiction.

This may seem like a contradiction to the duality-focused thinking human mind, however, because the thinking human mind deals exclusively with the world of the discrete. But the discrete, while real, is not fundamental. The manifest arises within the absolute. We could even say: The manifest is made from the absolute. The mundane is made of the miraculous.

Even as the absolute precedes the manifest, these "levels" of the absolute and the manifest are not discrete or separate.

The manifest includes a myriad forms of discrete experience: reality systems within reality systems, experiences within experiences. All That Is expands its nature through all manifest experience. Spirit simultaneously fully transcends any given manifest experience, and yet is fully within it.

In very crude dualistic terms, some manifest experiences or realities are experienced as "closer" (vibrationally) to the Source, and others are experienced as "farther." Yet simultaneously the spirit can never be far from itself, just as the wave can never be far from the ocean.

The human mind conditioned by duality tends to think in spectrums as if they were absolutes, but they are not. Beingness is richer and more complex than that, and what we crudely try to partition as the "absolute" and the "manifest" are not separate but One.

(158)

The Joy of the Truth

The truth feels wonderful! When we align with the greater truth, we feel great. Our true nature is the full bliss of Being, and so that bliss shines forth when we are not separating ourselves from it by being associated with thoughts, beliefs, or self-perceptions that do not align with its loving, connected, free, and creative nature. When we really know we are loved, we feel great. When we really know we are connected, we feel great. When we really know we are free, we feel great. When we really know that we are creative and powerful, we feel great. We feel great not just because these are nice ideas but because vibrationally within consciousness space they are a move closer to the truth of who we really are.

When you see the truth, you know it. When you feel the truth, it feels right. If an idea doesn't feel right, it either isn't the truth or it simply conflicts with your current beliefs, or both.

Spirit rejoices in the truth; the human personality struggles within the illusion of separation, because separation is not native to who the experiencer of the human personality really is. There is no separation.

In what is actually true, there is absolutely nothing to fear, ever. If in any given moment we are not feeling that, it means we are associating with something that is not the ultimate truth.

The truth is more wonderful than anything that can be said with words. Follow your deepest joy, and know it!

(159)

Yo – Have Fun!

"On one hand you take life too seriously. On the other you don't take play seriously enough." –Seth

Images and form are simply the tools and toys of creation. Physical life is like a highly realistic and specialized game environment – you are not only allowed to play in it, you are encouraged to do so! Fun is worth having for fun's sake.

The spirit is playful! Seriousness and fear are not native to what we are. On the other hand, fun, creativity, joy, expressiveness, spontaneity, and excitement *are* native to what we are.

So when we have fun, we are better able to sense what we really are. When we are acting in joy, others are automatically reminded of the joy in their own being. In this way, having fun itself is a form of service.

When we act in free joy, and when we follow the excitement that is within us wherever it may lead, we are aligning with the deeper power that has given rise to this whole experience of form. In other words, acting in joy and excitement is more than just fun – it is powerful!

(160)

The Peace of Non-Seeking

The very act of seeking itself can be a move away from peace. In a sense, in wanting something we are actually moving away from it, because pursuing it is often done in service of the idea that we lack it in the first place. In trying to become rich, we become poor; in trying to become free, we lose sight of the freedom we already have; in trying to become spiritually enlightened, we can become self-centered.

Pursuing something to satiate a need is ultimately empty; all things are already present right now.

There is no place we truly need to go. There is no thing we truly need to do. There is no object we truly need; no reconfiguration of the play is actually necessary. In knowing that fully, there is peace.

In hearing this, we may decide to even reject seeking itself (a new thing to pursue or reject). But rejection is not the way. The way transcends and yet can arise within all objects, all paths, all searches. That truth is actually not an abstract or far away thing – rather, it is the closest thing to us. We simply need: to Be.

Be. You are, and that is more than enough! Be today, be here. Give the world the gift of your attention, your full presence, with no seeking required.

272

PART 3 – QUESTIONS & ANSWERS

Q&A Introduction

What follows is a series of informal responses to a variety of spiritual questions, many of them appearing exactly as originally asked by fellow seekers. The responses are organized by topic. I would like to reiterate the following two disclaimers: (1.) words cannot possibly speak successfully to the nature of many of these questions; and (2.) I am a fool, and I certainly do not claim to have all the answers – far, far from it! I am a flawed and largely ignorant student of Life. I am also learning and changing my understanding every day, as we all are. Still, fools can help fools, so I present this content just for consideration in the hopes that it may be of assistance to someone!

Purpose

See also: (001) (002) (027) (043) (048) (064) (078) (079) (116) (126)

Q: What is the purpose of human life?

We come for the purpose of the expansion of love and joy through the integration of experience. We enter the world of form to be something specific and see how we can better express and expand our true loving and creative nature in and through that context. And the context of being human offers a very specialized and unique opportunity.

Q: Why was our universe created?

Our universe was created to facilitate the expansion of Beingness through Creation, and to facilitate the expansion of joy and love. Sojourns into duality and form enable the individual and the collective to expand incredibly. Put another way: The fundamental truth of love is even more deeply known and can be even more powerfully actualized when we actually engage ourselves into challenging constraint-sets. The bigger the "vibrational distance" from our Source that we can go and integrate, the more expansion can occur, and the more that can be added to the eternal joy. The physical universe is an environment that was created to fulfill that purpose.

273

Q: If we are spirit and our earthly lives are just some kind of game or play, then does that mean our earthly lives don't matter?

No! Our earthly experiences and relationships are extremely valuable indeed! Just because the ultimate reality transcends the earthly experience does not make the earthly experience unimportant. In fact, everything we do here is very important!

Q: You say we are here to integrate experience. What does that mean?

To integrate an experience is to fully know it and assimilate it into what one is, so that one fully "gets it" at the being level (not just the intellectual level). When an experience is fully integrated, it no longer prompts fear. An integrated experience is one in which the individual can comfortably say with familiarity "oh yeah, I've been there, done that!"

As a single very simple example: When my father was a child, he used to be afraid of his closet. Every night he would lie in bed, tormented by his own imagined fears about what the closet might contain. Eventually he concluded that whatever was in the closet, it couldn't be worse to experience than the fear itself. So one night he got up from bed, pushed his way into the closet with determination, and sat down on the floor. Nothing happened. He realized that there was no real danger- it had all been imagined. Having gone and done that for himself, he was no longer afraid of closets. Physical reality can be a bit like this: We experience fear as we impose our own negative meaning on our unrelenting and often painful experience of separation, and then eventually, after we are sick of being afraid and suffering, we face those fears head on. Once we do, we have been "been there, done that" – and we are no longer afraid.

While fear can be a sign of un-integrated experience, integrating experience does not always involve fear. Learning a skill, becoming familiar with a way of living, or performing a certain role are also types of experience integration. Just about every experience we have in the world of form is always contributing towards its integration (even if in the very long term). Integrating experience is what we do, so it is happening constantly.

274

God

See also: (019) (037) (114)

Q: Is God real?

Yes. God (Source) is real, and in fact is the "Most Real." But God is not like a man; rather, God is the conscious living Source of all being, the living sentient foundation of love upon which and through which all reality and all experience is built.

Q: Is God a light? A man? A force? An energy? What is He?

To ask "which object is God?" is to mistakenly assign fundamental existence to the objects – as if "light" or "man" were fundamental things and God is some other thing, and we're trying to figure out if He's "this" or "that." Objects only exist because of that which gives rise to them. It is not that That Which Is has to be labelled as one or more objects, places, or sets of ideas. Rather all objects, places, and ideas exist within and because of Beingness itself. (114)

Q: Does Source have a personality? What are the characteristics of Source?

I feel that answering this type of question will immediately and inappropriately pigeon-hole Source. The human mind thinks in terms of forms (objects and ideas), and thinks reality can be deduced by figuring out which form this thing is and which form that thing is. So the questioner probably thinks that he or she can determine what some higher reality or being "actually is" by figuring out what forms it is and what forms it isn't, what characteristics it has and what characteristics it doesn't – such as, does Source have a personality? But Source transcends and gives rise to all form. In a sense we could say that personality is "made of" Source. Caring is "made of" Source. Source is Life itself, Beingness, and *all* things that exist arise within it. By asking which form applies, you are assigning fundamental existence to the forms, rather than that which actually has fundamental existence. (114)

275

Q: Is Source's love personal or impersonal?
Both. You are personally known and completely cherished, celebrated, and adored; and simultaneously Source's love is vast and forms the bedrock of all existence.

Q: Who created God? How did God come into existence?
Because we currently live in a world of duality and linear time, and because that's all we typically remember while human, the human mind believes that duality and linear time are fundamental; so it assumes that all things, even ideas like "God," can fit into that understanding. They can't. We assume everything has a beginning and an end like in our world, but that is not the case. In fact, duality and linear time are not fundamental. They arise within that which *is* fundamental. The questioner is (naturally but incorrectly) trying to take his or her locally learned "virtual" constraints (linear causality) and trying to impose them upon that which gives rise to that entire local experience. That Which Is needs no cause; it is that which exists. This may not satisfy the human intellect, because the human intellect is trying to fit everything into its "local" assumption-set so it can understand with its form-based (local object-based and idea-based) thinking. But indeed the entire world of form and duality exists within that which fully transcends it, and that "thing" has no beginning and requires no beginning.

Q: Is God simply the collective consciousness of all individual beings or is God a separate self-aware entity capable of existing apart from those individual beings? If God is only the collective consciousness of all individuals, then who is the creator and who is the creation?
Any time we talk about this we are immediately going to fall short, because language and ideas are form, and God transcends all form. Also, that means when we say things about God they may sound paradoxical, when they aren't.

Regarding "Is God simply the collective consciousness of all individual beings or is God a separate self-aware entity capable of existing apart from those individual beings?" God is both, except not separate. Nothing is separate. God is both all the drops in the ocean, and also the ocean itself,

276

which is far, far more than a collection of drops. In other words, the ocean is more than the sum of its parts. This is difficult for us to understand because we think in terms of matter and components, and we expect spirit to break down discretely like that, too, but it doesn't. Spirit gives rise to matter, not the other way around.

Regarding: "Who is the creator and who is the creation? Is there even a creator?" Beingness just is. It doesn't need a creator. The idea of creation (requiring a beginning) only exists as the idea is considered by a character (human) in a linear-time system where linear time is assumed to be fundamental, whereas in fact it isn't. In other words, because we deeply believe in linear time, we assume things need to be created and start somewhere in time like they do in our reality system, but that assumption is not correct. Linear time arises from Beingness, not the other way around.

Q: I am afraid of offending God. How can I avoid offending God?

You cannot offend God. Offense is an ego thing, and God's perfect Love and Beingness transcend all fear and ego. It is the human ego that strives to think in terms of duality and judgment. Perfect Love transcends duality and judgment.

Q: You say "for or against God" type thinking is earthly thinking. Why is "against God" earthly thinking? I feel most spiritual religions on Earth are actually against the existence of a creator. Doesn't God care about that?

Do you think that Source has an ego problem with religions not giving Source a name and identity? Or that Source has an ego problem with not being recognized or praised? And another question, this one metaphorical: If you really love your child, when they get into a difficult situation and become grumpy, and if you completely and totally understand why they are grumpy, do you love them less? How about if your child lost all their memory and didn't remember you for a while (as happens in physical incarnation), would you be upset that they didn't remember you? In that last question, pretend that you possess eons and eons of wisdom and oceans and oceans of love – would you be upset? We live in a world of apparent duality

277

– hot and cold, night and day, for and against. We think the higher realities must be so, too. But Life itself has no opposite. Consciousness itself has no opposite. It has no opposite even as it experiences stark opposites for a while.

Q: Did God create evil?

At the deepest level, the most fundamental thing is Beingness (also called consciousness or spirit). That Beingness is perfect, unblemished; it just shines with the light of its own being, which is love. Beingness then chooses to expand the depths of what it is – to expand the possibilities and the joy – through manifestation and the experience of defined creation. This choice is an additive service. Through that experience, any given soul (any given "piece" of the Source) is only "so good" at any given time at reflecting its true loving nature within a given context and set of constraints. Some contexts are very challenging – and the human condition, which includes the experience of separation, is one of those potentially very challenging contexts. Fear happens when through those challenging contexts the individual buys into perceptions that are not in alignment with the truth (perceptions such as "I am shameful" or "I am powerless" or "I can be destroyed"). As the individual seeks to cope with the unnatural state of being separate and experiencing fear, the ego arises to protect the individual and to try to "reclaim" the power that seems to have been lost. When the individual makes choices from fear and ego, rather than the underlying truth of love, that is what we call "evil." *Evil* is our word for the ultimately fear-based intent which arises out of the response to this non-native state of separation. "Evil" is what happens when a loving consciousness is acting from fear and ego because that consciousness is engaged in an experience that it has not yet fully integrated. (111)

Thus God did not create evil; rather, God gave the soul the opportunity to grow and expand in love and joy through choice making, and that opportunity included the opportunity to be challenged to such a degree that even fearful choices were possible. We are a part of Source, and Source is unconditionally loving, just as we are completely free – so we are permitted to choose even an experience in which we may make imperfect choices. Our true nature cannot change; none of us are ever truly in danger. But in the process of working through that extreme experience of apparent separation and vulnerability and making choices within such a rich context, we add

278

incredibly to What Is, and we help expand the joy and love of what we really are! That service is incredibly valuable and worthwhile.

The Soul
See also: (015) (056) (123) (127) (144) (150) (152)

Q: What is the "higher self?" What is the soul?

The higher self is *you* – the real and complete you – unconstrained by the limitations of the physical experience, the you that knows its oneness with all, the total you with all the experience you've had (as opposed to the "smaller" you, the human personality, which is the portion of you who identifies almost exclusively with the local human identity). The soul is metaphorically the drop in the ocean, the "fragment" of the Whole that is both connected and individuated and has free will. I am using the two terms *higher self* and *soul* interchangeably.

Q: Is our soul or spirit energy?

While we are human we believe reality is made of things. So, when we want to know what one thing (e.g. our soul/spirit) is, we ask, is it this other thing (energy)? All discrete things – all forms – arise from that which is fundamental: consciousness (or spirit) itself. Spirit is the fundamental substrate of everything. Spirit does not have a precedent; it is That Which Is. And all forms – including concepts like energy or experiences of energy – arise within it.

Q: Do all beings have a soul? What's the cutoff for souls? Plants? Mold? Bacteria?

Bodies don't have souls, souls have bodily experiences. Think of consciousness as the fundamental substrate, which transcends form. It can then utilize (or "be") various forms within creations of form that exist within itself; and the extent to which it can utilize those forms – have the experience of being them and growing experientially through them – depends heavily on the nature of the form and the rule-set of its local reality. So for instance a human with a brain is capable of a much different cognitive and intellectual experience than, say, a mouse. But spirit can be (is) the mouse, too, and can experience the universe from that very different perspective. Indeed, spirit is experiencing every aspect of its Creation, in this universe and beyond, and it is all Life. What we tend to think of as "alive" is an extremely narrow definition, since we tend to think of Life only as a physical form, whereas in fact consciousness itself is not physical but contains all physical forms within itself.

Q: Does the soul have qualities? Or is individual consciousness a neutral thing?

There are multiple levels involved here, which are almost impossible to speak about with language. These "levels" are not discrete or separate, but we might talk about two broad levels: First is the absolute, second is the manifest. (157) On the absolute level, Awareness itself transcends all thoughts and feelings, which are forms. Simultaneously, on the manifest level, each soul has had its own vast set of experiences on many levels and has its own unique "qualities." There are many levels within this manifestation – some very deep and "close" to Source, others very "far" and in extremely discrete levels of existence. This is almost impossible to describe with language, though. The human mind conditioned by duality tends to think in absolutes and in spectrums, but Beingness is richer and more complex than that, and all things and experiences are not separate but One. Very simply, though, we can speak about Consciousness/Awareness itself, and we can also identify then the many qualities of any individual soul, or any environment of form.

Q: If our souls are already perfect and already know everything, why do we come into this life for experiences and "growing up"? After we die, if we will wake up and understand everything, why do we need to have earthly life experience, and why do we need to wake up again to that which we already know?

Those first two statements sound paradoxical, but actually they are not. The soul evolves as its "experience vocabulary" expands. It comes here to have this experience and expand its nature (of love and joy) through that experience. Meanwhile, the soul is simultaneously perfect, and at the soul

280

level has access to all information (which is not the same as all experiential evolution). The learning we come to do is experiential, not intellectual.

Q: If our souls are already perfect, why do we need to come and be physical and work towards ascension? Why do we need to evolve?
Beingness itself is already perfect; there is nothing the soul "needs" to do. Then, as the soul chooses to engage realities of form (realities of duality), at any given "time" it is only "so good" at actualizing its true loving nature within a given context of form (within any given biological and circumstantial context). As the soul integrates experience and evolves its ability to wield intent (make choices) based on love rather than fear, a tremendous expansion of capability, joy, and love occurs. All That Is becomes more. That process is not required, but it is chosen because the soul decides it is worth doing. To participate in the expansion of joy is not required, but joy is its own reward. (113)

Q: What do you mean when you say that the soul expands? That sounds abstract – what does it mean specifically?
The expansion of Being cannot be accurately described in words. As a crude metaphor only: Imagine spirit as an energetic substance that can be "refined" through exposure to experience. The stresses of physical incarnation cause a "high-pressure" environment that permits a "processing" of that substance. It is not simply the pressure itself, though, that causes the change; it is in *how* that living substance chooses (wields intention) through that experience, how it meets and deals with that pressure in every moment. Even more crude metaphors might be: Dough needs to be kneaded in order to be made into bread; or, a tree needs to be exposed to wind and the elements to grow strong; or, coal needs to be exposed to high pressure to become a diamond. As the soul evolves, its ability to personally know, understand, and – importantly – experience certain things grows. In knowing extreme depths, it knows extreme heights, forever. In being able to meet extreme depths with rightness of spirit, it is able to apply that rightness of spirit in incredible ways in reality systems with fewer constraints. Depending on the reality system and the "rules" of that system, that ability may mean powers of creativity that are comparatively "godlike" to less-evolved beings. Ultimately, though,

the journey is not about power but about love and joy – for love and joy are the ultimate power. The level of refinement "achieved" by another being is clearly perceivable in other reality systems as that being's "qualities of essence" that can be seen and felt through telepathic evaluation.

Q: I still don't get it. How can such a difficult experience be helpful?
The expansion of Being is a refinement and increase in a great many different aspects of personal and collective experience. One way it is important to consider this is through emotional understanding rather than intellectual understanding. The following crude metaphor may be helpful. Imagine two movies. In one of them, people always love each other and care for each other, and they create beautiful things all day. Most people would find that movie "nice", but perhaps boring. In another movie, a hero struggles and fights her way through lots of extreme challenges – particularly facing her own fears – and ultimately masters them, driven by a spirit of love and compassion that she defends against all odds and that she uses to help and save others. Even if certain parts were difficult to watch at the time, the second movie is far more compelling and yields a much larger experiential result. Metaphorically, we are in the movie right now. And after having processed the extreme contrast of Earth, we experientially know something that we may have never known before. What's more, we *become* more, and All That Is becomes more, as we do that. That process is ultimately additive.

Q: I've heard the Rumi quote, "This is a subtle truth: whatever you love, you are." What does that mean?
Pick something that you love. Your form is not its form, but your nature is the same as that which you love – that which has been expressed as the wonderful thing that you love. I think that last sentence is the most succinct way to put it. But to put it another way, when you look at that thing and love it, the love that is shining forth is really, ultimately what you are, too. Take nature, for example: When you see a glorious sunset and love it for its beauty, beauty is *your* true nature, and you are appreciating the deep What Is and how it has here expressed itself as a beautiful sunset. You relate to it because it is your true shared nature. That beauty, now expressed, is what you are, too – and that's why it feels like love and beauty, because it resonates

282

with what you really are. The form (your body, or the image of the sunset) is not fundamental; but Beingness, which is full of life and expresses itself in so many wonderful ways, is what you are, too; and you are appreciating it in the form that you love.

Near Death Experiences
See also: (016) (027) (032) (053) (116) (123)
Disclaimer: I am not a near death experiencer. As with all these thoughts, I share these comments from my own perspective for consideration only.

Q: Why do some people have NDEs and others who get close to death don't?
The question is, why do we not remember our greater nature every day? Why do we only remember being human? When we come to be human we have to accept the "veil" – the constraints in consciousness space that go along with being human and having a body. The veil makes it so that we do not remember all of what we are, which allows us to focus on the human experience and have the full experience of separation. All of us have nonphysical experiences while our bodies sleep, but because of the veil we also do not remember those. When the body dies the veil is removed. But many either don't get close enough to actual death to have an NDE, or they have an experience and don't remember it because of the veil.

Q: Why are near death experiences unique? Why isn't the content of NDEs always the same?
The reason NDEs are so different is because the thing that is actually fundamentally real is consciousness (spirit) itself. The forms that consciousness experiences – the objects and environments and even ideas – are not fundamental. They change. In our own reality on Earth, we have an apparently shared objective reality (technically it's the *experience* of a shared reality rather than a fundamental place). But other reality systems have different "rules" and are more responsive to the nature of the individual. They are generally much more responsive to belief, thought, and intent. In the course of an NDE, differences in individuals and their human experience

become apparent in the environment of those more responsive reality systems and in the content of the experience. The higher realities speak to the earthly personality in the "experience language" of that personality. They are very real experiences that are in many cases custom-made for the individual, until that individual "steps past" the local personality (past the "point of no return"). Put another way: Higher reality systems are thought-responsive and belief-responsive, so while earthly assumptions and beliefs still define reality for the individual, the apparently external environments of those realities will interact with the personality in a way that is the best physical "translation" for that individual. Note: That doesn't mean they're not real! Indeed, experiences of higher systems are commonly perceived as far more real than the experience of our physical world.

Still, NDEs do share many characteristics. According to Dr. Jeffrey Long's book *Evidence of the Afterlife*, in which he studied the NDEs of 613 experiencers, 75.4% of NDErs experienced a separation of consciousness from the physical body, 74.4% experienced heightened sense perception, and 76.2% experienced intense positive emotions or feelings, just to name a few characteristics.

Q: OK I get that NDEs and other nonphysical experiences are unique. But some are totally unique. Why do people who have returned from bodily death occasionally report significantly different experiences about the afterlife? If the other side is real, shouldn't everyone see the same thing?

Consciousness itself is the fundamental thing, and it can engage many different reality systems. When we are freed from the local human constraints, there is a huge variety of possible experiences because, among other reasons: (1.) The "larger system" is nearly infinite in its variety and capability; (2.) We often need to process our recent, highly unique Earth life and are often engaged through the "experience language" of that life; (3.) Our "higher natures" are also exceptionally unique; (4.) There are higher processes ("laws") at work that help direct us according to a myriad of factors; (5.) There are often "plans" at work, both plans we have made beforehand (even if we've forgotten) and those "higher up" that can affect

284

what is experienced. In general, we should be careful not to take our locally learned assumptions – like the assumption that what is "most real" is this shared, apparently objective external environment of matter – and apply that to how we think the "higher systems" should be. They are far more real, yet not limited in the same way as our own. This means hugely varied experiences are possible.

Q: If NDEs aren't the product of the mind, then why do people often see the things they believe in?

The experienced "form content" of NDEs (objects or people seen) often reflects the beliefs of the individual, because thought-responsive environments often interact with us in the "experience language" of the local human personality. Consciousness is fundamental, not form – but in interactions with the form-believing human personality, rich form can be used. That doesn't make it not real – in fact, it is more real than the pale form of our own world by comparison. The "reality" of the higher realms is completely self-evident when you are there.

Q: Some NDErs have experiences so profound that it shatters their previous worldview, and they experience nothing like what they previously believed or conceived. In light of the fact that some others have experiences that are in alignment with their beliefs, how can this be explained?

The larger context vastly transcends the relatively limited beliefs of the local personality; so if the individual is ready, new information (even to the point of shattering someone's previous worldview) can certainly be conveyed.

Q: Why do NDErs often not remember their mission when they return?

Our missions that we fulfill here on Earth must be carried out within the earthly context. And that context includes operating on this side of the veil (forgetfulness), and within flesh (human limitations). I feel the issue about not remembering one's mission is generally not specifically about the withholding of information; rather, the lack of information is a natural and largely necessary byproduct of operating within our reality. Also, our missions, by their very nature, gain their value by having to be performed within our context and constraints. In my own case, though I had pre-birth memory as a child, I forgot it as I aged, and then I suffered trauma in my early 20s, which was necessary for my fulfilling my intention for coming here. I did not know that at the time – at the time I only suffered. Years later, though, after engaging and healing much of my darkness, along with committing to a path of personal ownership, only then did I spontaneously regain memory of that part of my mission. Because otherwise, it would have been impossible to do so! Often our missions involve needing to experientially learn to operate in some way by exercising valuable (loving or fearless) deep intent (not by superficial thinking or even by performing certain physical actions); and we must do that within the context of only "knowing what the human knows." Even though the thinking mind may not know, the deeper being certainly knows, which is one of the reasons it's important to follow our intuition and the spirit within us.

Q: In my research I have found significant examples of veridical evidence that NDEs are real. How do doctors and scientists dispute NDE veridical evidence? Isn't this proof enough that our souls do leave our body?

Most scientists are working with a deeply held belief in materialism. So when new evidence shows up, I suspect that, like most of us, they try to fit that new information into that existing belief, or quickly dismiss it. Belief is a powerful thing, and the ego is its proud warden. Consciousness is fundamental, and consciousness assigns the meaning – so when the meaning is firmed up in belief, it can take quite a bit of new data – and/or a significant amount of courage – to change one's interpretation.

Q: Are we meant to have NDEs? Is it a flaw in the system to see behind the veil (assuming the veil is there for a reason)? Are NDEs an aberration?

I'm not an NDEr, but from my pre-birth experience I can at least mention the following comments in case they are helpful. (1.) Yes, the veil is there for a reason. (2.) The veil is extremely effective and consistent, but it's not a "simple rule"; it is a complex mechanism and it is tailored to each individual

286

uniquely. I suspect that leaves room for differences in experience. (3.) I think the "system" is extremely good at predicting outcomes, but things can play out in "unforeseen" ways – there is a whole lot of free-willed choice making going on. The spirit is incredibly strong, and things can happen when the "pressures" of physical existence play out; so I do suspect some returns to the other side are premature in a way. Others, I feel, are much more intentional and sometimes even planned. For instance, I am aware that people often have various potential "exit points" (possible death times) that are known beforehand. So I don't think I'd categorically answer the question with either/or. I think the system is very rich and complex, and as with all manifest things, everything is ultimately used for the good (for the evolution of spirit and the expansion of love and joy).

Q: I see some NDErs that say God is love, that it is important to take each action out of love, and that our actions create ripples that spread out and affect the world; but then I see other NDEs say there is no sin or evil and all is well. How can everything be OK if each action has consequences but people are taking actions that are not out of love, causing unnecessary suffering for themselves and others?

All is well, even as through experiences of form we wield intention that is often not in alignment with our already OK true nature of love. Intention that is in alignment with our true nature we call "love"; intention that is in alignment with (illusory) separation we call "fear." Fear causes more "distance" for ourselves and others, which is (temporarily) painful – sometimes very painful. There is no paradox in saying there is no evil, all is well; and also, choosing love is very important and meaningful. It is all a huge adventure, even as it is important that we love each other and reflect the truth of love to each other. Only the human thinking mind conditioned in duality thinks (incorrectly) that these two things must be opposed. It tends to do that because it believes duality and form are fundamental when they are not. Duality and form arise within that which is fundamental, in which all is always well.

Q: Why do some people who have NDEs or other nonphysical experiences come back with negative interpretations? For instance,

they might interpret that the Light is trickery, or put other negative spins on something that I have experienced as being wonderful and beyond any such spin.

Two pertinent points: (1.) Non-physical systems are not all necessarily high vibration. Some individuals with strong fear patterns may visit relatively low vibration thought responsive realms for a time. (2.) When we return to the physical reality system, we are often firmly rooted back on this side of the veil and in the environment of the current collective consciousness. That "consciousness environment" is one of very stark duality: We tend to interpret things within a rigorous perspective of duality (good and bad, light and dark, and interpretations of struggle), and we have a lot of "belief momentum" built up in our consciousness from doing that. In other words, the local self can take remembrances of the other side and immediately frame them within the local context. In both cases it is important to remember that the entire "stage" (of both this physical reality and even other low vibration reality systems) is not fundamental at all – the complete love and freedom of Being fully transcends it. And there are many who do come back to successfully retain that deeper message.

Q: Some people see Godlike entities in NDEs. Are they seeing God?

I cannot answer "yes" or "no." There are many different levels of the self, or others, or the Whole that we can interact with in various ways. But regarding "Godlike entities," we are *all* powerful beings. When we die, a guide or friend or very powerful being may appear to us in a way that appears godlike for one reason or another, or we may see the true powerful divine nature of another, or the "greater system" may indeed create an avatar to interact with us. But ultimately, Reality is far more than what can be seen and accounted for in a sensory experience, as if the larger systems were just like our own with objects and beings and one of them over there is called "God." No, Beingness "rises up" in many ways. The Great Spirit of life that is within and at the heart of it all, the living loving power that is so amazingly perfect and to which we all individually aspire, is what we very crudely call "God." There are no words we can put on that to truly name it, for it is beyond all names and beyond all boundaries and descriptions.

288

The Afterlife Experience

Q: Is the afterlife just one place or state?

The "afterlife" is staggeringly vast; it is not just one place or one state. In fact, there are many, many different reality systems, and what one can do in them varies significantly.

Q: What is there to do in the afterlife? What activities can we perform in Heaven? For instance can we eat dinner, go for walks, and enjoy a sunset?

Yes, we can engage earth-like environments, where we can perform activities that are very "normal" for us on Earth, including eating dinner, going for walks, or enjoying a sunset. However, there is far, far more available to do than the human portion of us might conceive of. We are powerful, creative beings, and so we can create and enjoy an extremely wide variety of very real environments and activities. There are huge numbers of ways we can express and enjoy our loving and creative natures with one another. In general we might say that our "activities" are centered around serving others and the whole, expressing creativity, participating in the expansion of creativity and beauty, and experientially "learning" and evolving the quality of what we are. It is more than just activities, though; there are also states of being available that are profoundly amazing, including states of joy and bliss that far transcend what we commonly experience while performing earthly activities! There is a profound amount of freedom, and that freedom is exercised in multitudinous ways, many of which are not even imaginable by the human mind.

Q: Can you give examples of activities that are possible when not in the body?

There is far more possible than what can be listed in earthly words. That being said, in my pre-birth memory in the system "above" our own I recall doing what we might call traveling, talking and playing with others, training, participating in complex creative endeavors, relaxing, participating in games of consciousness, and even just spending a great deal of time "frolicking"!

289

But there are actually far more possibilities than we might imagine while human. For instance, many realities are immediately thought-responsive, so you can do all sorts of fun things just by thinking. As a simple example of that, during an OBE I had a few years ago I decided to figure out if I could taste in that reality – and I immediately created a rich peanut butter frosting. I was delighted to discover that not only did it taste and feel very real, but in fact tasted even better than I had expected – it was the "perfect" version of peanut butter frosting! (Though it lacked any "surprise novelty.") Anyway, in general I don't feel the activities are what is most important, I think it's ultimately more a question of being than doing. That is, what we are is unto itself wonderful and full of joy. And then, what we are expresses itself in a myriad of amazing ways and within a myriad of reality systems. We can even be entire other forms of existence that are purely blissful, without even having to deal with objects or bodily actions.

Q: When we die, are the reality systems we can enter other objective places that are already inhabited by other beings?
In general terms the answer is often yes, but I think the following qualification is pertinent. Reality is not primarily comprised of fundamental places where one can go and see things. (We learn that assumption here, because that's how Earth seems to be.) Reality is primarily comprised of consciousness, or spirit itself. Consciousness engages reality systems with various "rule-sets," some like our own that are apparently shared places, and others that are extremely different (but still real). With such a huge array of possibilities, it can be quite difficult, or even impossible, to explain a given experience, speaking from Earth-side. That being said, there are other shared realities like our own that we can visit. In fact, that even happens while the physical body is alive – we can and do visit nonphysical places, especially when our body is asleep, and often without the local part of us remembering! But again, since "places" are not the fundamentally real thing, I feel it is not an optimum habit to try to understand the higher realities as just places (that is, to think in Earth terms). We tend to immediately tie up the idea of an objective place with our definition of reality – and that is not a good assumption. Linear time (linear causality) and singular location, and even the experience of separation of the self from an "outside" world, are all

290

assumptions we tend to believe in because of what we experience here on Earth, but none of those are fundamentally necessary. In fact, the experience of stark separation that we are experiencing now is not only not fundamental, it is often perceived as one of the most highly alien and unusual experiences within the Big Picture, undertaken by only a relatively small number of very unique (and brave) souls!

Q: NDE experiencers mention things that are common to earthly experience – languages, clothing, etc. These things are human creations and constructs of society, so I wouldn't expect to find them on the other side. How could things that are based on our human experience exist in a world beyond? That is, why are there reports of the afterlife having earthly objects in it, like bodies, clothes, and green grass?

Consciousness is what is real (not things); and then consciousness, when it incarnates as a human personality, learns to understand all of reality from the learned earthly perspective. There are other reality systems "above" our own where the "thought objects" of all participants of Earth are quite real and can be experienced in new environments. Also, the larger system uses the "experience language" of the individual to interact with them, since that is what they know. Truly, reality does transcend all the relative objects of Earth; but to the local portion of the self that knows nothing else just after death, earthly contexts are most appropriate, comforting, and enjoyable. Meanwhile, many NDErs do experience transcendent states, but they typically have a very difficult time describing them in words (since words are also of our world).

Q: If we are all One and are all connected, will I lose my individuality when I die?

There are many states of being available to be experienced; but no, we do not lose our individuality when we die. Our individuality is precious and preserved. In general, we will be simultaneously aware of both our individuality and our oneness with all. We can go to various extremes across that spectrum, but the precious individuality is never lost.

Q: I've always wondered, if you meet your friends and relatives in the afterlife and spend eternity with them, what about all their friends and relatives, and *their* friends and relatives. You couldn't spend all your time with the people you know, if they're spending time with the people they know. Do we exist in all places at the same time?

When we consider higher realms from within our local constraints, our intellect can come to all sorts of weird "duality-rules-based" conclusions. That is, when we assume local constraints apply to higher realms, things can seem logically confusing. We are all ultimately One, even as individuality is preserved. And there is a very, very wide variety of ways in which we may spend our "time" – even with individuals, or with the All, or as individuals who know we are one with the All. Those relationships are not like they are here on Earth, bound by physical, biological, and space-time constraints. Our "true" relationships are enjoyed with far less limitation.

Q: Are there any instances where someone is bored in Heaven because all the things they like aren't available there and the only things they can do are things that don't interest them?

One is not truly made happy by the things one likes. One is made happy by the true knowing, experiencing, and expressing of one's being (knowing and/or expressing the connectedness, freedom, creativity, and love of one's being, which includes serving others). Meanwhile, many heavenly environments are thought-responsive, and all manner of "things" (forms) are available for enjoyment. Yet there is a certain something that only the call of real challenge provides, so many return to be re-engaged in new ways within a universe of constraints (like ours) so as to expand the nature of their being through manifest experience.

Q: I've read that a person who was restless in this Earth life will probably remain the same in the afterlife. Do we not get peace when we die?

Peace is native to the Being. A given level of the self, though, may have certain patterns that lead it through various manifest experiences, whether in this reality or others. With death, the constraints of biology are always relinquished, and much of our current hardship is in those constraints. It is

292

possible that fear can continue to lead the individual into certain manifest experiences for a time, perhaps even a long time. But one way or the other, ultimately all people always return to the love and joy that is their true Being.

Q: As we age, we begin to develop mental illnesses of all sorts. When we pass over, will these mental illnesses affect us on the other side?
Having a body is like wearing a biological constraint set. When the biology dies, the biological constraints vanish with it. When the body dies, all is healed! From my PBE I remember reviewing the precious, wonderful quality that a certain spirit had developed as a result of experiencing a long neurodegenerative disease as a human. In other words, the rigors of mental illness or other neurological challenge are actually an amazing opportunity for the spirit to... how to say it... "refine" the way it interacts with and experiences reality. (This is extremely hard to describe from here, and I acknowledge that it can be a very hard pill to swallow from the human ego's perspective.) It can be seen from that perspective that the rigorous challenges of living in a deteriorating body or mind, though extremely challenging at the time, are actually more than worth the difficulty.

Q: If one has shed the body and is now "energy," how can one feel anything physically at all? Aren't physical nerves required for the sensation of physical touch?
Even your physical body is an experience! The experience of the physical body occurs within and is "made up of" consciousness itself already. So, you don't need to be in this physical reality to experience a very real body. In other words, the body doesn't "cause" physical experience, as if it were fundamental, but rather the physical body is a part of the significant "constraint set" of this local reality, where you "wear it" as an experience. And you can "wear a body" in other reality experiences, too.

Q: I have trouble having close relationships with people in this life. If I am the same person after I die, will I continue to have trouble connecting with others in the next life?
In the nonphysical, interactions are much more genuine and communication is full and known. Exchanges take place through telepathy, by which no

misunderstanding is possible. You have very dear relationships with many, and they with you – even if you have forgotten those relationships while human. Those beings love you for exactly who you really are – no pretenses required! They know you in a way that you may have never been known while human. When freed from the constraints of a reality system like ours, you will have no problem connecting with them. Meanwhile if you have interactions with others where their nature and yours are dissimilar in some way, that is no problem at all – you might naturally just not spend time together, but there is no social pretense at all. Love and understanding are commonplace, and everyone's true unique nature is recognized and valued.

Heaven
See also: (085) (138)

Q: Is Heaven a real place?
Yes. There are numerous reality systems of such creative expression, beauty, and bliss that you could not possibly articulate them with human language, or even imagine them with the human mind. Beingness itself is always full of bliss, freedom, and love, because that is its enduring true nature; and it expresses that nature through incredible reality systems that are overflowing with bliss, freedom, and love.

Q: Where is Heaven located?
This may be a useful metaphor: Imagine you sit down at your computer to play a video game; but as you play this game, you completely forget the "real world" and only remember and know about the video game world. Then, later, while still in the video game world, as your character in the game, you ask: "Where in our video game world is the real world?" The question cannot be answered, because the real world is a higher dimension that is giving rise to the video game world. So it is with Heaven: We are already there but are metaphorically asleep as we walk this human journey – and we can never, ever be far from Heaven.

Q: Is Heaven a state of mind?

294

A positive, selfless, appreciative, and loving state of mind automatically moves us into a vibration that is more in alignment with the joy and love that we already fundamentally are. That feels heavenly. Also, that joy and love that we already fundamentally are manifests places (reality systems) of unspeakable beauty, creativity, and bliss. So "Heaven" is both possible to know in a given relatively high-constraint reality system such as our own, and also within other reality systems "higher up" that are much less constraining (have completely different "rule-sets") and are already vibrationally much "closer" to our true nature. Simultaneously, however, no explicit reality systems are even required in order to experience the bliss of Being. So to put all that another way: Joy is native to what we are, and that joy can be expressed or known in many different reality systems to varying degrees, or even beyond them.

Hell
See also: (016) (068)

Q: How there can be a hell, or hellish experiences? Surely these exist. How can we explain this?

The unconditional love of Source transcends all the reality experiences of form. But within experiences of form (whether in this reality or others), great contrast is possible. When we go "far" from Source, we can experience great fear, and where there is fear, "darkness" happens (ego, selfishness, greed, etc.). We are powerful, creative beings; and so, whether in this physical reality or in other more thought-responsive realities, we can create hellish experiences due to our fear and because of our beliefs and expectations. All of that, however, is contained within the great transcendent Beingness that gives rise to it all. In other words, the unconditional love is first – and then within that love we are even given the opportunity to experience environments of stark contrast in this and other reality systems, some of which can be hellish – until we evolve past that fear and expand the love and joy in due measure.

Q: Is hell real?

Temporary hellish reality experiences can happen both in other nonphysical realities and also here on Earth. The highly constraining Earth experience is sometimes perceived as a hell – not because it is fundamentally charged, but because of the meanings incarnate consciousness has placed upon it and bought into about it. Nonphysical environments are often thought-responsive and will instantly reflect the personal nature and beliefs of the experiencer in an extremely real way. Also, sometimes a "hell" is experienced as a "wake-up call" – a way to get someone's attention and show them they are on a path of fear or selfishness.

None of those hellish experiences are fundamental. The fundamental Beingness that gives rise to all experience is of love and joy and freedom! It ventures from that state into discrete experience – even what may end up being a potentially hellish experience – ultimately for the sake of creativity, joy, and love. Nonfundamental hellish experiences may occur as we wield fear-based intent (intent that reflects the illusion of separation); but they do not last, because they are not fundamentally real, just as the Earth environment is not fundamentally real. The experience is real, but the Beingness having the experience is more real, and that Beingness is always one of love, freedom, and joy.

Q: Is hell a place?

Extreme vibrational distance from Source, which is very roughly synonymous with living in fear, is hell. And that can happen in both our reality system and others. Thought-responsive realities can become extremely hellish when one's fear is allowed to run wild. But ultimately fear has no true power. The true power is Love! There is never ultimately anything to truly fear! It is of great benefit to remember our true power and to shine, rather than to live in fear.

Q: Is there such a thing as eternal punishment?

No. The very idea of eternal punishment is not one of unconditional love; it is an earthly, fear-based idea. Eternal punishment is an idea we came up with that represents the extreme imagined end of a perceived "duality spectrum":

296

It is the extreme of what our imagination can concoct as a result of our real experiences of pain and suffering that happen on Earth. Even if it seems to last for a long time, actual suffering is always finite, because the physical constraints, separation, and fear that give rise to suffering are not fundamental to Being. While nonfundamental hellish experiences happen when fear-based intent is wielded – including here on Earth – the deeper fundamental truth is love, joy, freedom, and unity.

Q: Is there punishment in the afterlife at all?

We are all completely and totally responsible for every single choice, thought, action, and intent. Our past choices, thoughts, actions, and intents can lead us into various experiences, whether in this world or in another. And some of those experiences may be extremely painful or dark. But the enduring truth that transcends that entire process is unconditional love, and that love is completely and totally accepting and understanding.

Q: I feel so separate, and it is like a hell! Is Hell a place of total separation?

Separation is not native to our Being, and so it can feel like hell. Yet, there is no such thing as true separation. We do visit various reality experiences where separation can be experienced, but even those experiences are ultimately based in unconditional love, and arise within lasting unity of Being. In other words, we are never, ever truly separated from anyone we love, and *all* of us are completely cared for, supported, and adored. (016)

Q: If the veil is what enables us to "wander far from God" and experience life, which can result in fearful or hellish experiences in this realm or the next, then wouldn't it behoove us to not experience the veil and to not exercise our free will in an environment like this one?

The veil allows us to have *this* type of experience, not to "experience life." Consciousness can have many, many experiences that are not so veiled (reality systems where our true connectedness is known). But being veiled permits an extremely unique form of experience. We are so creative, and we are so freely curious, and we wish to expand our native joy and love in such

297

extreme ways, that we accept the earthly veil to have this highly specialized human experience. Free will is not a thing to be avoided. Free will adds huge amounts of creative expression and preciousness to What Is, and it is cherished and protected. Perhaps the asker is thinking that the goal is to do anything we can to avoid the negative – but that is not the goal; the goal is to expand love and joy and All That Is; and that can be accomplished by *overcoming* the apparently negative, which was not fundamentally real in the first place. (002)

Q: I know people who have seen hell. Since they report on it, we know it is real, right?
Nonphysical realities can present themselves in a myriad of ways, depending on many factors that are personal to the experiencer (including beliefs, expectations, intent, fears, and thoughts of the experiencer). Thus, the objects seen are not always indicative of the nature of the environment itself (as we might assume with our world) but of the individual (of their fears and form associations).

Since we are used to being human, we think reality is ultimately made up of objects and places. In the physical world, if I go to a place like, say, New York City, and I see something there and report it to you, you can gain some knowledge about that place secondhand. But higher realities do not necessarily follow the same rules as our world. Higher realities – which are incredibly real indeed (often even more so than our own) – are often very personal. And the way a given personality experiences them is often personally symbolic – even if painful. So it's not simply a matter of saying "someone saw some objects" or "someone visited places" – as if reality is primarily comprised of objects or places. Rather, in order to understand many of these experiences, I feel it is important to recognize that consciousness is first, and then form is second. (132)

Q: Are demons real? Are there evil spirits?
Generally speaking, the idea of "demons" may fall into two categories: The first is actual fellow free-willed beings who have fearful or selfish intent and who are operating in other reality systems of form, and the second is the

298

lively "thought objects" that arise from the human collective consciousness and that can be interacted with in nonphysical environments but are not actually free-willed. In both cases: Spirit (consciousness) transcends duality itself. And spirit is fundamentally loving, free, powerful, and joyful. Spirit can then "opt-in" to have discrete free-willed experiences of form and duality, whether in this reality or others. Now, there is such as a thing as any given spirit only being "so adept" at expressing its true loving nature within a given set of forms or a given constraint-set. That is, each of us is only so evolved in love, and each of us yet has fear. Indeed, part of what we are doing here is working to evolve the quality of our intent such that we can be successfully loving and creative within a very wide array of experiences. This choice making occurs both in our physical system and in other systems – there is imperfect choice making happening both on Earth and in other realities of form. So the wielding of fear-based intent is possible even by beings in certain other reality systems. But "evil" is not a fundamental force; it is only the expression of our yet-unevolvedness; it is where we express fear, within whatever context. As creative beings, we give birth to all sorts of experiences (choice-making opportunities) and living thought forms, all sorts of ideas and objects and names. That includes things we consider "dark" – things that help add to the depth of possible manifestation by providing contrast. Are those things experienced as real within a given reality system? Yes. But are those things – even things like demons – *fundamentally* real? No. What is fundamentally real is loving consciousness itself; and that consciousness engages in all sorts of wonderful and terrifying free-willed experiences of form in the ultimate name of joy and love!

Q: If there is no hell, then what happens to those who are wicked and evil? Where is the justice?

The following two statements are both true and do not contradict: (1.) The love of Source is completely and totally unconditional. That unconditional love is fundamental and can never be lost. (2.) We are 100% responsible for every single thought, word, action, and intent. There are "divine laws" in place that facilitate a natural and complex energetic cause and effect through which we each experience the results from our choices (the results of "who we are" or "who we have been"), whether in this physical reality or other,

299

nonphysical realities, so that we can grow past fear and towards love. That process is ultimately additive and ultimately serves love, even if a given portion of the self may experience long periods of suffering. In that process, which is founded in inconceivable wisdom, there is always justice – and that whole process is built on love. The true justice is that *all* are loved and accepted, and that *all* are healed. Only the ego wishes less than that for someone else.

Q: Why do so many NDErs feel so adamantly that there is *not* a hell but others say there definitely is?
Hellish experiences occur in our world and in other, more thought-responsive reality systems, but many NDErs come to understand that the fundamental ("more real than that") truth – the bedrock from which all reality arises – is unconditional love. Love is at the foundation of all activity that occurs; and ultimately, everything is used for purposes of love, creativity, and joy. Put another way: What is fundamental is consciousness (spirit) itself, and it is fundamentally loving and free; and consciousness chooses to engage and commit to various limited (nonfundamental) experiences, some of which can be very high-contrast.

Judgment
See also: (035) (038) (068)

Q: Does God judge us when we die?
From the vantage point of the other side and with full access to all information, we judge ourselves. Or perhaps more appropriately: We assess ourselves. Who we are becomes clear: We can see exactly how we affected others, and there is no hiding. We still have some choice as to how to use that awareness and how we will respond to the "energetic results" that are now a part of us. In other words, wisdom is not automatic. Meanwhile Source loves us completely and unconditionally! And we are encouraged on our long roads of expansion, even as those roads often include many very challenging experiences that may result from our own fearful or selfish choices, and our own imperfection.

300

Q: Does this mean even Hitler is loved and accepted? It seems he deserves punishment!

We are 100% responsible for every single thought, word, intent, and deed. We absolutely do not escape what we have been (or more accurately, what we actually are), and we are completely accountable for it. Simultaneously, we are unconditionally loved and accepted, always. These two things do not conflict. So even the soul who "played" Hitler is completely loved and accepted, too. True justice is that all are healed and loved and grow together as they are completely understood and accepted; while wishing for harm to another (even in the name of "justice") is yet ego.

Q: If our souls are "pieces" of the Source, then why do we judge our earthly actions either positively or negatively during our life review? Aren't we blameless? Furthermore, as humans we are limited by our human abilities, which are largely a function of what we are born with: genetics and life circumstances. How can we be held accountable for those?

The following two statements are both simultaneously true: We are perfect just as we are, and also, we are only so good (so evolved) at reflecting that perfect loving nature in a given limited context and constraint-set (which is often, in fact, a context and constraint-set we sign up for beforehand). From the other side, that context is seen completely and fully. It includes all the biological constraints (genetics, brain chemistry, etc.), circumstantial constraints (family situation, etc.), societal constraints, economic constraints, etc. What we "judge" (assess) in our life review is how well we actualized our true loving nature through those constraints – even as we understand that they were often very extreme constraints. We always have free will in choice making, even when the circumstantial pressure against us seems overwhelming. Despite the extreme circumstantial pressure, we can see clearly in the life review how "well we did" because we see the true nature of our intent and exactly how others were affected by us. The soul in its depths of power and wisdom can often, then, understand how it could have done "better" – that is, how it could have more lovingly and less fearfully wielded its free will intent, even within that highly constraining or difficult context.

301

To put all that simply: While it is recognized that the fear and pain of others has passed to us, and that has made earthly life hard for us, we always have a point of power in our free will choice making, and we seek to use that point of power well, even if it doesn't appear to be much on the physical surface.

Suicide
See also: (093)

Q: What happens to a soul after suicide?
Suicide is not an "out." That must be definitively said first. Also, the results of any particular physical action certainly cannot be easily identified or categorized. That being said, no matter the cause of physical death, all are completely and unconditionally loved and accepted. We do always have responsibility for all we have been – we are responsible for all we have thought and intended and done. So sometimes we need to have future experiences to "heal" parts of ourselves that we have not yet integrated. In that important sense, suicide is *not* an escape – the fear that led to the act must still be confronted. But, that process exists within and is transcended by unfathomable love, compassion, and forgiveness.

Incarnation & Reincarnation
See also: (066) (088) (106) (112) (137) (141)

Q: Is there reincarnation?
Yes. The soul is so great that one incarnation experience does not suffice for its purposes. You always remain you – the you that feels like you to you. That you has the experience of being and doing various things in its quest for the expansion of Beingness, creativity, love, and joy. Some experiences necessitate the temporary forgetting of the rest of what one is, because there is incredible opportunity and potential in that unique, specialized experience. The soul develops as it integrates experience. The soul evolves and retains its ability to express its true loving nature – that is, to make love-

based rather than fear-based choices – as it proceeds through various experiences, including experiences of highly varied context.

Q: Do we plan our lives beforehand?
Yes, but not every detail. The soul may choose to experience certain contexts or themes in order to facilitate the expansion of being. The individual is free to make free-willed choices within the planned contexts. The contexts that are agreed to may sometimes seem extreme from the human vantage point, yet the greater the contrast, the greater the opportunity.

Q: What kind of things might we decide to experience before we come to Earth?
Generally speaking, all aspects of earthly life are possible choices of contexts to experience. We may choose to experience: a certain gender (or unique gender), a certain sexual preference, a certain economic situation, a certain type of relationship, a certain biological limitation, a certain form of abundance, a certain form of hardship, or any other aspect of earthly experience. Meanwhile, it is important to remember that while the context may be pre-selected, we always have free will once we are here, and we are free to do our very best within, and even "overcome," any context. In other words, no context, regardless of the level of challenge, can automatically "overcome" the spirit (though it is possible for the human personality to be temporarily "overcome," such that it cannot psychologically endure an experience). Spirit may choose a great challenge, but that is because it knows its true nature is one of unspeakably vast love, power, and freedom. And so love, power, and freedom *can* actually be known within and expressed through any earthly context.

Q: So do we come to Earth to do just one thing primarily? Or many?
Our time here is full of opportunity, so we are not narrowly restricted in how we may participate in the process of evolution or the love of others. Love is indeed the higher theme always at work in its many expressions, and there are innumerable precious ways we might serve that purpose in any lifetime – even in any single day!

Q: If Heaven is so great, why do we come to Earth?

The application of the free-willed spirit against a rigorous context is an opportunity for the permanent expansion of joy and love through choice making and experience integration. We are curious enough, and confident enough in who we really are, to take the risk of diving deeply into this rigorous context.

Q: If we live many times, which identity will we associate with in the afterlife?

The state that one experiences immediately after death is not the same for every individual because each soul is unique and is at its own point of evolution. Some people, for instance, may continue as their latest human personality for a while in a non-physical environment that can appear very Earth-like. But ultimately, the you that feels like you to you isn't actually your human identity or human associations. You may think your human identity is what you are right now because all you may remember is being the human – all you may remember is your name, your body, your physical associations. When you are done experiencing this human condition-set, you will still be you. In fact, you will be *more* you! The other characters you have played weren't "other people" – you were (are) those characters, too! And if you go into a new set of constraints and a new context, you will still be you there as well. In other words, in the higher states you know that you are you – you aren't the forms or associations of various experiences. You aren't ultimately defined by those forms. You may love and appreciate those forms, and indeed they are precious to the soul; but you don't need to differentiate between them or pick one over the other, because *you* played them all.

Q: Is it our choice alone to come here or does another being talk us into it?

It is our choice. It is the individual that chooses to experience a given life, and that choice is made from a much higher vantage point than the earthly one. Yes, there are guides who might make suggestions or "nudge" us (reminding us of our own growth intentions), but the choice to incarnate is always up to us. The soul has sovereignty; the choice to be "bound" into the physical experience for a while must be entirely our own. I feel it is possible for some

304

who are yet quite "wrapped up" in the incarnation cycle to make such a choice with much less deliberation, but ultimately the choice is always ours.

Q: Not everyone chooses to have kids, and a soul has to find parents who are conceiving. Does this give the soul limited options? Do they or God know who is going to have kids and who isn't?
Yes and yes. In my pre-birth experience, the guides and I worked out what would be an optimal experience for me, and then they (in their huge wisdom and vast experience) reviewed the "databases" and came back with an option that would fit well for me for certain reasons (experienced from that side as a broad and complex energetic match). They can only select from available life opportunities (in this case, children being born). Because there are a limited number, being given the opportunity to live a life on Earth is an *enormous* honor and incredibly precious gift of an opportunity! Yes, the "system" can foresee where children will be born with varying points of certainty "beforehand" (it's typically extremely good about knowing "ahead of time"). However, since that realm is not restricted to our own version of linear time, it gets strange to try to speak to that from here.

Q: If reincarnation is real, then how could individuals be there for their loved ones when they die many years later? Wouldn't they be otherwise occupied?
This is very hard to talk about in language, but I think this may help. We might very crudely say there are two "layers" to the individual – the local self and the higher self. The local self is the human personality, and it can only "be" one place and "do" one thing a time. The higher self, however, is not bound to linear time or any given reality frame, and it can "play" any of its "characters" at any time, even simultaneously. After a given human character dies, it is possible that the once-human personality of a loved one will be occupied off in some other experience. But, the loved one's higher self can still "play the character" of the loved one as it desires. In other words, the higher self is not constrained to be "only here and not there." Each of us in fact exists in multiple reality systems simultaneously right now!

Here is a crude metaphor that may help. Imagine that you sit down at a computer to play a video game, and while you are playing you forget you are sitting at a computer and are playing a character in a virtual world. The "real you" is not in the game, and when your character dies you "wake up" to the real you who was playing the game. Other players are also sitting at their computers playing. Now imagine the real you who sits at the computer can actually play more than one game at once. When another player's character dies, you can still go see them by playing as your previous Earth character (the relative they know) on a different server (different reality) than the Earth server, if you wish. This is a very complex process, one that I am not really qualified to speak to, but I hope that idea may be helpful.

Q: Do we come to Earth to get a "gold star" or something? I don't want to come back to this nightmare!
We do not come for a "gold star" (not an accolade or trophy or something). Imagine all the pain you've known in this "nightmare" reversed, and now better understood forever. Imagine the deep chasm of the suffering you've dug for yourself in this lifetime now filled with light and joy. Imagine all the wantings you've given birth to, fulfilled; all the loves you've had in this life, now celebrated unfettered. We are participating in an expansion in being, an expansion in what has been experienced and will forever be a part of you (and a part of All That Is, too).

Q: Having to come back over and over to make things right sounds like "saved by deed" theology or "work-based" acceptance. Isn't Grace freely given? Isn't it true we don't have to earn our way into Heaven?
We are loved unconditionally – Grace is *always* freely given – even as we then freely choose to commit to various incarnation opportunities. We come back because we choose to, not because we have to.

Q: What is the purpose of reincarnating over and over again? What is the point? What is the end game?
The expansion of joy and love – the expansion of Beingness – is its own lasting reward. The soul develops as it integrates experience, and various experiences yield various opportunities which ultimately serve that

expansion of joy and love. The processing and overcoming of fear is synonymous with the expansion of love. Incarnation offers opportunities of perspective, growth opportunities, and opportunities to integrate fear or express love. Regarding an "end game": The human mind, which perceives reality as being linear, tends to want to understand a "beginning" and "end," but Beingness has no beginning, and it creates as it so chooses in an ever-evolving symphony of expansion and refinement.

Q: Would the soul ever plan to take part in something harmful? For example, would a soul ever agree before coming to Earth to be a person that rapes and abuses others, or is that the human side of us? Conversely, does the soul ever agree to be the "victim" of something horrible and tragic? If a soul does decide to be a part of these circumstances, what is the purpose of these experiences?

First, souls do sometimes agree to commit to experiences that have a high potential (it's never a requirement but a potential) for the experience of harm (being a "victim"), which can possibly lead to them causing harm to others on the stage of a given "play." Souls do sign up for "roles." From the soul's perspective, the incredible opportunity of those experiences is apparent: It is an opportunity for the refinement of being through the actual knowing of something extreme, and seeing if and how one can "shine love through" or "refine themselves through" even that experience. That is, we are provided with the valuable opportunity to meet even that experience with love or bravery, to see if we can actually make loving or brave choices even in that circumstance. It is also valuable in that we can permanently develop our ability to actually know something by knowing its opposite – for example, we can forever know and enjoy freedom more if we have actually experienced real lack of freedom. Also, we often yearn to apply ourselves in a way that can actually help others, even within difficult circumstances – so we might sign up for living a difficult experience so we can be there for someone else who was also going to experience it. As to whether or not we sign up to harm others, I did not experience this in my PBE, as *love* is our nature and aim, not intentional harm – but we do sign up for certain "roles" that from the human perspective might seem negative but that can actually help those we love to develop in ways that are important to them. Even in those cases, I feel

307

it would never be a case of being *required* to cause harm. Rather, we sign up for highly constraining, highly challenging circumstances, and then we strive to bring light through those experiences – even knowing that many times we may end up being "overcome" by those circumstances once we're here, which may mean that a temporarily rather damaging personality can result.

Q: If the little light is part of the bigger light, why doesn't the little light know darkness if the big light knows darkness? In other words, why does the little light have to walk its own path and incarnate into physical existence at all?

An incredible amount of creative potential and love potential is added when the big light can differentiate itself into free-willed individuations (souls). Those individuals are free to choose what they will. They each have the potential of the Source, but in order to actualize that potential, they must walk their own journey. The "goal" (poor word) of spirit here is to refine itself and add to That Which Is through the process of experiential evolution. That evolution is not something that is simply passed on; it happens precisely in accordance with the depth of "real" experience and the choice making that happens.

Q: How can we be a fearful and damaging person in one life but a nice person in the next? If the being experiencing those different roles is the same spirit, how can that one spirit express so differently in different lifetimes?

It is the same self. But two things: (1.) The self "evolves" and grows past its fear, and as it does so it is better able to express its true loving nature into contexts where it previously would not have been able to do so. (2.) Contexts have a huge variety of constraints and challenges that go along with them. Many people can make a loving choice and not be motivated by fear when the constraints are low and all is easy; fewer can make a loving choice and not be motivated by fear when the constraints are high and things are difficult. In our physical reality we deal with so many constraints: biological constraints, psychological constraints (psychological patterns of the local human personality portion of us, which the deeper "I" works through and within), societal constraints, physical constraints, and many others. The

308

human experience is a "high-challenge"/ high-constraint game – and the player, who remains the same, may be able to shine her true nature of love into the constraints differently, depending on her experience and state of evolution, and depending on the nature and severity of the constraints she is working with in a given experience.

Q: Does Source have need? If it doesn't need anything, then why do we need to incarnate?

Source doesn't "need" anything, and it doesn't "need" to do things out of love, but it loves the souls it has created of and in itself with unspeakably profound and powerful love, which we might say is its very nature! Love is giving! It loves so much that it gives the soul the opportunity to have discrete experience so as to participate in creative expression and the expansion of manifestation. We love to do that, so we do it. Also, we are curious, so we do it. We could also say: If there is to be creation, then it must be created and experienced. None of that is about need – need is an earthly idea.

Q: How could one actually want to return to the physical? How could one get bored of heaven?

When the counterpressure of challenge is not available, the soul sometimes "yearns" for it again so as to actually have the opportunity to grow. In other words, myriad very pleasant experiences are wonderful, but there is a certain something that only challenge can provide.

Q: So many people seem to live terrible lives on Earth. For instance there are so many children born into starvation and poverty, or war, or abusive situations. How could any soul want to choose to incarnate into such circumstances? Or is it that the soul "has to" do so?

Extreme experience yields extreme opportunity. The soul is bold and brave in its decisions to take on extreme challenges, because it knows the lasting expansion of joy and love that is possible through them. Even though it knows those experiences may seem very hard at the time (in the physical), it also knows the truth of what it always really is, which is far greater and far more enduring than those potentially crushing contexts. The soul knows that ultimately all is always well, and that it is immortal and unharmable, and that life on Earth is but a limited sliver of experience – so it may choose to engage even a very challenging sliver. Even those very challenging experiences are not a "has to" – not something required that one must endure – they are a profound and precious opportunity to commit to a defined (even if sometimes painfully unrelenting) experience within a high-density (high-opportunity) context.

Q: What is the point of the veil of forgetfulness? Why is it necessary?
I remember knowing that the veil was basically necessary to be human, for several reasons, all of which are very difficult to articulate from here, but I will try to put it into crude language. (1.) The veil allows us to have the very specialized experience of creaturehood, and to make choices from this very "deep" and convincing perspective (to make choices "as if" we are only the human personality – which is the very crux of what makes this experience so valuable). In other words we get to make choices almost completely from what is in front of us, even as we don't remember our higher nature; and that is a powerful opportunity for personal and collective expansion. (2.) The veil allows us to focus on the physical (to not get directly distracted by other realms or other portions of the self). (3.) The veil protects us from extremely painful homesickness, which might even cause complete physical dysfunction. (4.) The veil allows a clean slate each time – the ability to build up a precious new (human) personality that is free from certain old patterns and to "play anew" (though certain deeper patterns do carry over from lifetime to lifetime). The veil is thus additive to the higher self in that a fresh new personality can be experienced and "added" to what it is and knows.

Q: I've heard the physical universe described as a "play," and that we are just players upon the stage. I've also heard about soul contracts, and about how spirit seems to know how physical events will likely play out. Does this mean the play is scripted and there is no free will?
There is always free will – always. And free will operates within a given defined context, like Earth. The "soul contract" is more like a commitment to a path, and then once on that path we make free-willed choices in every moment. In that lies the unpredictability and value of the "simulation." It is true that we can only chose from so many things, but within those things we

310

are completely free every moment to wield our intent as we see fit. And how we do that is very, very important. The asker might also be thinking that since events are "seen beforehand" as to how likely they are, that might imply there is no free will and that the play is scripted; but actually, it is just that spirit is very good at predicting the likelihood of billions upon billions of possible outcomes, because it has all the "data" (see Tom Campbell's *My Big TOE* reality model for more on this). But at any given time that prediction is "likelihood only," because the outcome is *not* pre-scripted – it is free will-based, and novel. The unique free-will decisions of the personalities we become are exactly where the beauty, novelty, and creative power enter in, and that is precious.

Q: Does every spirit incarnate physically?
No. There are many beings who never choose to incarnate into a physical reality like this one.

Q: Does spiritual evolution have an end point? Do we ever stop the incarnation cycle?
No and yes. The spirit ever grows and evolves toward greater heights of Being, towards greater expression, and towards deeper joy and love. Meanwhile the physical incarnation process is just one method of evolution available, and eventually a given soul may choose to not pursue it further.

Karma
See also: (007) (036) (063) (068) (115)

Q: Is karma a system of punishment? Or is karma self-imposed?
We are energetically accountable for all we have been and done. From the other side, we can see exactly who we are (who we "have been"), and we wish to expand our understanding and work through our own weaknesses and failures. Basically, we cannot escape what we are, so we choose to engage our own failings so as to evolve past them.

Q: Are we judged by our actions, or our intent?

We judge (assess) ourselves. While the product of our actions is important, our actual intent is of primary importance and is "first." The quality of our intent in all things is plainly seen. So our purity of heart – or selfishness – is plainly seen. In other words, there is no hiding the "real why" behind the choices that we made. And that "real why" is what is important. We are here so that our "real why" may become love rather than fear.

Q: Do we end up in Heaven or Hell solely based on our actions? Or also our thoughts? If I have evil thoughts but never carry them out, would that have any impact?
We are always unconditionally loved and accepted – always. Meanwhile the "energetic results" that we may experience in other realities or in this one are a result not just of thoughts or actions but of our deepest intent. Our local thoughts are both biological and spiritual in origin, and ultimately some layer of intent gave rise to both. The "real why" we did what we did is important; the "real why" behind how we interacted with our internal and external environment is the active ingredient. And from the other side we have a chance to fully review how our own "whys" – our own fearful and loving intent – affected every other being. We are responsible for ourselves and for how we affected others. And even as we are responsible, and even as that responsibility will lead us towards certain experiences in this reality or others, we are ultimately always, always fully accepted and loved; and every choice we ever made is understood from a place of profound knowing and wisdom.

Q: We are not our thoughts, right? If we are not our thoughts, how can we be "energetically responsible" for our thoughts?
We are not our thoughts; we are the consciousness experiencing the thoughts. We are responsible for our intent, which is the primary movement of our being. Our intent is either love-based or fear-based, and intent gives rise to all sorts of forms, including thoughts and actions. Thoughts can also occur as a result of other factors, including energetic factors and biological factors (state of the nervous system). What we are responsible for is our intent, what arises from it, and how we utilize and interact with the forms that are in our experience (including thoughts). Put another way: Intent

312

operates even with and through thoughts, and even with and through the biological context which may give rise to them.

The "Akashic Records"

Q: What are the "Akashic records"?
The data regarding every occurrence in our universe is recorded and maintained in what can be imagined as an immeasurably vast "database" in spirit. Data is maintained not only for actualized choice-making but also for a huge number of unactualized outcomes. All of that can be reviewed and experienced directly as a tool for experience review and learning.

Q: When I view information within the records, it appears completely real and "live." Is there free-will choice making taking place in these recordings?
The Akashic records appear completely real because all data is maintained about all situations in our physical universe, both actualized situations and an incredible number that are unactualized (never ended up happening but could have happened). That includes all sensory data about a given environment and moment in time (sight, sound, smell, feeling, and taste), and so when it is reviewed, it can appear completely real. Regarding whether there is free-will choice making taking place, very broadly speaking, there are two levels of spirit interaction to consider: (1.) There is free-will role participation when a soul actually incarnates (or "plays") as a given being in a given "live" system; and then (2.) there is what we might call a "dwelling" experience, where a soul can experience a certain form as something that is more like a recorded movie than a novel free-will experience (for instance, "view" a free-will experience executed by another soul, or even "view" a context that was not actualized). Broadly speaking, the first is novel, the second is not. Accessing the data of the records is typically an example of the second one.

313

Soul Contracts
See also: (140)

Q: Are soul contracts a real thing? Who would we make a soul contract with?

The soul contract is basically an agreement and commitment to fulfill some role or attempt to integrate some experience. Doing so is a profound act of love and a gift of service. In my pre-birth experience I signed up for a certain path this life. I don't think I'd call it a "contract" in the human sense of the word, but there was definitely a reverent agreement and holy commitment to "bind" myself into a certain experience, attempt a specific "fear integration," and to try to be of "energetic service" in a certain way. (This is very hard to describe, though.) From that perspective we really love the opportunity to serve each other, and the whole, in certain ways. Sometimes that service requires the gift of a deep commitment.

Q: Can soul contracts be changed or modified while we are physical?

Yes, but that is done from the soul level, not from the level of the human personality or its ego.

Q: Many NDErs talk about a soul contract. But how does that reconcile with the principle of cause and effect, or karma? Why would contracts be needed if karma self-regulates the challenges based on our previous learnings?

A soul contract is a commitment. "Karma" is the natural "cause and effect" of "who we are and were." In my own case, in a previous life I was completely overtaken by a very deep fear, and because of that I ended up being a very hurtful person in that life, and I caused damage to many others. Because of that "karma" – that "energy" that remained a part of what I have been – I voluntarily and excitedly chose to sign up for (be committed to) a very difficult experience this time, with the intention that I could re-experience that fear. I did that so that I can now integrate it, because I knew in doing so I would be greatly contributing to personal and collective expansion (expansion of being and of joy and love).

314

Suffering

See also: (010) (042) (045) (049) (077) (083) (093) (096) (128) (138) (140) (142)

Q: Why is there pain and suffering? Why do bad things happen to good people?

Pain and suffering naturally occur in a free-willed system of form in which imperfect beings are making choices from fear, which are not in alignment with our native love and joy. The opportunity for choice making within a universe of form ultimately serves the expansion of lasting love and joy, even as temporary experiences of extreme pain are possible. The Being is (even more) extreme in its fierce love and creativity, such that even extreme experiences of pain can possibly be manifested for ultimately creative purposes.

Q: There is so much suffering in the world. Why does life need to be so hard?

There is no need to blame life. The physical universe is just a very rigorous, consistent, unyielding context. It is *we* who are imperfect enough to suffer deeply when we are applied against that rigorous context.

Q: Is it necessary that we suffer in a physical incarnation in order to evolve?

It is not that suffering is a necessary ingredient. It is that suffering is a natural consequence of free-willed choice making within a rigorous context (by beings who yet have a way to go in their evolution towards love). And many times we only evolve when "pushed" to do so through results – including painful results arising from fearful choices.

Q: How can love be the true power, with so many terrible things in the world (like child molestation, genocide, etc.)? How can we possibly come to terms with the fact that these terrible things exist?

This question is far too broad to sufficiently speak to with a simple response, but I will offer eight brief comments, in the hope they may help, even if just a little:

(1.) Everything "negative" serves as a point of contrast to help establish the experientially known depths of what is "positive." In other words, love can be better known, forever, when the spirit has actually known and experientially understood separation from love.

(2.) "Negative" experience, even unanticipated, offers a "counterpressure opportunity" for the spirit to exercise loving or brave choice-making through. Put very crudely, if you can play the video game on a harder difficulty level, you develop mastery more quickly and can then later apply that mastery in other games (other realities) in other ways. Put another way, while it may not be apparent in the midst of suffering, our journey is extremely meaningful and important. It is important because real, lasting expansion and growth is possible when we successfully engage such an extremely challenging context.

(3.) This is subtle and difficult to articulate: By experiencing challenge, even unanticipated challenge, the system ends up "discovering novelty" within itself and adding potential. In other words, creative manifestation begets more creative manifestation. Put another way, even in destruction, more things become possible than may otherwise have been possible.

(4.) Our world is us. We have a long way to go to actualize and become the love that is native to our being. Our world is what we've done with our free will within our very challenging constraint-set. We do have the power to change it.

(5.) No matter what the circumstances, as consciousness we always, always have the power to place our own meaning and interpretation on any given circumstance. In other words, as hard as this is to accept, there is no circumstance that is fundamentally charged.

316

(6.) We are never, ever alone. Countless beings watch over and help us, even in the most difficult moments, and especially in the most difficult moments. And God's (Source's) unconquerable love is always, always present, always upholds us, and always protects, even as we wail and rage.

(7.) Ultimately, we are all healed! Every single one of us is healed. Ultimately there is no disease, there is no pain, there is no suffering. Those things are temporary experiences that we engage as we dive deeply – and bravely – into a universe of form and apparent separation.

(8.) For every pain in our world, there is far greater love and light, and the love and light endures while the pain does not. Pain and damage are temporary; joy, love, and bliss are our true, enduring nature. Our human journey can be an incredibly challenging road – yet even as the beauty of that road sometimes seems completely lost in the misery, please be reminded of the above, and take heart, and take hope! (128)

Q: If what created us and put us here was loving, why is existence here sometimes so horrible?

We aren't created just prior to our Earth experience, we exist long before it and we choose – purposefully – to come and experience this context and constraint-set. We are not "put here" by someone else. This place is one that is very "distant" from Source (vibrationally), and so we have a very significant amount of "challenge potential" here. That "distance" offers a significant opportunity for the expansion of being through loving choice making (even under fire) and through the conquering of fear. (002) This place also offers the opportunity for the knowing of discrete perspectives and interpretations, each of which is ultimately valuable. While we know our immortal nature prior to coming, we understand that there is ultimately nothing to fear by signing up for this very real "game," and we do so because the benefits outweigh the potential temporary hardships (that is, what are seen from the local perspective as hardships). Very generally speaking, the reason the world can often be a mess is, we are not "grown up" enough to be able to actualize our true loving nature here under these biological and physical constraints. We each have a lot of fear. We have a lot of room for

317

personal and collective evolution. That evolution is happening, even if it may seem slow from a given human's single-life perspective.

Q: Since there is definitely suffering happening, how can all experience be rooted in love and joy?

Loving and joyful Beingness gives rise to manifest experience (defined experience within constraints like ours), and suffering only happens as that "distance" away from the Whole is experienced and the individual "buys into" and loses himself in the form (association with the discrete objects or stories) and/or wields fear-based intent within that limited context. The suffering happens through the stories that we buy into and think are so real (but that aren't fundamentally real), and as we interact with reality in ways that are not in alignment with the deeper truth of love (when we act from fear). Even pain is not already charged (it does not automatically have a negative meaning) – it is, at its root, a (potentially extreme) sensory experience. Meanwhile the depths of Beingness itself always remain present (consciousness doesn't go anywhere), and that Beingness is always of love and joy. The separate self and its ego may protest and say, "No way – I am suffering and I reject it!" – but suffering is only possible through such a separate self (who rejects), not the true self.

Q: I'm questioning why spirits would voluntarily elect to enter a body that will suffer untold physical pain, trauma, and horror. There are dark corners beyond imagination all over the world. If I were a spirit, I don't think I would willingly participate in this kind of existence. I don't think I could elect to forget everything I know and enter into a life of unimaginable torment and suffering. What sense do you have (if any) of the purpose of this system?

This question is not one that can be sufficiently addressed with many words, let alone a few. But I will at least say this. The spirit's goal is not to avoid suffering at all costs. Rather, experience is precious to the soul, and it knows there is absolutely nothing to fear, so it makes bold ventures into discrete experience to ultimately expand the joy of Being. It does that even when temporary deep suffering is possible, knowing that nothing truly can ever go wrong, and knowing that its own Being and the love of Source is far deeper than any suffering, and can never be conquered. The earthly ego rejects this mightily, but even in the suffering that occurs in that rejection, there is opportunity for expansion! (002)

Q: I can't stand to see other people or animals in pain, and pain seems to be everywhere. The world is so very dark, how can we do anything but reject it?

While it is admirable to desire that our brothers and sisters be spared from pain, a rejection of reality is often driven by ego and not spirit. When we reject or denounce "what is," we are automatically aligning with the separation. That does NOT mean we have to "be OK with the bad"; rather, we should *fully* meet every present moment, and act accordingly. In that there is both peace and healing of the circumstances. In other words, there is a difference between a rejection of reality and the decision to act from love and presence wherever you are, to work to heal something you see that needs to be healed. That latter approach is actually harder to do, because it means fully feeling, fully meeting the experience, and accepting ownership for all the messiness of the whole world, rather than denouncing the world. Yet also, underneath all the thoughts and judgments, the Peace of awareness itself always, always remains unharmed. Put yet another way: When we reject the world, we lose our peace, and then we are a part of the problem.

Q: Is depression a physical ailment, or a spiritual one?

We cannot dissect the various levels of the being; they are connected and affect one another deeply. The body arises within the spirit, and also affects the spirit; the constraints of being human and biological are high. Neurochemical imbalance can be rooted either primarily in physical mechanisms (physical lifestyle choices like diet and exercise), psychological mechanisms (learned response to trauma), or spiritual mechanisms (being level fear). And each affects the others. While the physical health and biochemical condition of the body often seems foremost in what physical emotions are experienced, and while they do very much "frame" how one's consciousness is capable of perceiving the physical world at any given time, the spirit is always first, and the body always listens to the spirit. There is a direct and constant connection. So spirit has the primary power, and thus

319

healing is always possible. And also sometimes, when the spirit "heals," or fear is faced, an external physical solution will make itself known. I have personally experienced extremely painful neurochemical imbalance, and I feel it is very important for the experiencer to remember that it is not who they are. We are not the feeling; we are not the pain. It is powerful when we do not to assign meaning or a "story" to the pain; rather, neurochemical pain is like any other pain – it is just a (sometimes exceedingly strong) sensation. When we can see it as just a sensation rather than a story, and fully allow it to just be present, it will be able to leave on its own. The consciousness of the experiencer remains, always. And no matter the depth of depression, therefore, the peace of our true Being is always present. There is no experience, even the darkest depression, that takes place truly separated from the underlying bliss of Being. While that bliss may seem impossibly far away at times, we do always have true power to take a step back toward it – not by rejecting the pain, or indulging in yet another story about it, but rather by bravely going *through* the present moment exactly as it is.

The Nature of People
See also: (016) (038) (046) (065) (133)

Q: I see greed and selfishness everywhere. People are just so mean to each other. Is this not evidence that we are bad and sinful creatures?
We all have a lot of fear (yet-unevolvedness), and where there is fear, there is ego and all of its workings. Yet the true nature of every single person is one of love, even as we seem to become lost in the illusion of separation for a while. (016) Every person is a part of God. Meanwhile we see in the world what we believe about the world – so oftentimes the way the world appears to us is more a reflection of us (what we are and what we believe) than it is an accurate view of the world itself. (031) (086)

Q: It sometimes seems that people never change, and their faults remain with them for a lifetime. Why is that?
Our fear yet runs deep, and so the ego remains strong. Thus it can sometimes take many experiences, sometimes even many lifetimes, for us to work

320

through fear. We are all, always, working with and through our own imperfection. Regardless of how much physical time that process may appear to take, and while the road may be long and winding, all are naturally working through their experience, which facilitates the evolution toward love in one form or another (whether they are consciously aware of it while human or not).

Q: Why do people need to be atheists (or have any other religious or non-religious affiliation)?
The question is a bit like saying, "Why do people need to come to their own conclusions?" or "Why do people need to respond in ego?" The conclusions people reach are not the truth of their being. That is true even if the subject of their conclusion concerns whether God exists or not. The truth of our being transcends the forms and context of our world, and our personal conclusions about that world. God (Source) is absolutely real, in fact more real than the dream of earthly life. Why then lament when the dreamer goes along with the dream, which itself occurs inseparably within God's unconditional love?

Q: Isn't even love done ultimately for selfish motivations? Isn't everything humans do ultimately selfish?
Loving choices made out of genuine loving intent are not selfish. The self exists. It exists, and it is good that it exists. Put another way: The self is What Is. That self is far more than just the local apparently separate human personality. So love – service of the Whole, and service of all other parts of the Whole – is a service of What Is. The part can serve the other or the Whole with true altruism, with no need or desire of any reward whatsoever, even as the other is actually another part of the self. The desire to experience joy and reflect one's true nature (love) through action is not selfish – it is native to what we are! There is no shame or selfishness in thriving in your native joyful true nature. It is natural and good to serve others, it is natural and good to take care of one's self and to love one's self, and it is natural and good to feel great and to want to feel great. Yet we should also be aware that the ego can very easily get ahold of these ideas and seek to serve the separate self in the convincing guise of something more altruistic. Love is always

321

about the service to the other and the Whole (of which you are also a precious part) – and while it is often very difficult to wield intent that is pure and not in any way in service to the ego of the separate self, it is indeed possible.

Q: I wish to communicate what I learned during my spiritually transformative experience – that love is the answer and there is nothing to fear – but I find most people reject it. Why do people reject it? What can I do to communicate it better?

Even the following truth is rejected by many, and often in the name of earthly learned "righteousness": "We are loved unconditionally and accepted, no matter what." Here on Earth, what we wish to communicate must make it through the thick filter of the listener's beliefs and ego. Do not fault the listener when that happens, for they are yet another brave spirit who is finding their way through this obfuscation known as the human condition. The attempt to "proselytize" others is usually futile. I feel we should be patient, tolerant, and present. If you are keen to make yourself available, that may be enough, as your intent will allow windows of opportunity to share the love that you know.

Life on Earth

See also: (008) (023) (026) (030) (035) (043) (047) (049) (061) (063) (069) (076) (091) (104) (108) (115) (116) (121) (131) (140) (145) (146) (151) (156) (159)

Q: Are we here to learn, or simply to experience? I ask this because I would assume our souls are far more knowledgeable and perfect than we are as physical beings, and therefore have no need to learn anything.

The "learning" we do is not intellectual or behavioral, it is experiential. There are some things you can only "know" and "be" by actually being them. We deeply integrate experience, and that expands the soul. The change is in the quality of what we actually deeply are – ultimately towards love – not a conditioning or intellectual learning of some kind. In my pre-birth

322

experience I chose to come to this life primarily to face a very old fear that had "bested" me previously. I came to experience an extremely low vibration on purpose, because I knew that if I could integrate that, the expansion of personal and collective power and joy would be unfathomably beautiful! I knew I was serving both myself and the whole by agreeing to undertake this experience. (137)

Q: Many NDEs speak of telepathy, but now I am hearing that we all have telepathy. Why aren't we using it? Is it too difficult?
When we come to experience this local universe, we are bound by the constraints of being human. They include the constraints of the veil (limited memory) and the human biology. Technically, though, one's consciousness always retains its native capacity, so telepathic communication is still possible, though most humans are generally exclusively focused on the "dense" physical world objects and thoughts, so conscious telepathy is not common here. (It is very common in other reality systems.)

Q: Many NDErs talk about the importance of love. If we plan before coming to Earth to engage in painful or even potentially harmful scenarios, why do we bother with compassion, kindness, gentleness, patience, and love? Why do we go through the trouble of such choice making if our true nature is already love? Why practice love at all?
I think the short answer is: Joy is wonderful. So the expansion of being (which is an ultimate expansion of joy and love) is its own reward. In other words, the expansion of potentials through choice making (even difficult choice making) by definition yields its own fruit. Love (compassion, kindness) best reflects our true nature, and as creative beings we love to expand that true nature. That process is served when we choose compassion, kindness, gentleness, patience, and love. Conversely when we act from fear and ego, we only add to the difficulty for ourselves and others.

Q: I've heard we're living in a computer simulation. Is that true?
The "computer simulation" is an analogy. It is not a literal computer. But this reality is what Tom Campbell calls "virtual" – that is, constructed within

higher systems for the sake of the players having unique experiences. A part of that "game" is forgetting the rest of what we are while we are here.

Q: Are negative emotions derived from consciousness itself only?
No. Bodily emotion occurs biochemically. The consciousness then has to deal with that (wield intent/ make choices based on the new constraints). For instance, if you have depression in the form of low serotonin, the entire world will seem grey or sad. However, also note that biochemical emotion arises not just from physical things (like diet, genetics, state of health, sunlight, nutrition, etc.) but also from the consciousness (intent, choice making, other aspects of the self that are arising, fear, etc.) and how that consciousness is utilizing or interacting with its local personality's "mind structures" that it has come to build and experience over the lifetime (thought patterns, interpretations, beliefs). The body and its emotions are highly responsive to consciousness, so consciousness is generally more responsible than we might think.

Q: I don't like not remembering! Why do we have to have the veil?
Four pertinent comments: (1.) The veil permits us to focus "down" fully into the human experience. You couldn't very well have the full experience of going to work and using the bathroom and all that if you knew you were, say, the sun! (2.) The veil prevents very painful Homesickness. (3.) The veil permits new self-discovery free from past identities. In that sense, the veil is additive, not subtractive. (4.) The veil forces you to deal with an intensely rigorous environment that can prompt a lot of fear, and there is opportunity in facing and healing that fear and making loving choices even in that context.

Q: How seriously do we need to take life?
In short: We don't need to be too serious! The spirit is fundamentally joyful and loves experiencing things for fun and just for the sake of experiencing them. It is only through human conditioning and the rigorous physical constraints of this world where physical things live and die that we end up adopting our "serious" local perspective. But we always have the choice to alter our perspective, and we do not have to take things too seriously. (009)

Q: It seems to me we are here to grow spiritually, not just to experience. This seems like a serious endeavor, not just a playful one. For instance you came to face a fear – that sounds serious to me.

There are different levels here. On the most fundamental level, even my choice to come and face an extremely challenging fear was not done out of seriousness but out of excitement and joy. But living here as humans, it can indeed be important for us to be focused and to try hard. Sometimes the word *serious* to us just means "trying" and "focused," attributes that are indeed often useful and even critical for us to fulfill our intention. Loving intent can and does operate *through* many different perspectives, actions, objects, and even moods – even seriousness – even as it transcends them all, and even as simultaneously, fundamentally speaking, nothing is ever wrong and nothing needs to be taken too seriously! (113) (115)

Manifestation

See also: (014) (048) (059) (086) (101) (109) (130) (135)

Q: I once read about an NDE where the experiencer learned that we have the power to speak things into existence. Is this true?

Since we are a part of the Source of reality, reality responds to our intention. Our local physical system is a lot more "dense" and "inert" than other systems (which are often immediately thought-responsive), but even here our intent always has an effect – and words are formulations of intent. Manifestation will occur within the "rule-set" of whatever reality system the individual is participating in (see Tom Campbell's work).

Q: How are we already powerful creators?

For a moment, forget that you are in a dense shared physical reality and imagine that your consciousness has the ability to create whatever it thinks about or intends. That is how it is in many other reality systems. Our dense physical reality also responds to our intent, but just much more slowly, and it is being "nudged" by all participants collectively (not just individually), too. The "firmness" and "denseness" of our physical reality is one of its unique

325

qualities that helps us experientially learn some very "in our face" experiential lessons. More evolved beings tend to have more "love capability" or "experience capability" – so mastering the dense physical universe experience ends up yielding extreme capability in other systems. In other words, if you can master the rigors of being human, your capability to express yourself is greater, especially in less constricting systems.

Q: I read that we are beings practicing to be able to create god-like creations. Are we practicing to be gods?
As pieces of Source we are already powerful creators. As the spirit evolves towards love and past fear through discrete experience, that power increases. From a human perspective, capabilities that are very common in higher-vibrational realities can appear very god-like indeed, even though they are the nature of every soul. Those "powers" increase as we actually conquer fear and grow toward love.

Q: If I desire something, I sense intuitively that means it is possible for it to be attained. Why?
If you can conceive it, it is possible. All is possible within All That Is, and All That Is enjoys expanding What Is. One of the valuable things we are doing by being physical is "creating desire" – setting what we want so we can fill into it. Would God (and you are part of God) have something that is unattainable to It? No. (Except that God, through you and me, may experience the perspective of something not being attainable for a while.)

Meditation & Awareness of the Higher Realms
See also: (011) (015) (044) (050) (054) (098)

Q: How do I meditate?
See the "Meditation: How to Start" section in Part 4 for just one idea. But unlike an action within form, meditation is not just a specific, prescribed activity you can sit down and do. Meditation is the focusing of intent away from the "focus momentum" and "thought momentum" of physical reality, towards awareness itself. As we do so, the momentum changes. Over time

326

the thoughts that arrive to us have less and less velocity, and gradually our ability to perceive reality from a clearer "supra-physical" perspective gains traction all on its own. It is not something we "go do"; rather, it is a practice of focus such that our larger nature can rise back up all on its own. That larger nature is one that is more alert, clear, and real than the experience of any given local thought.

Q: How can we experience higher reality systems? How can we meet and dialogue with our spirit guides?

In general, awareness of nonphysical environments and interactions can be promoted by practicing meditation, because meditation promotes personal familiarity with the part of you that already transcends the physical: your awareness itself (consciousness itself). Put another way, awareness of the nonphysical increases as you gain the ability to relinquish your focus on sensory data and thoughts, which are aspects of our local reality and the local personality, and surrender into the depths of alert conscious Being that you already are beneath the sense data and thoughts. The "frequencies" of the higher realms are initially very subtle and refined (from our vantage point), so "tuning in" requires one to be able to "sense past" or "focus past" the comparatively dense thought-forms that typically occupy human attention. Once we "tune past" the local dense form to the higher form, that higher form is no longer perceived as subtle but emerges as extremely real – in fact even more real than lucid physical waking life!

Another approach that works for many people is dedicated OBE techniques. The Monroe Institute has credible OBE programs, and certain practiced OBE explorers have published works on the process – for instance see the works of William Buhlman.

Q: Is it possible to have direct experience of the higher realms through meditation?

Yes, that is definitely possible, though practically speaking it is often very difficult to achieve. Imagine your consciousness as receiving a "data stream" of the physical world (see Tom Campbell's *My Big TOE* reality model). That is, your consciousness already is right where it is, and the physical experience appears within it as a consistent stream of sensory perceptions and thoughts. Meditation is using your fundamental power (your intent) to shift focus away from those perceptions and thoughts toward the clarity of alertness itself. Since your higher nature already exists "outside" the physical reality, as you train yourself to let go of the physical "data stream" towards the present moment for exactly what it is without any labels, experiences of your higher nature can automatically rise back up to you on their own. You can't "go get" those experiences as if doing so were some physical activity. But you definitely can gain increasing familiarity with what you really are – your awareness for exactly what it is, rather than your many thoughts – and as you do this, you do clear the way to naturally experiencing the larger reality, and for wielding your intent to do so. You are already that larger reality right now – you are already transcendent consciousness, capable of engaging in many other realities. So if you are willing to completely let go of all the forms of the physical that you think are you, and just experience the real you (your awareness) with absolutely no locally learned requirements or expectations, you may spontaneously experience the larger reality in a tangible way. As the guide Seth says, "Physical reality is like a bright point of light you never look away from." But we can look away from it, with willingness, humility, and practice.

Q: Why do we "have to do" things (like meditation) to get awareness of higher realms?

The reasons are complex, but the short answer in the broad sense is, the experience of Earth involves a set of constraints upon consciousness that facilitate this specialized experience. In other words, that is the very nature of this physical experience we are in: We volunteered to engage an experience where we do *not* know, because that prompts in us an unbelievably real and challenging internal and external experience. The "veil" is rigorous and very consistent. Spiritually there is nothing we "have to do," but from a "technical" standpoint, the sense data and local thoughts seem completely real and convincing once awareness "loses itself" in them. So to regain a higher vantage point, we often need to train ourselves to let go of or look away from all those thoughts and forms of the physical universe that seem so real. Our belief in their being real helps to make them firm.

328

Q: I've heard the phrase "It's all inside you already." Can you please elaborate on what this means?

The "you" that is experiencing everything – your awareness itself – is what you really are, and that "substance" already actually has everything within it and is connected to everything else. This can be fully and blissfully experienced when one fully lets go of all the physical references and associations. Everything is then experienced as very tangibly within you – as if your (real) body itself (your aliveness) was full of all things.

Q: If there are spirits, angels, etc., why don't they just show themselves clearly to us? Why don't the guides guide us in a way we can perceive?

The veil is effective. The guides do guide us every day, actually – in fact, I believe there are more guides at work than there are "players in the game" – but we are often not consciously aware of it, so that help can seem nonexistent. Indeed, even as our guides help us, their role is centered around maintaining the veracity of our conscious free will choice making: They respect the "rules" we have signed up for, because from their vantage point they can see how our independent choice making is beneficial to us and to the whole. The guides help us in various ways that may on the surface appear to be subtle – for instance they may provide energetic or mental "nudges" in the forms of feelings or fleeting thoughts, may send us messages in the form of dreams, or may gently "guide" small probabilities to help things align in a certain way.

Q: Many people have reported seeing or interacting with religious figures, such as Jesus. What is happening here?

I think there are four general categories of how we can label an experience where someone sees a religious figure: (1.) If a person has a belief in a religious figure, a nonphysical environment itself might portray itself to the experiencer using a religious figure as a part of that environment, because the religious figure is the best translation in the "experience language" of the experiencer. (2.) Guides (nonphysical friends or helpers) may also utilize the appearance of a certain religious figure so as to best and most effectively

329

interact with somebody if that aligns with their beliefs. In other words, a guide may appear as Jesus, a saint, or an archangel if that is what is best understood by the personality. (3.) Religious figures like Jesus are very well established "thought forms" with great history and energy – and the thought form can be interacted with directly in a very physical way in other reality systems. (4.) It is possible that the soul who played Jesus could indeed play him again – that is, a direct interaction with the person of Jesus is possible.

Q: If the veil is real, shouldn't it restrict "greater awareness" all the time? Why would there be any differences between people?

The veil accurately restricts what it is meant to, and focuses the local consciousness to the physical "data-stream" extremely consistently. But it is not a physical thing like a blanket, or like a simple human law. It is – and please forgive the significant limitation of language here – a set of personal energetic modifications and restrictions that occur on and in (and are accepted by) the very unique spirit so they can "be" the human. I believe the nature of those modifications/restrictions is largely shared among most participants, but it is not exactly a uniform thing. Rather, the veil is a personally tailored set of restrictions applied to consciousness that permit the chosen physical life.

Q: If there is an afterlife then how come when we receive anesthesia or go to sleep we just experience nothing?

While you are human, your cognition is limited to the constraints of the body and biology. When those constraints change, your local cognition changes. The deeper you never wanes; but while you are "bound" to this side of the veil, the physical is typically all you remember. That will change later when the constraints lift. In other words, when you pass, you will regain awareness of nonphysical adventures you have had even while physically alive. Meanwhile there is an important hint in the following: Note that your awareness itself never vanished during anesthesia or sleep, only the context changed: You experience "before" falling asleep and then "after" falling asleep, or you experience "before" falling asleep and then something in the middle (dreaming), but you never experience not experiencing. Everything occurs in ever-present awareness, even content such as physical context changes, which include things like sleep. The reduced or missing memory of dreams or other non-physical experiences is also important to keep your daytime identity stable and consistent.

Q: Can those who have passed communicate with those who are still on Earth?

I feel there is not one categorical answer, but very generally speaking, yes, the now unconstrained individual can visit their loved ones and friends. Regarding communication: There is a significant vibrational gap between those on Earth and those who are no longer Earthbound, so communication often requires a vibrational "meeting point" – we might describe that as moments when the earthly personality is not consumed by dense Earth-thoughts and is in a low-resistance and/or higher-vibrational place. We are always all connected, and communication may occur that the local portion of us is not aware of: The limiting factor for locally identifiable communication is often how deeply we are focused into the denseness of the physical and our labels of it. For many people, the mourning process may only increase the "denseness" of their focus, which might make recognizing such communications difficult. Nonetheless, love is a very powerful bridge, and so where love exists, communication is possible.

Q: Is channeling real?

When consciousness is engaged in the physical, it retains its connection with higher portions of the self and other selves that exist. So it is possible for a physical individual to "channel" another portion of the self, or another consciousness, whether individual or collective, through into the physical. However, for most individuals, the "path" to do so is exceptionally cluttered by thoughts, beliefs, and associations with physical assumptions. Also, whether to a greater or lesser degree, the channel always has some effect on the information coming through. Furthermore, concepts apparent to beings in other dimensions are often not translatable into earthly language. So while effective channels do exist, I feel that generally speaking, healthy discernment is required when evaluating channeled material. Personally, I enjoy and would recommend for consideration the channeled work of Seth (channeled by Jane Roberts in the Seth Speaks book series), and Silver Birch (channeled through Maurice Barbanell).

Prayer

Q: Does prayer work?

Intent always has an effect. When consciousness moves, there is a result. Every thought and intention is always "heard," always sending out ripples, whether we call it prayer or not. But much of that thought and intention that we wield is "sloppy" – that is, done unconsciously, or done in alignment with some earthly pattern or belief we have learned. Prayer is pointing intention "upward" – it is a purposeful focus, and a shift in focus-momentum. As humans we often "perform" that prayer through the forms we know – through names, or rituals, or beliefs – and that is fine. But it is the deeper "being level" intent (Tom Campbell's term) that wields the power. When our intent is one of focused love for another, or toward connection with the divine, there is indeed power in that. The power is not in the ritual or the action itself but in the intent, in the love, in the reaching of Beingness, in the reaching of Life. Focused love is powerful! (And by contrast, lukewarm thought-mutterings are generally not powerful.)

The constraints of the physical universe are often very firm – it can often be extremely difficult or even nearly impossible to change certain physical outcomes. But on the other hand, the physical arises within spirit, and so spirit has the power; and many, many things are possible in the physical that we might typically believe are physically impossible. Meanwhile it is often the ego that demands a circumstance be changed, and ego (fear) has little power in consciousness space.

One other comment: While we are "veiled" as humans and believe so deeply in the human drama, there is value in our consciously and genuinely turning towards the "divine," in whatever form that may take for us. There is value in clearing space in our human focus and taking human time for the divine – because the divine is what we really are.

332

Form vs. Spirit

See also: (008) (069) (073) (075) (080) (082) (118) (124) (132) (136) (137) (155)

Q: But I love form! I love music and beautiful places, I love my family and the fun activities I get to do. If all that form isn't fundamental, I don't feel good! What do you say to someone who is afraid to lose all that?

What you love endures, because love is of you (not the form), and because you are a part of the I Am that assigns the value and enjoys the form. That which we create and love arises from Beingness, and is not lost, but ever enjoyed! (153) Meanwhile you are also not the forms; you transcend them.

Q: If there is life after death of the physical body and consciousness goes on, then why isn't there definitive proof rather than only a lot of supporting subjective evidence which is mostly human-reported experiences?

Consciousness is fundamental, not the context of the world of matter. Can you point to anything anywhere that occurred separate from someone's experience of it? Experience is the report, because consciousness is experiencing things – even things that transcend the entire local dimension. The following is a crude metaphor but it may help: Imagine you are playing a massive multiplayer online role-playing video game like *World of Warcraft,* and while playing it you forget that you are sitting at a computer somewhere, so you think you are the elf. Then one day as the elf who believes almost entirely in just the video game world, you ask, "If there is a world outside the computer, then where is the proof of that in the video game?" There are clues in the video game, but generally speaking it is impossible for that "higher" dimension of outside the game to be communicated within the game using game ideas and game words. In order to know, the experiencer would need to return to being the player at the computer rather than the elf. Similarly, you are far more than your human character – and, metaphorically, you are sitting at the computer right now! When others have

333

such experiences in the higher realms and they return into this physical game, what can they offer, other than reports?

Q: Is there really such a thing as spiritual growth? Is enlightenment a thing or have we got it all from birth and it's just about practice?

There are no "things" unto themselves – there is Beingness having an experience of things. And as it works through those experiences of things, it evolves its ability to reflect its true nature into and through those things. We have perfect Beingness even before birth; and simultaneously, evolution of love and joy then develops through manifestation as that Beingness applies itself through choice making into defined experience.

Q: Why can't out-of-body experiencers always see objects in our world exactly as they are?

There have been quite a few cases of NDErs who have experienced verifiable physical world events while their physical body was clinically dead. Common veridical reports of NDEs include activity in the hospital, the confirmable actions of other people at varying distances, and sometimes even things like objects on the roof of the hospital. However, I think it's important to release the assumption that the shared apparently objective physical world of Earth is "*the* reality" that is the only gauge of veracity. We have been trained to believe that external and repeatable results are the only way to confirm something is real. While I wholeheartedly hold up the scientific process, and while it is indeed important to objectively test what reality is, this materialistic assumption limits our total understanding, because reality is not ultimately based on an objective world of matter. Rather, the apparently objective world of matter only occurs as it is experienced by that which *is* fundamental. That which experiences it – consciousness itself – can and does engage many other reality systems, too. So it is not sufficient to only look in this one system for the answers. That being said, to more directly speak to your question, OBE states are not limited to this local physical reality frame – there are "layers" of realities, some very "close" to our own that are indiscernibly similar, but not always the same. Many OBEs happen in those "layers." I have experienced this: One time I was out of body walking around my house, and the experience was so real, normal, and lucid that I was questioning whether I was out of body or not. I actually concluded that I was *not* out of body – in fact I felt foolish for even questioning whether I was – until I walked through a wall! I did not pay attention to the location of small objects in my house when that happened, but I suspect they would not have been located in the same exact places as in the "real world." I think part of why that happens is that even those "layers" that are "closer" to the Earth reality are more thought-responsive and individual-responsive, and the rigorously consistent "object placement" that we are used to on Earth is simply much less important.

Q: I feel like nothing should exist. But actually everything exists. And that blows me away. This creates endless and obsessive thinking, because I feel compelled to seek the answer! Why?

Perhaps when you take the leap into beholding that which does exist, you are assigning it fundamental reality. In other words, since there is form, you believe it is mightily real; so then you feel incredibly compelled to work your way through all that form (think all the thoughts, experience all the things, erect the understandings, debate this and that to arrive at some new place of understanding, etc.). That is natural and good! It reminds me of a Seth quote I love: "Consciousness rejoices in sensation and creativity. You cannot understand what you are until you understand these things." Yet, simultaneously, believing in the apparent fundamental realness of form is precisely the action that is the confusion, because the formless "I" falls asleep into the form when it does that. In other words, when you believe you are human, you become the human; when you believe the identity, you become the identity; when you believe the thoughts, you become the thoughts. When you believe the thoughts are fundamentally real, they seem fundamentally real. You become "nothing more" than the associations of the forms, the innumerable relationships among thoughts and things. That is very stimulating! But, as you can likely agree, you do not find pure joy and utter satisfaction in beholding the multitude of thoughts and things. They always lead to more. The joy of being can and does shine as it appreciates its creations in the world of form, including its intellectual creations, but it can quickly lose itself in being "only them," in being separate. The separate self seeks endlessly within the world of form, looking here and there, under every

335

rock. There is no rock you can look under to find what you seek, because the rock appears not as All There Is – rather it appears as only a rock. Looking under the rock *is* looking away from what you really are. This Eckhart Tolle quote comes to mind: "Become at ease with the state of 'not knowing.' This takes you beyond mind because the mind is always trying to conclude and interpret. It is afraid of not knowing. So, when you can be at ease with not knowing, you have already gone beyond the mind. A deeper knowing that is nonconceptual then arises out of that state." The Tolle quote is about moving towards being OK with not knowing, not understanding, not grasping. That is, there is power in not looking under the rocks, and being OK with not even looking at all. Ironically, even though that feels like a move *away* from understanding, it is actually a move *towards* understanding! Because in so doing we take a step back towards that which *is* fundamentally real – life itself – and all things arise in perfect order within that, and are known within that.

Q: I am frustrated in my search for answers. It seems like the constant questioning and search for answers is never enough. Should we just accept we can never know so that we can get some peace?

Thought is a form experienced by consciousness – and "form" never ultimately satisfies, because by definition a form is a form and not the whole truth (which transcends and encompasses all form). The thinking human mind only deals with form and understands with form – but it will never find the peace and full knowing within the world of form (within thinking), no matter how many forms it looks through. Meanwhile, the peace of Being is native to what we really are! As we let go and actually experience our aliveness and our awareness itself without thought or label, the thought momentum slows, and that peace returns all on its own. (And then, interestingly, the true knowing of Being contains all the answers we were seeking anyway.)

Q: In physical terms, what is love? Is it a field or some other physical force?

The human mind tends to try to associate everything with forms from this local world. We think in terms of "things as being most real" – even ideas of things like "a field" – and then we try to identify higher truths with those things. But things arise within Beingness, not the other way around. Another way to say it is: The spirit is of love, and then a universe of things and ideas of things (like fields) arises within it. The question we should ask is not, then, "what thing is love?" Rather, we should engage in a search for Being and for what our life itself is! The answer to that is far deeper than any local idea the intellect can throw on it. Love and spirit cannot be defined with words. When we try, we might say: Love is the living attribute of consciousness; it is the expression of our native unity, our calling, our desire, our goal, and our very nature.

Q: Does the brain produce consciousness? We can see that when a person's brain is altered in some way, their physical consciousness is affected. Doesn't this prove that our consciousness is a result of the brain?

No, the brain does not produce consciousness. (124) The brain (and body) is more like a "reduction valve" – it is a significant physical constraint that the pre-existing living consciousness has agreed to experience for a while. When the brain is altered the constraints change, and what the individual may physically do or locally experience may change, because the brain is an integral part of the human character's body. But the larger parts of the self always remain deeply alive beneath any local biological result, and the local human consciousness can and will return to that deeper awareness when the constraints of having a brain are released.

Fear & Ego

See also: (033) (034) (038) (051) (053) (074) (084) (096) (104) (111) (129) (143) (149)

Q: Why do people live with so much fear? What is the core root of the fear?

Fear is a response when consciousness is exposed to a constraint-set or context that it has not yet fully integrated and mastered. In that sense, fear is just a natural symptom of "unevolvedness." (111) Fear is reflective of the

337

non-native separation, whereas love is reflective of the native fundamental unity. Fear occurs as consciousness "buys into" perceptions that are not in alignment with the truth (which is unconditional love and power and connectedness), and as one's biology (neurochemistry) then reflects that interpretation. Ego is the personal construct that happens as the individual attempts to address the fear and "reclaim" his or her power. And belief often arises from ego as a way for the individual to "settle" what is going on, rather than having to face and feel the full unknown. Ultimately there is nothing to fear – the very context of separation is not fundamentally real, so neither are the apparent causes of fear. The true cause of fear is not in the contexts, even if they are very rigorous, but in *us* – in our own "yet unevolvedness." As we grow towards love, fear vanishes!

Q: I have a terrible fear of death. What can I do?

When you think about the idea that you are going to die, can you locate the negative self-perception you are buying into that seems so real? Perhaps it is: "I am going to be destroyed," or "I am powerless," or "I have no control," or "I am unworthy of love." I think it is worthwhile to locate the negative self-belief that you think the world proves to you, because it's important to identify the fear-generating perception, so that you can actually go and *feel* (yes, feel!) that *feeling itself*, rather than getting lost in countless thoughts about it. Why is this helpful? Our actual, true nonphysical nature is one of immortality, and power, and joy, and love. That is our lasting true nature. While we are physical, when we buy into perceptions that are not in alignment with the actual truth of that, we suffer. We are terrified when we buy into some identity or perception that we aren't. For example: In truth, it is absolutely impossible for us to be destroyed, so when we buy into the perception that we can be destroyed, we suffer. In truth, we are incredibly powerful beings, so when we buy into a perception that we are powerless, we suffer. In truth, we are absolutely deeply loved and adored and can never lose that, so when we buy into a perception that we are unworthy of love, we suffer. Finding the actual negative feeling itself, going right to the root of it, brings the "light" of awareness to it – and that is incredibly powerful! Because always, always on the other side of the suffering and fear is the truth of our powerful immortal nature. And if we want to actually know that

338

experientially, we need to be willing to feel what we are actually feeling. That is, we need to be willing to go towards what is actually real in the present moment – *including our feelings* – rather than just avoiding what we actually feel and spinning our wheels in the endless ideas of the local mind about our circumstances. We need to be willing to see past our own ego's many stories and strategies and actually feel what is down there. We need to be brave enough to actually meet reality and meet our actual experience, including all the feelings that are down there – because ultimately, underneath all that we are rejecting, reality is rooted in hope and joy, not loss and death. (034) (096)

Q: I am constantly thinking about all the bad things that are happening in the world. There is so much suffering, and it constantly occurs to me how many other people or animals are being hurt. The only thought that keeps me sane is that "suffering is always temporary." But it's not enough to give me peace of mind. I'm often able to think through negative thoughts with logic, but I can't "logic my way out" of this, because it's clearly true. How do I cope with this?

Start with your experience itself, before you've thought anything at all. Look at reality exactly for what it is, and at your present moment for exactly what it is – before the ideas are applied. If you do that without labeling anything, you will find that even when certain sense data is happening or when certain feelings are in your body, there is no distress yet. Distress occurs only when the thinking mind arrives to serve you with an interpretation you have previously labelled as important: a "yeah, but!" thought. Give yourself permission to even let that go. Why do that? To "logic your way out" is an activity of the local thinking mind, and the peace of Being that transcends form isn't found in the local thinking mind, it is found in exactly what you really are and what the present moment really is. That peace doesn't only serve to deeply relieve you, it also permits you to regain power to actually help this place for the better, because when you are connected to what is true (actually true!), you can and will help heal the world, almost automatically. Otherwise, while in distress, you are "lost" as a small part of the problem.

Q: Should we focus on resisting pride and lowering ourselves so that the ego doesn't grow and try to distract us from doing our best?

This comment is subtle, but I feel might help someone. Trying to control the ego or resist our negative impulses does most certainly have its place, but doing so can also often be ego. In my own case, the walk has not primarily been about resistance but about acceptance and surrender. It is helpful to remember that duality itself is not fundamental. It is thus not just a matter of "pushing really hard" in one direction – even in the direction we think of as "resisting pride." (115) If we are resisting something, usually if we look deep enough we can find the fear that compulsion is striving to cover up – for instance fears associated with negative self-perceptions such as "I am not good enough" or "I am powerless" or "I am trapped" or "I am unworthy of love." Those fears need to be met and fully felt, not covered over or fought with great vigor. They aren't fundamentally real anyway – but when we don't know that, we resist them like crazy. As we fully feel and integrate and process those fears, the compulsion that we were once striving against vanishes on its own. Until that happens, intentionally resisting our negative impulses – sometimes mightily – has its place. But true peace lies deeper than the fear that gives rise to the struggle.

Healing
See also: (010) (013) (018) (024) (033) (042) (045) (076) (094) (097) (151)

Q: Is healing always possible?

Yes. While we are heavily limited by the "rule-set" of the physical universe and the constraints of biology, and while that limitation does effectively limit when healing may occur, it is technically always possible to heal, because the physical expression arises from something deeper, and that something deeper has the true power. Nothing is truly impossible.

Q: Do you have any suggestions on how to heal anxiety, depression, and pain?

This question is incredibly unique for each person. At least in my own walk, I feel that true healing is not simply the kind where you realize a physically better or more homeostatic state (though such a state tends to naturally result when deeper spiritual healing occurs). I feel true healing happens at a deep personal level: the "I have integrated that part of experience" healing, the permanent kind, where you are forever more because of it. That kind is very hard to speak to or make suggestions about– but I'll still make one suggestion for consideration. Rather than trying to achieve some state or some configuration of circumstances, bring your being to bear on your relationship to the present moment itself – and that means your relationship with the pain itself, too, when it is there. What are you? Are you the pain? No, you aren't. You are the experiencer of the pain, not the pain itself. When you are in deep depression, the pain feels like it will never end – but that is a lie. Meanwhile, since you are not the pain but rather the experiencer of it, you do not have to resist or fight it. In fact, you can even welcome it when it arrives! Let it in for tea. Don't identify with it – just be with it fully, feel it fully, without labeling it. It is an experience of form, passing through your awareness. It does not need your judgment; it does not need your action – it needs your love, your willingness, your understanding. Just watch it, be with it, feel it fully, and allow. Be loving and patient with yourself as you feel what you feel. Feel it to heal it. (013) I feel the goal should not be to "escape the pain at whatever cost." Rather, healing is a natural byproduct of your willingness to fully *be with* whatever darkness or pain or fear you are resisting. Resistance causes pain; acceptance relieves it. Being fully with whatever darkness or pain or fear you have been resisting when it arises requires a *lot* of bravery and willingness to feel, willingness to be weak, willingness to be... whatever you are right now. Are you brave enough to be present with that deeply? Are you brave enough to really feel? It can't kill you to feel – though it may feel like it might. True healing is not primarily about fixing up the boards of the house of your story to survive the terrible tornado of your circumstances and feelings, it is about walking into the tornado, letting it toss you through the sky, landing, and then – without your doing, but because of your willingness – the tornado has lost its power. Once you hear the message of your pain, and honor it with your willingness to feel it, it can go. And you will be forever more as the great Experiencer that you are – for truly, you are greater than any darkness or pain that may arrive into your experience, no matter how incredibly extreme it may seem in any

341

given moment! (034) (096) Take heart, be strong, and fear not! This moment is powerful.

Apparent Paradoxes
See also: (055) (062) (113) (139) (147) (157)

Q: How can there be both free will and predestination? Are both true?
We always have free will. But that free will must work within the available "decision space" (Tom Campbell's term) – within the context and constraints, within the possible choices available. The "binding" of the local decision-making self (the human) within the firm, consistent structure of the physical universe is done intentionally. The simulation of the physical universe follows certain rules for its operation, and while the free will of all participants operates within the context of those rules, the system is extremely good at predicting outcome, even very far in advance. That can appear like predestination, but free will always remains, so unanticipated outcomes do happen.

Q: I can't grasp the idea of eternity. How are we eternal? Eternity seems like such a long time!
Considering eternity from the physical vantage point seems overwhelming because we are doing so from within structured linear time. Consciousness itself is not bound to that time. Beingness is not beholden to some "thing" called "time"; Beingness creates systems with linear time for its own purposes. So eternity is not a burden, but rather time is a manifestation of the abundance of Being.

Q: You say that linear time is specific to our local physical reality system, but also that you experienced a progression of events in nonphysical realms. If linear time is specific to our reality, how can there be progression in those higher realms?
This is another question that is almost impossible to speak about from the Earth perspective, since we are operating from within linear time right now.

342

But I'll just say this: Local physical linear time is a construct that exists within a "higher time," and sequence exists in that "higher time." Meanwhile, simultaneously, everything everywhere is happening in the one Now.

Q: Are we separate or are we One with All? Which is it?

From the human perspective, the following statement can seem like a paradox, but it's not: You are *both* one with all and also simultaneously individual. In higher realms both of these truths are simultaneously known, and they do not contradict. Right now you may sense deep down in you the yearning for connection with others and with nature and a yearning for love (the unity), and also sense the deep preciousness of you as consciousness and as an individual (the self) – both of those are simultaneously fully true and known in higher realms. (Though there are states of being we can enter that are "further" in one experiential direction for a time – for instance the human condition is quite a deep experience of separation, where no separation is inherently true.) (123)

Q: Some NDErs say we are a part of Source, and others say we were created and are separate. Which one is it?

Individuality and oneness with Source do not conflict, they are simultaneous. That is true even as individuality was Source-initiated, and even as experiences of extreme apparent separation (like being human) have been created. (123)

Q: I've heard we are each a small fragment of God, yet I've also heard that we each have the power and/or potential of God. How can these both be true?

Because when we are human we only remember being human, we use the assumptions learned in our local system to then try to understand all of reality. So for instance we think of "less than" and "greater than" as being fundamentals. In other words, we believe duality (spectrums like "lesser than or greater than") is fundamental, and/or we believe other local characteristics like linear time or discrete location (distance) are fundamental. They are not. You can't use duality logic (the basis of a local subordinate system) against that which transcends it – even generates it – and succeed in understanding

343

that transcendent truth. That being the case, it is almost impossible for us to speak to this topic successfully with words. Yet I think this question is best addressed by this Rumi quote: "You are not just a drop in the ocean, you are the mighty ocean in the drop." These two things seem paradoxical but are not paradoxical and are in fact both true. We might say, the drop in the ocean is not the whole ocean but is still the ocean and has the potential of the whole ocean.

Q: It never seems to dawn on nonmaterialists that the very act of proposing that any "thing" is nonmaterial is an act of differentiating it from its surroundings. And the only way you can differentiate anything is via material difference – properties of some sort. If a thing has properties, then by definition it cannot be nonmaterial, as properties are the very definition of material! So nonmaterialists find themselves stuck in an absurd loop. They propose that nonmaterial things exist, yet the only way something gets to be a thing is by having material properties. Something with zero properties is equivalent to "does not exist." There is no difference between a thing with zero properties and nothing at all.

The following comment is only true to the local thinking mind: "Something with zero properties is equivalent to 'does not exist'. There is no difference between a thing with zero properties and nothing at all." The differentiation the questioner is referring to is specific to duality, and Beingness transcends duality. When Beingness knows itself in its fullness – beyond all form, and beyond all individual properties in our universe – it is *full*, not empty. I can't say it any other way. This is not an issue of human intellect (which deals with discrete forms and uses thinking to try to understand them) but of Being. So to know the truth of what I am trying to say, you must experience it as Being, not as an earthly intellectual thought. As long as local human thought alone is being relied upon, the greater truth is not findable, because human thought deals exclusively with discrete form and with the rule-set of duality, and the truth transcends and contains *all* form and precedes the rule-set of duality.

Q: When we hear that form arose from formlessness, does that mean existence come from nonexistence?

Consciousness is. Put another way: "That which is" exists. Then things – forms – arise within it. That includes systems of duality like our own where conflicting ideas like "existence" and "nonexistence" can be considered intellectually, or systems of linear time like our own where serial causality ("this came from that") can be considered intellectually. So to put it another way: Consciousness exists, and ideas like nonexistence arise within it.

PART 4 – BRIEF COMMENTS ON PERSONAL INVESTIGATION

HOW CAN WE KNOW OUR GREATER NATURE?

While each person's process of investigation will certainly be unique, here are just four simple ideas to consider. Disclaimer: I have no interest in telling anyone what to do or how to live; I present the following ideas for consideration only in the hope that they may be helpful to someone!

First, deeply investigate your own awareness. Consider committing to a long-term meditation practice so you can actually experientially discover what you really are beneath the thoughts and ideas. Don't settle for thoughts or beliefs – rather, remain rigorous in your alert investigation of what the present moment itself actually is, what your experience actually is, and what your awareness itself actually is, beneath the thoughts and judgments. This process can potentially take years, but the pursuit is more than worthwhile. See the "Meditation: How to Start" section below for just one possible simple but effective exercise. The human portion of you is just one small portion of you: Your consciousness already exists beyond the physical reality system right now! By becoming increasingly familiar with your alert awareness itself, the larger parts of your being can naturally rise back up to you on their own.

Second, be completely open to what the spirit and the deeper parts of yourself are trying to show you, even if what you are shown is difficult or contradictory to your current viewpoint. The spirit has a much higher vantage point than your local human character. Be willing to be intuitively shown, even if you do not intellectually understand.

Third, be willing to actively search out and reevaluate your beliefs – even your core beliefs – and to take ownership in how the meaning and interpretation you have bought into is affecting yourself and others. Our experience on Earth is deeply colored by what we believe. When we are able to consciously identify our own beliefs and the meaning that we have placed on the content of our life, we are able to see more clearly. Personal belief

346

identification and evaluation can be an important part of the investigative process.

Fourth, be brave enough to actually face and feel everything – both everything that is happening "outside" of you, and everything happening within you. Allow yourself to feel everything you actually feel while you are human – even your deepest darkness. Be willing to feel, be willing to take ownership for yourself and for your world, be willing to be vulnerable, and be willing to completely surrender your need for control. Be authentic. Spiritual growth is a growth of the being, not a change in ideas. As your full experience is fully encountered, the greater parts of yourself will naturally reveal themselves.

In all four of these, as with all spiritual pursuits, it is important to take the "long road." Spiritual growth is not a "quick accomplishment": The expansion of the Being often takes time. Be willing to allow the process to take as long as it will. You actually are an immortal being – you have all the time you need!

Meditation: How to Start

Meditation is a fantastic pursuit, the rewards of which are not apparent until it is practiced. Not everyone will benefit from a journey of meditation at a given time, and that is completely OK. But for those who are ready, it is a life-enhancing practice and a very powerful investigative tool.

There are many different "ways" to meditate, and different methods will work better for different people. What follows is just one that helped me, and I feel it has the potential to help others. The main exercise provided below is conceptually identical to the meditation exercise recommended by Tom Campbell in the aside of Chapter 23 (pages 171 to 179) of his *My Big TOE* trilogy.

Note that while a certain set of actions is described below, meditation is not ultimately about performing an action. Rather, meditation is an exercise in awareness: focusing awareness, directing awareness, knowing awareness, being awareness. When the self is lost in the world of form and lost in the thinking mind, that awareness can seem to be lost. Meditation is the practice of using intention to move back towards the awareness that underlies all of the form.

It is important to set aside the time to perform the meditation. The human personality works in time and typically has built up a huge amount of "thought momentum" and "feeling momentum" in time; so to move "past" that form association and "toward" awareness itself, it is very important to routinely set aside time. An instantaneous return to deeper awareness is certainly always possible, but most humans require the use of time to achieve it, because the association with form is firm.

Also, as you practice meditation over time, if you feel frustrated, you are probably trying too hard! While "effort" may be required in the early stages, ultimately the process is not one of effort but of ease.

A Recommended Meditation Exercise
Sit in a quiet place, close your eyes, and pick a neutral object of focus to think of in your mind. It could be a visual object like a table or a triangle, or alternatively an audial repetitive sound, or even a combination of both. Whatever object is chosen, stick with it. Visualize (or otherwise mentally focus on) the object and keep your concentration focused on it. Thoughts will come to you and you will find yourself suddenly off thinking about something else. When you do, just gently redirect yourself back to focusing on the neutral object. If thoughts come constantly, make the object more active. Do whatever you have to do to keep your focus on the object! It's OK that thoughts come. Don't judge yourself as to whether you are "doing it right" – just keep redirecting your focus over and over. The form of the neutral object that you are focusing on in your mind is irrelevant; what is important is the action of using your intent to focus on something neutral that you are choosing, rather than being lost in a stream of thought. You'll find that doing this for just 10 minutes is very difficult at the beginning. But you'll also find that in just 10 minutes you can probably slow down your "thought momentum" noticeably. Repeat this practice regularly – it is

important to "train" yourself to be able to focus just on something neutral. Set aside time every day, at least one 30–40-minute period, or two 20-minute periods, just sitting there focusing on a constant neutral image, or possibly a neutral sound, in your mind.

Eventually, after consistent practice and over enough time, you will find the thoughts coming much less frequently and intensely, and you can eventually – but not too soon – drop the object of focus and instead just focus on your alert awareness of the present moment itself for exactly how it is. It is important to remain purely and intensely alert. Over time you will learn to become aware of what thoughts feel like when they come and go, and more and more you will grow awareness of what *you* (the real you – your awareness) are when not constantly focused on the "dream of form" that are your thoughts.

Throughout this whole process it's important to *not* judge yourself or your progress. You may find yourself thinking, "Am I doing it right?" or "Am I meditating?" Meditation is *not* an action within form. It is learning to deprioritize listening to thought, and it is a shifting of intention away from form to your own alert awareness itself. That awareness has no definition, and it cannot be "done." You can, however, put yourself in a state where suddenly – as Mooji puts it – "Peace will come and kiss you"; and truly, what an amazing experience that is!

Eventually it is also possible to become familiar enough with your personality's thought-stream that you can willfully "look away" from this physical reality to other "reality data streams." You may find those realities can be way *more* real than even this one! But! First things first – take the time to put down everything in your mind and focus on a boring neutral object! Do this daily for at least six months before judging the results. As Tom Campbell suggests, it is important to take the long-term approach to this.

One other comment – as you are focusing on the neutral object, try to "think with your body" while you do it (even though meditation is not ultimately about thinking at all). That is, allow your whole present alert

Part 4 – Brief Comments on Personal Investigation

bodily experience to focus on what you are doing, not just the thinking mind.

Alternative Meditation Focuses

The above exercise begins as a rather active intellectual activity, which can be helpful in initially slowing the thought momentum of the mind. However, there is also great benefit from less intellectually active approaches. Rather than focusing on the mental image of a neutral object, the following focuses can be practiced. Each of these can be very beneficial in the exploration of consciousness:

- Practice focusing purely on your breath.
- Practice focusing on the living awareness of the body, feeling the formless aliveness that is always present "in" the body. (Actually, the experience of the body is arising within that formless awareness, but the search can start by directing full attention to the body itself and to the feeling of aliveness within the body.)
- Practice completely "letting go" of absolutely everything – all physical, mental, or emotional tension – with full intention. Practice full surrender.
- Practice allowing the body to rest fully, even to the point of sleep if it wishes, while keeping the mind awake.
- Practice "body scans" – that is, shifting one's attention across the body from the top to bottom and back, like a scanner passing through the body.
- Practice intentionally connecting and surrendering to the divine, in whatever form or symbol is genuinely meaningful to you.
- Practice directing awareness back to awareness itself in any given moment, without any in between focus.

As you progress, any of these exercises can be practiced in any physical condition. That is, they can be practiced while you are lying down, sitting, or standing, or even while other activity is occurring in the environment.

A Brief Comment on Mindfulness

The practice of moving away from thoughts and labels towards reality exactly as it is does not have to be limited to meditation. While we are operating in the physical world, there is benefit to being as fully present and alert as possible with whatever we are doing and with whatever is occurring. For instance, when you wash your hands, feel the water, feel the soap, and remain keenly alert to the experience itself for exactly what is happening within your consciousness. Be vigilant in your rigorous attention to exactly What Is! No matter the activity or the context, practicing mindfulness in our daily physical life helps us to automatically move closer to what is real: Our willing and alert attention automatically shifts us in consciousness space toward the constant underlying bedrock that is the peace and joy of Being in which all things occur.

HOW CAN ALL THIS BE PRACTICALLY APPLIED IN OUR WORLD?

That is up to each of us! *You* know where love is needed in your life! *You* feel where you are called! As the quality of your intent improves towards love, the actions must follow. Loving thought and action flows from us naturally when we overcome our fears and more fully allow the power of Life to flow through us!

Made in the USA
Monee, IL
18 January 2023

25520625R10201